This Ain't Chicago

THIS AIN'T CHICAGO

RACE, CLASS, AND REGIONAL IDENTITY
IN THE POST-SOUL SOUTH

Zandria F. Robinson

The University of North Carolina Press / Chapel Hill

This book was published with the assistance of the
Fred W. Morrison Fund for Southern Studies and the Authors Fund
of the University of North Carolina Press.

Set in Utopia and Aller types
by codeMantra
Manufactured in the United States of America

Library of Congress Cataloging-in-Publication Data
Robinson, Zandria F.
This ain't Chicago : race, class, and regional identity in the post-soul South /
Zandria F. Robinson.
pages cm. — (New directions in Southern studies)
Includes bibliographical references and index.
ISBN 978-1-4696-1422-9 (pbk.) — ISBN 978-1-4696-1423-6 (ebook)
1. African Americans—Tennessee—Memphis. 2. African Americans—Race identity—
Tennessee—Memphis. 3. African Americans—Social conditions—1975- 4. Memphis
(Tenn.)—Race relations—History—20th century. 5. Memphis (Tenn.)—Social
conditions. I. Title.
F444.M59N488 2014
305.896'073076819—dc23
2013041271

18 17 16 15 14   5 4 3 2 1

To
DeMadre Kareem Lockett
(1979–2004),
who believed all southerners
rode horses and buggies

Contents

Preface

During the first several months of fieldwork for this research, when my ability to channel anthropologist and folklorist Zora Neale Hurston was far more unpracticed than I like to imagine it is now, my interview sessions had notoriously bumpy takeoffs. Careful not to assume an insider status and cognizant of my position as a young, middle-class black woman, I painstakingly went through the institutional review board consent form with respondents. Invariably, one glance at the form and the Northwestern logo it carried would bring my spiel to an abrupt halt, as the respondent would interrupt me and say some version of the following: "Northwestern? [Side eye.] Well, I hope you know this ain't Chicago. [Eye roll.]" At first, I assumed respondents thought I was from Chicago, or had been Yankeefied and therefore corrupted by my time there. Since I went to great lengths to interview persons whom I had not known personally or known of through social networks prior to my research, respondents may not necessarily have known that I was from Memphis. Often their declarations were followed by colorful explanations of *why* "this"—by which I assumed they meant the city of Memphis—was not Chicago. These explanations ranged from the usual distinctions between South and North, like "Things are more family-oriented here" or "People are backward here," to things like "This is where the real black folks are here" or "This is where it all began."

I also thought respondents might have been making an observation about social distance and that their admonishment was a warning to me not to make certain class-based assumptions. This line of thought was largely fueled by my desire to flatten the social distinctions between respondents and myself. I believed controlling my unacknowledged biases and blind spots as a black southerner from Memphis investigating black southern identity in Memphis was essential to the integrity of the research. Managing class and experience distinctions that might have influenced respondents to be less than forthright with me was part of that process.

As the research continued, however, I realized that "this ain't Chicago" was not about respondents' reactions to me as the researcher. Nor was it about Memphis or Chicago, those fabled stops on the City of New Orleans Amtrak line that runs from the "Jazz City" to the "Blues City" to the "Windy City" with stops in between. Rather, "this ain't Chicago" was akin to OutKast rapper André 3000's now famous utterance—"The South got something to say"—made amid boos from East Coast and West Coast emcees when the duo won big at the 1995 Source Awards. The admonishment was against conceptualizing black identity through a northern lens, which, for respondents, included not only Chicago but also New York, Los Angeles, Philadelphia, Detroit, and anywhere else outside of the former Confederate and Border States. It was about compelling recognition of a distinct southern black experience and reclaiming a space for southern black identity in the broadening landscape of black identity articulations. Nearly twenty years after André 3000's representing for the region, my respondents would argue that the South *still* got something to say and, moreover, that we had better listen.

My southern rearing in Memphis is a reflection of what my respondents herein argue is the "best of both worlds" interplay between urban and rural sensibilities in the contemporary South. Though for many of them, I have not spent enough time in the country to be comprehensively southern, I am nevertheless heeding the ever-echoing call to "tell about the South." In *This Ain't Chicago*, I tell about the South with attention to the multiple levels on which the South is constructed, experienced, and performed, especially for and by post–civil rights generations of black Americans.

Acknowledgments

This project would not have been possible without a community of family, friends, mentors, and colleagues. Wanda Rushing provided support for early versions of these ideas and continued to champion me throughout my early career. At Northwestern, Wendy Griswold, Mary Pattillo, and Chas Camic believed deeply in this project, even when I could not, and always pushed me to ask and address difficult questions about the empirical and theoretical nature of culture and identity. The opportunity to take part in Northwestern's Culture and Society Workshop helped me test and develop these ideas, and colleagues Jean Beaman, LaShawnDa Pittman, Mikaela Rabinowitz, Nicole Martorano Van Cleve, and Yordanos Tiruneh were always especially supportive. Wonderful friend and colleague Marcus Hunter was and is my undying ace in innumerable ways, and I quite literally would not have made it without him. His personal strength, generosity, and intellectual tenacity made me a better scholar and person, and for that I am eternally grateful. Steadfast friends and advocates for regional analysis Dave Ferguson and John Eason at the University of Chicago plotted with me to bring the South back into sociology, and our interlocutions were especially important for shaping my ideas about sociology in and of the South.

I am grateful to my wonderful colleagues at the University of Mississippi in the Department of Sociology and Anthropology and at the Center for the Study of Southern Culture. I relished being loud with Barbara Harris Combs and am especially thankful for the unerring support and friendship of Kirsten Dellinger. Charles Reagan Wilson's belief in this work undoubtedly buoyed it in the lean times. Conversations with graduate student I'Nasah Crockett about the South, hip-hop, and expressive cultures pushed my cultural analyses forward, compelling me to consider representation, performance, and lived experience simultaneously, however tricky that endeavor might be methodologically.

Several funding sources also made this work possible. I am eternally grateful to the American Sociological Association's Minority Fellowship Program, Northwestern University, Rhodes College, and the Consortium for Faculty Diversity at Liberal Arts Colleges. The College of Liberal Arts at the University of Mississippi and the Office of Diversity at the University of Memphis also provided important sources of support.

Perhaps most important, kin and friend support networks, and my sister and parents especially, worked behind the scenes to make this project possible, providing tangible support as readers, practice interviewees, sounding boards for ideas, and care providers for my daughter, Assata, when I was in the field. Unbeknownst to me, my parents' country mouse/city mouse skirmishes provided me with an experiential background in the issues I explore in this book. Through it all, I am most appreciative of Assata and my partner, Robert, who plied me with hugs, kisses, and brownies until this project was done.

Finally, I am thankful to the dozens of Memphians who sat for interviews with me, let me follow them around, and allowed and implored me to share their realities. Without their critical perspectives, this book would not be possible.

This Ain't Chicago

Region, Race, and Identities

Ruth Ann, a thirty-two-year-old returning college student and server at a chain southern home-style cooking restaurant, had become exasperated with me during our interview session at a coffee shop in downtown Memphis. She feigned annoyance at my line of questioning, in which I asked her to elaborate on what she had called black southerners' "superiority" to non-southern blacks. Popping her gum and carefully moving her hair behind her shoulder, she summed up the sentiments of many of my respondents, black Memphians whom I had interviewed and exchanged ideas with for five years between 2003 and 2010. "We just do things better down here, you know. Bigger. Better. Better hair. Better loving. Better singing. Better churching. Better cooking. We look better. Just better. We just all around better black folks." Delivered without an air of judgment and as a statement of verifiable fact, Ruth Ann's assertions underscore ongoing debates about racial authenticity and identity, about great migrations and reverse migrations, and about the place of the South, past and present, in African American social memory. This notion that the South, and in particular southern cities, represents a best-of-both-worlds blackness, or even a better blackness, is not one confined to black southerners' backyard barbecue or kitchen chatter. Claims of black southern superiority are also framed and articulated in a powerful segment of popular culture coauthored by competing and intersecting black, white, corporate, and national interests. From the plays, films, and television shows of writer and producer Tyler Perry, to commercial advertisements for Popeyes featuring Annie, a properly buxom southern black woman selling the Louisiana-spiced yardbird, to hip-hop music's definitive turn toward crunk and the Dirty South, the South has risen again as the geographic epicenter of authentic black identity.

Although popular culture is replete with varied explorations and constructions of contemporary black southern identities, and southerners like Ruth Ann are thinking through, fashioning, and reconstructing those identities in their everyday lives, social scientists have been slower to consider region as an important dimension of the multiplicity of black identities in the twenty-first century. However, this has not always been the case. Sociologists and anthropologists took great interest in the South and black southerners before World War II, exploring how black people thought about race as well as how race structured their lives politically, economically, and culturally. A range of scholars, including Ida B. Wells-Barnett, W. E. B. Du Bois, Allison Davis, Burleigh and Mary Gardner, John Dollard, and Howard Odum, took up the southern question. What were the lived experiences of black folks in rural and urban contexts in the South? What were the features and long-term implications of the South's racial caste system? How could a region dictated by rural crops and seasons thrive in an urbanizing, industrializing nation? What distinct forms of cultural expression emerged from the region, and how did those expressive forms reflect socioeconomic conditions? How did the cyclical flow of people from rural communities to cities in the South affect culture, structure, and place? How did the South's poverty affect class and race relations, economic prosperity, and the ever-elusive pursuit of "regional convergence," through which the South would reach economic and social parity with the North?

After World War II, these questions were pushed to the margins of sociological investigation. As sociologist Larry Griffin[1] has pointed out, declining conceptual and empirical interest in region among sociologists meant southern questions that could not be generalized to larger national or global issues were deemed unworthy of scientific consideration and attention. Further, "the Negro Problem" had moved to the urban Northeast, Midwest, and West during the second half of the Great Migration. Sociologists therefore shifted their focus, following the train lines from South to North, exploring black identities and lived experiences as they were constructed in the new urban environments of Chicago, Philadelphia, and New York. Urban and suburban homogenization and shrinking communication and commerce divides have yielded periodic declarations of the declining significance of place since the 1970s. Although a robust and sociologically driven advocacy for the continuing significance of place has challenged these declarations with varying levels of success, we still have little sociological knowledge about how place—region, city, suburb, town, or rural community—matters in the South. Moreover, beyond surface demographic descriptions about segregation levels and morbidity rates, we have scant information about how place is implicated in the socioeconomic and cultural outcomes and experiences of African Americans in the South.

Today, two generations after the second wave of the Great Migration, our social scientific understanding of black identity is still largely shaped by studies that take place in those early twentieth-century migration destinations. Recent attention to the South inspired by return migration to the region has not explicitly focused on black southern identity. Rather, this literature has sought to explain and understand the broad implications of urban demographic change vis-à-vis the lure of a mythical South of sweet tea, warm weather, and hospitality and the decline of the industrial Northeast and Midwest. In short, sociologists' tendency to focus on moving populations has obscured our vision of the people who have always made up the numerical majority of African Americans—black southerners.

This Ain't Chicago analytically separates black southerners from their migrating cousins and fictive kin, as well as from their white counterparts, to explore how region intersects with other axes of identity and difference in the black South. It is set in Memphis, Tennessee, the first big city stop heading north out of the Mississippi Delta, and uses the city as a grounding site and case for exploring race, class, gender, and regional identities. Traditionally, case studies take place in a field site that is relatively confined by space, place, and temporality. The ethnographer rigorously investigates all aspects of a place to understand social interaction and structural processes, whether that place is a barbershop, a corner, or a neighborhood. Yet, while my research physically took place in Memphis, the city shared the spatial and geographic spotlight with the South as a region as the research site. I do not suggest that the South is monolith. Indeed, there are multiple Souths, and I do not intend to gloss over the distinctions between southern places, in particular the differences between African American experiences in these multiple Souths. However, Memphis, a city that is "neither Old South nor New South,"[2] sits at the physical, temporal, and epistemological intersection of rural and urban, soul and post-soul, and civil rights and post–civil rights. As such, it is a fitting proxy for a conversation with the varied instantiations of the South, past and present.

With the proliferation of representations of black southern identity in television and film, from Bravo's wildly popular *The Real Housewives of Atlanta*, about dubiously wealthy Atlanta socialites, to the independent film *Mississippi Damned*, based on the true coming-of-age story of three young women of color in the rural South, it is difficult to treat identities on the ground as separate from popular representations. To extend the conversation about the South beyond Memphis as a physically located place, I turn to popular culture, and popular film in particular, to ethnographically explore other black southern spaces. I contrast the recent concerted production of southernness as the "new black" in popular media, including film, television, and music, with everyday southerners' understandings and articulations of regional identities. I make use of content analyses of contemporary films about the black South, including *Idlewild, ATL, Hustle & Flow*, and *Welcome Home Roscoe Jenkins*. I draw on these films to offer critical evaluations of regionalized performances of race, class, gender, and authenticity as presented in popular media. As such, throughout the book, I move between ethnographic analyses, film analyses, and analyses of broader public conversations that signal the changing statuses of race, class, gender, and region in contemporary America. My examinations of filmic representations and interpretations of the black South, Old South, and New South are drawn out relative to themes emergent from participant observation and interviews with black Memphians. Conducting a meta-ethnography in and through these films, I expand the role of viewer to that of participant-observer, taking inventory of the black southern worlds created by writers and filmmakers and putting those worlds into conversation with my respondents' discourse as well as into broader narratives about the contemporary black South.

The ethnographic data and voices in *This Ain't Chicago* straddle tensions between multiple notions of the black South—one created and inhabited by respondents, one reflected by culture producers and popular culture products, and one imagined by corporate advertisers and reality television producers. Because of the powerful and enduring nature of the black South as representation, stereotype, and metaphor, my respondents' voices cannot, in some ways, exist on their own terms. As Faulkner famously instructs us, the past is neither dead nor past; further, media representations are neither completely fabricated nor accurate reflections. Even as I endeavor to present a modern-day narrative of black southerners' everyday experiences, I am attentive to the ways in which the past—in varying forms—both *is* and *interrupts* the contemporary South.

I explore narratives of black southern identity, articulated by respondents as well as in popular culture, with particular attention to the generations that came of age after the South's most sweeping cultural, sociopolitical, and economic changes took effect, including the passage of civil rights legislation and the expansion of federal, private, and international investment in the South. I use the term *post-soul*, an idea popularized by cultural critic Nelson George that signifies the temporal and cultural shifts from past to present and back again that characterize post-1960s African American cultures. Extending George's ideas, popular culture scholar Mark Anthony Neal focuses specifically on the cultural and aesthetic features of this shift, describing a *post-soul aesthetic* through which contemporary black cultures sample from and signify on the cultural and political ideas of previous generations. Both

George and Neal situate post-soul as pointing to a cultural moment influenced and framed by the social, political, and economic paradoxes that have characterized African American life since the civil rights movement: mass incarceration, wealth stagnation, and the entrenchment of HIV co-occur with unprecedented educational attainment, skyrocketing wealth for a small but expanding blue-chip elite, and the first African American president. Post-soul accounts for cultural generational differences between the hip-hop generation and black millennials and their civil rights generation predecessors, as well as for structural and theoretical shifts in how black identities are understood.

Conceptually, post-soul encapsulates several central themes of this work. In the context of place, the term highlights Memphis's literal and figurative relationship to soul, soul music, and black American soul cultures. Additionally, it highlights the city's political relationship to the civil rights movement, particularly after Martin Luther King's assassination, and the ongoing battle for social justice in the city. Temporally and culturally, post-soul connotes a moment that is chronologically after the soul era—after the heyday of Al Green, Stax Records, and Mavis Staples—but that is constantly signifying on soul, remixing it to create something both new and familiar. While I sometimes use post-soul and post–civil rights interchangeably, the two terms have slightly different analytical connotations, with the former referring to culture and the latter to political and socioeconomic matters.

This work focuses on post-soul southerners, the generations of African American southerners who came of age after the assassination of King and in the shadow of glacial desegregation, resegregation, increased Latino immigration, and primary and return migration by African Americans from outside of the region. These southerners have been actively engaged in remaking the cultural significance of region to racial identities and in carving out new ways of being southern, being black, and being black southerners in the twenty-first century. While vocal segments of previous generations may have eschewed a regional identity because of its links to racism, forced subservience, and a violent and painful past, post-soul southerners boldly and defiantly claim a regional identity as a distinction, a significant nuance to their racial identities. This identity work has been ongoing while sociologists have been looking away from the South and continues to happen while we focus on migrants to the region's rural communities and urban metropolises. Attention to how black southern identity is lived, theorized, and experienced by black southerners allows us to explore broader questions about shifts in black identity and the cultural makeup of the region and the nation.

This Ain't Chicago enters the ongoing discussion of the increasing complexity of black identities and racial authenticity in the post–civil rights era, adding black regional identity to the constellation of possible black identity configurations. Examining African American southerners' evolving relationship to and with the region illuminates new intersections of race, class, gender, and black solidarity in the post–civil rights era. As more African Americans without southern roots or experience move south, and as the region becomes increasingly multiracial through increased immigration from a number of ethnic groups, the boundaries of black southern identity—and in some ways, native black identity more broadly—are contested and reified. Rather than assuming a monolith black southerner or black southern identity, *This Ain't Chicago* highlights tensions between ubiquitous myths about the black South, representations of black Souths in the popular media, and black southerners' ideas about their identities and experiences in the region. Rather than focusing on African Americans in rural or small-town communities, civil rights generation African Americans, or black migrants to the South, I focus on the people who constitute the majority of contemporary black southerners: urbanites, largely born after the baby boom, whose mothers, grandmothers, and great-grandmothers lived a majority of their lives in the South. Through the voices of these respondents, I explore how black southerners' race, class, and gender identities are mediated through a prism of regional distinction. I also explore black southern identity as constitutive of a set of intersections: between urban and rural, at the nexus of race and region, at the meeting place of soul and post-soul, and at the complex junction of Old South and New South. I find that black southerners' recent reclamation and less apologetic expression of a regionally marked blackness is born of a genuine desire—as residents, progeny, and co-creators of the South—to defend the region from naysayers who lambaste the South's perceived wholesale rurality, fundamentalism, and provincialism.

To be sure, respondents and popular culture elite are not uncritical of the region. In fact, some of the most poignant and thoughtful condemnations of the region come from its African American sons and daughters. Yet, in the spirit of the underdog tradition embodied by southerners since the Civil War, black southerners rescue the region from the scrutiny of outsiders even as they turn their own critical gazes on the South's persistent ills and their southern brethren. In the process of defending and critiquing the region, black southerners forward claims of authenticity that implicitly—and sometimes explicitly, like in the case of Ruth Ann and other respondents—privilege the black southern experience, effectively affirming the roots of real blackness and a better black experience in the post–civil rights era.

This book addresses several questions about the relationship between region, race, class, and gender identities.[3] How does regional identity intersect with and reinforce race, class, and gender identities in the post-soul South? As the geographic and cognitive epicenter of American blackness shifts southward, how are the boundaries of black identity reshaped and challenged? That is, how does the Americanization of black Dixie affect the formation of black southern identities? How do black southerners, located on the margins of both southern and black identity, reconcile regional and racial identities? By exploring the tensions between the myths about the black South and black southerners' ideas about their identities and experiences, *This Ain't Chicago* aims to address these and broader questions about the relationship between regional and racial identities as played out in media representations and through the everyday experiences of post-soul southerners.

New South Soul Cities

The intersections of race, class, gender, and region I explore occur with and against the backdrop of the southern urban landscape. While southern cities are certainly varied, they share a regional, topographical, demographic, and social history that renders them more similar to each other and in some cases more distinct from non-southern cities. Out of this similarity and variation, two relatively distinct urban Souths have emerged on the twenty-first-century horizon, both of which inform the mediated modern black South and black southerners' lived experiences of race, class, gender, and region. The first is the *new urban South*, which has experienced white, Latino, and most notably black population growth, driving the region's increasing racial and ethnic diversity. The new urban South includes Dallas, Atlanta, and Charlotte, all metropolitan regions that have experienced considerable growth and demographic change from migration and immigration. The second is the *historic urban South*, which has experienced modest Latino population growth, declining white populations, and steady or increasing black populations. These cities' stubborn black/white binary population and power arrangement is counter to the United States' coming tri-racial society, or the theory of "Latin Americanization" forwarded by sociologist Eduardo Bonilla-Silva.[4] While some attention has been paid to the new urban South as a new and/or return migration destination, less scrutiny has been given to the arrangements of racial power in urban contexts in the "Soul Cities" of the historic urban South.

Memphis is a majority-minority city, one of several largely southern and southwestern cities with a majority-minority adult and child population. While a number of cities are on target to hasten "the browning of America" in the twenty-first century with both African American and Latino population growth, a cluster of the original cash crop southern cities, including New Orleans, Jackson, Memphis, and Atlanta, will for the demographically predictable future remain what funkmaster George Clinton has famously called "Chocolate Cities"—cities with dominant and significantly sized African American populations with multiple multigenerational black communities. These cities will retain their demographic Chocolate City status in part because of African American population growth, but largely because Latino, Asian, and white populations will not move into these cities in large enough numbers to shift the racial demographic landscape.

Yet, not all Chocolate Cities can demographically resist melting. Journalist Natalie Hopkinson has written about one such Chocolate City, the dubiously southern Washington, D.C., investigating its declining black population and the concomitant cultural and economic marginalization of its black residents through the history of its distinctive music, called go-go. The District's history as a twentieth-century migration destination, rather than an initiating point,[5] means it shares characteristics with other migration destinations whose urban landscapes were changed by an influx of black and white southerners from the lower South. Thus, although D.C. has a majority-minority child population, gentrification and other urban political and economic forces have contributed to the decline of the overall black population in D.C., just as they have in Rustbelt black metropolises Chicago and Detroit.

This Ain't Chicago is about a different kind of Chocolate City: the Chocolate City's southern instantiation, the Soul City. Soul Cities exist in the new urban South, like Atlanta and Houston, as well as in the historic urban South, like Memphis and Jackson. Their distinguishing features include their relatively large and usually dominant African American populations, Old South power relations, and cyclical connections with rural and small-town black communities as well as with other Soul Cities. The movement of people across these soul nodes, from New Orleans to Houston or Memphis, from Memphis or Jackson to Atlanta or Houston, solidifies black cultural similarities and differences across the modern urban South.

While Chicago, Detroit, Philadelphia, Los Angeles, and other migration-destination Chocolate Cities have experienced either declines in black population or stagnant growth relative to Latino population growth, Soul Cities like Atlanta, Memphis, Jackson, and New Orleans have either maintained their black populations, experienced black population growth, or are on track to increase their black populations as majority-minority child populations become adults. The numerical majorities of African Americans in these cities are uniquely positioned, in ways that would seem demographically inevitable relative to other Chocolate Cities experiencing black population exodus and decline, to influence the political and economic landscape of urban life. While issues of power and inequality in Soul Cities are not unlike those of black folks in metropolises across the United States—struggles over access to quality public schools in the context of education privatization; the destruction of historically black neighborhoods through gentrification or urban renewal; the displacement of poor black populations as housing projects are replaced with purportedly mixed-income housing; the political marginalization of middle-class blacks despite their relatively high income and wealth—modern manifestations of Old South power relations create regionally specific disadvantages that disproportionately affect black populations in the South.

The great paradox of the Soul City is that throughout the United States, and perhaps especially in the South, black urban demographic dominance and middle-class status do not often translate into broadly useful public political power. While Washington, D.C., is home to the highest percentage of college-educated blacks and a significant percentage of wealthy blacks, frustrations about access to quality public schools and other public social goods abound across class.[6] Atlanta, too, is representative of the Soul City paradox, as a powerful perception of a Chocolate City belies a relative lack of power over urban public goods. Still, the perception of black power and soul cultures pull black populations southward to the newly designated capital of black America. In the first decade of the twenty-first century, Atlanta's black population growth outpaced that of Chicago, which had long claimed the second largest black population after New York City. While the broader Atlanta region does not quite yet have a majority-minority population, it does have a majority-minority child population. Still, an impending demographic majority and growing wealth will not necessarily translate into better outcomes for black Atlantans.

On the western side of the Deep South, Memphis and Jackson, urban bookends of the Mississippi Delta, both have majority-minority adult and child populations. Yet, unlike their wealthier Soul City counterparts, Memphis and Jackson were among the last to have significant black municipal elected leadership in the form of African American mayors. While black populations slightly outnumber white populations in their respective metropolitan regions and outnumber whites by greater numbers within city limits, relatively high levels of poverty and social and economic disenfranchisement underscore struggles over access to resources in these southern cities. As I will demonstrate, this context affects how black people think and talk about race and class in the modern urban South.

Finally, though the devastation of Hurricane Katrina affected African American population levels in the Crescent City, New Orleans, too, has a majority-minority child population. In the aftermath of Hurricane Katrina with developers eager to cash in on devastation and displacement, then-mayor Ray Nagin proclaimed several times, and most notably in a 2006 Martin Luther King Jr. Day speech, that New Orleans would continue to be a "Chocolate City" with an African American majority. Among my respondents from New Orleans, there was a consensus that in response, Mitch Landrieu, who became mayor of the Crescent City in 2010, contended that "the top of the dome has always been and will continue to be white." Using the Superdome as a metaphor for the racial configuration of New Orleans's political and economic structure, this assertion—whether actually articulated by Landrieu or a product of black New Orleanians' desires to have someone white speak the bitter truth about the order of things—might be aptly applied to all Soul Cities: expansive and rich white canopies with wider, poorer black bottoms.

Current demographic realities in Soul Cities are the direct result of the political, economic, and social history of the urban South. As historian David Goldfield has persuasively demonstrated, southern cities developed and existed to serve the needs of crop production, and specifically to harbor and process goods and people at various ports throughout the region. In the nineteenth and early twentieth centuries, southern city life, especially in the Deep South, was in many ways dominated by the needs of surrounding rural communities. As such, southern cities have always exhibited the characteristics of metropolitan regions—geographic spaces that transcend traditional boundaries between city, town, and country to encapsulate all of the economic dependencies and exchanges of a set of different kinds of places. Urban sociologists, following Chicago School sociologists Louis Wirth and Robert Park, have long thought that city cultures extended outward to transform the hinterland. However, as Goldfield demonstrates, southern cities were ruled from the hinterland by both rural and natural forces.

Rural cash crop needs drove not only economic activity in southern cities but also the racial and spatial organization of these urban economic outposts. As southerners migrated to southern cities from rural towns after the Civil War and throughout the first half of the twentieth century, attempts to accommodate the growing black and poor white populations and simultaneously maintain a hierarchical biracial system resulted in a distinctly southern racialization of space. Political scientists Christopher Silver and John V. Moeser highlight the South's "separate city"[7]—a self-contained political, economic, and social space that reigned until the late 1960s—which was different from the iconic ghetto that characterized cities in the urban Northeast, Midwest, and West. The sheer size of the black population in southern cities, coupled with whites' desire to maintain a biracial hierarchy while also exploiting black labor, yielded multiple black communities throughout the cities in which black businesses thrived, in contrast to the concentrated and densely populated ghettos of the urban North. Such a separate city, Silver and Moeser argue, created the physical and social environment in which black people, operating relatively separately from whites, were able to organize the civil rights movement, build a tenuous black wealth, and maintain distinctly racial and regional cultural communities. Today, these southern cities exhibit the legacy of both the separate city and the ghetto, rendering them important sites through which to understand regional history, urban history, and urban change in America.

People and places have a dialectical relationship; we influence the places where we live out our lives, and those places, in tandem, influence who we become and our outcomes. Although the South looms large at the center and margins of American identity, we know little about how the regional character of southern cities affects southerners' culture and identity formation. Further, we know less about black urban southerners' cultural identities, obscured as they were by the Great Migration. Soul Cities like Memphis, Jackson, Birmingham, Atlanta, and New Orleans carry on the musical and political legacy of the civil rights movement even as they attempt to reconcile the racial and socioeconomic realities of the post-soul era. The historical spatial and racial organization of southern cities, and the continuing legacy of those configurations, informs the social, political, and cultural landscapes of southern cities. The legacy of these configurations, in and through which definitive American movements and music were divined, constitutes the urban backdrop of *This Ain't Chicago*.

Racialization and Regionalization: Boundary Making in Everyday Life

Race is an organizing and structuring principle of everyday life, a master status that fundamentally shapes one's interaction with the state, social institutions, and others and one's experiences of the world. Sociologists Michael Omi and Howard Winant refer to the discursive processes by which societies attach racial meanings to certain behaviors, practices, and groups of people as *racialization*.[8] Pointing to the constructed nature of race, they highlight how racial meanings are constantly being made and remade in state, institutional, and individual contexts. By encoding racial difference and discrimination in the American justice system—for instance, as critical legal studies and critical race studies—scholars have demonstrated that the state participates in processes of racialization that discriminate against racial and ethnic minorities. Even the state's seemingly neutral process of the decennial census erects, creates, and ascribes meaning to racial categories, sometimes responding to political pressures from individuals and groups to remake categorizations and other times merely reflecting state conceptualizations of groups.

Institutional practices—from redlining, to race-based employment discrimination, to the subtle but powerful differences in medical providers' treatment of people of color—delineate the boundaries of racial groups by privileging whites and disadvantaging others. These practices reinforce and reflect the state's construction of race and also facilitate the popular construction of people of color as lazy, criminal, unfit neighbors who make poor individual health choices by sheer virtue of their skin color. Rather than see institutional discrimination in housing, employment, health care, and the justice system as structurally embedded manifestations of an a priori discriminatory state, racialization encourages us to view racial groups and individual racial and ethnic minorities as deficient in a purported meritocracy.

It is within this context of racialization that individual ideas about identity are formed and the boundaries of race are given specific nuances on the ground. Racialization yields shared black political practices and other inevitable similarities in experience born of the construction of race, culture, and color in America.[9] Yet, the intersection of other structuring processes, like class and gender, with race produces different black experiences and identities that often rupture racial solidarity.[10] Even if race is the constant, these differences and their concomitant distinctions in power highlight the importance of an intersectional approach,[11] one in which we recognize the ways in which race, class, and gender are mutually constitutive and reinforcing. Perennial intraracial class wars, for which comedian Chris Rock's bit on "niggas versus black people"[12] and Bill Cosby versus Michael Eric Dyson[13] serve as shorthand, make clear that although blacks are joined by the structural categorization of race, class matters just as much, if not more than, race.[14] Enduring racialized gender cleavages, played out in arenas from interracial dating to domestic violence, from misogynistic rap to baby daddy/mama drama, and from pimp places to pulpits, create significant differences in discursive positioning between African American men and women. Despite the galvanizing of black attitudes toward gay marriage when President Obama announced his support for gay marriage in 2012, strong divides over sexuality leave African American LGBT communities to choose race or sexuality and ensure their obfuscation in both gay rights and African American equality discourses. In matters political and social, then, the monolith blackness imagined by whites—and constructed by African American leaders with a vested interest in a unified black community—is tenuous at best.

Class, gender, and sexuality differences among African Americans do not give us leave to fly the banner of post-blackness, however. Where black diversity seemingly threatens black unity, racialization and the consequent fact of blackness still mean a shared experience of oppression; African Americans are frequently reminded of this linked fate. The 2012 murder of Trayvon Martin, a teenager shot to death in an altercation with a Latino/white neighbor, compelled many black parents to rearticulate the lessons of racial socialization. These lessons admonish black people, and black boys and men in particular, to be aware of the caprices of white authority and to remember that they are not equal in the eyes of whites, regardless of class status. Yet, black diversity need not be challenged by a unifying tragedy or oppression to evoke the vitality of blackness as a cultural concept—a concept that we as a society are not and may never be beyond because of the persistence of racialization.

In this study, region operates as another intraracial difference that is given meaning through individual and small-group interaction as well as through popular media. My respondents, as well as the popular culture elites and corporations invested in constructing a black southern identity, participate in a process of *regionalization*, in which exclusive regional significance is attached to certain behaviors, worldviews, and outcomes. Black and white southerners alike are invested in processes of regionalization, which include manufacturing regional histories, memories, and identities, albeit to different ends. Although undoubtedly southern regional identity is grounded in the historical and cultural differences of slave society, Jim Crow segregation, and the consequent organization of people, space, and place in the South,[15] regional identity is always already racialized, making and responding to cues from the state and social institutions. Further, region signifies and conjures ideas about class, gender, and sexuality as well.

Processes of regionalization reinforce and reproduce racialization in ways that root black American identity in the South. In short, region subsumes differences of class, gender, and sexuality among African Americans in service of one racially authentic black identity. I explore how the boundaries of race, class, and gender are both challenged and reinforced when region operates as a nuancing and mediating feature of the ongoing process of racialization.

When regional differences are created or exaggerated, they are often used to approximate something else, like race, rurality, class, or culture, without directly engaging the messiness of systems of oppression or inequality. For instance, ABC's 2012 midseason replacement *Good Christian Bitches*, which was quickly changed to *Good Christian Belles* and later to simply *GCB*, uses arguably hyperbolic southern white women to approximate the values and lifestyles of the white American wealthy more generally. Performative regional differences endure as meaningful interpersonal boundaries even in the face of the supposedly homogenizing forces of globalization and corporatization. In this context, southern identity is by far the most commodified regional identity—from Aunt Jemima to Paula Deen.

Despite the effects of globalization and corporatization on the relationship between places, place differences endure. That is, places continue to have a distinctive character even after the institutional origins of these differences can no longer be readily identified. In America, region is a more slippery form of place, despite official attempts to confine and define it for measurement purposes, because of widely contested opinions about its boundaries and characteristics. Although there is a sign, for instance, for the Mason-Dixon Line, the line itself is only symbolically accepted as a regional boundary. Still, similarities across the region, products of the region's demography, history, and structure, are evident in the cultural and social landscape of the South, especially in medium-sized southern cities. Yet, where does the South's influence, particularly as a cognitive artifact, end? Even with the number of migrants and immigrants entering the region with distinctive cultures, the idea of the South endures, however its boundaries are defined.[16] This book takes seriously the differences produced by place distinction and endeavors to demonstrate just how those differences influence black southern identity.

Inasmuch as processes of racialization and regionalization are structural manifestations of the will of the state, social institutions, and powerful elites, individual social actors are also involved and invested in these processes. Individuals both challenge and reinforce existing social structures through their performances of organizing categories. For instance, individuals might "do" gender, as Candace West and Don Zimmerman have argued,[17] repeatedly performing sets of established behaviors that mark one's membership in a gender category and thereby reinforcing the structural boundaries of gender through our everyday interactions. Individuals might also refuse to participate in established gender behavioral norms, create new norms, or blend men's and women's norms to challenge, reject, or remake hegemonic performance requirements. Yet, whether individuals ascribe to or challenge dominant norms, "doing gender" is a strategically negotiated *accomplishment* that requires deliberate effort. Rather than conceptualize distinctions—between places, people, and things—as self-evident and natural occurrences of difference, sociologists examine how distinctions are achieved, or accomplished, through deliberate practices instituted by cultural elites and other social actors. Theorizing performances as accomplishments allows us to examine the processes through which things, people, and places imagine themselves as distinct and are recognized as such.[18]

Much of the process of identity performance is focused on the erection and maintenance of symbolic boundaries. When people perform an identity, they are not only reflecting and responding to social structures but also drawing lines of cultural difference between themselves and others. These differences often take on value, which results in some form of what sociologist Pierre Bourdieu calls social or cultural capital, either through added positive value or by distancing oneself from something that is negatively valued. Bourdieu argues that this cultural boundary work is a fundamental tool of class perpetuation and therefore social inequality.[19] This social boundary work—maintenance of the boundaries between races, classes, genders, and sexualities—yields symbolic boundaries, meaningful behavioral and epistemological distinctions between people and groups that are not explicitly based on overt markers of difference like color and gender.

Building on Bourdieu's work and Tom Gieryn's notion of boundary work,[20] Michèle Lamont demonstrates that the symbolic and social boundaries of class and race are created and maintained through complex social and psychological strategies that name and ascribe meaning to social difference.[21] Symbolic boundaries almost always function to reinforce a social boundary, though tracing the breadcrumbs back to the particular social boundary, whether race, class, or gender, may be difficult. Still, the varied symbols and behaviors that stand in for difference, like the kind of wine one orders, the way one hails a taxi, or the absence or presence of a southern drawl, eventually lead us back to systems of oppression erected by the state, reinforced by social institutions, and dramatized in the interpersonal interactions of everyday life and popular media.

People's performative investments in southern identity, as everyday identity practice and as commercial product, are thus vast and serious. Resurgences of southern regional identity as ideology and product usually point to increasing class and race anxieties among middle-class white southerners, whose vision and versions of the South are challenged by the growing *Nuevo* South, an expanding African American middle class, and the increasing urbanization and racial and ethnic diversity of the region and the nation—processes that certainly do not bode well for the iconic (white) small southern town. The Old South persists in the region's white suburban enclaves, replete with subdivisions whose names at once hearken back to a pastoral plantation past and reify the race and class boundaries of the rapidly changing region. These suburbs serve as a refuge from an encroaching Yankee liberalism and urban cosmopolitanism. Indeed, for whites, southern identity is more than an "ethnic option" exercised on special occasions, like temporarily articulating one's Irish heritage on St. Patrick's Day.[22] It is the performative and ideological glue that holds contemporary American whiteness together as a distinct and superior culture, rooted in ideals synonymous with the highest national and Western principles.

Black southerners, too, have serious investments in performative southern identities, although they are largely spurred on by different motivations. As the category of African American becomes increasingly diverse, region becomes an important space for boundary work, the interpersonal and sometimes structural labor of delineating differences between oneself and others. Performing delineated roles and acting out identity-consistent scripts is the primary method by which boundaries are reified. These scripts are decidedly different across race, although in many ways, black and white southerners are calling upon similar tropes of southernness to draw a line between themselves and regional outsiders.

Region has long functioned as an intraracial symbolic boundary, especially for African Americans. Despite the cyclical nature of black migration in and out of the South, region has operated as a site of identity distinction in tandem and intersection with class, gender, and sexuality. Whether it was the green country women or 'Bamas from down south who needed to be socialized into their new northern environments in the early twentieth century, regional difference mattered for how African Americans categorized and understood one another. Regional distinctions of these sorts continued and evolved throughout the twentieth century, in tandem with a broader Western interest in the demise of the folk in the inevitable progress of modernization.

In the wake of the most significant gains of the civil rights movement, the South was moving more definitively toward regional parity with the rest of the country, progress spurred on by federal investment in the South since World War II. As Madhu Dubey has argued, anxieties about this progress led to rapid white regression to signifiers of a "simpler past": one in which plantation power was still the norm and African Americans were subjugated under the physical and social rule of whites.[23] African Americans, too, turned toward the South, toward "home," and specifically to the region's rural spaces. The convergence of these two divergent reasons for recasting and repositioning black folks in the South—on the one hand, for white folks to manage their anxieties about desegregation and black progress, and on the other, for black folks to manage their existential disappointment in the urban North and longing for their southern upbringing—yielded a fierce, region-based set of authenticity politics among African Americans: regionalization.

In black folks' collective search for an ancestral American history in which to escape the contradictions of the promised lands of Chicago, Detroit, and New York, the South stands in for a cognitively and geographically distant African homeland. Blues, soul, and gospel are the soundtrack, Alvin Ailey is the choreographer, and Atlanta is the urban motherland. Any instantiation of blackness, from punk to goth to Afro-futurist to backpacker, can be culturally rooted in these originary soundscapes, bodily expressions, and spaces/places. Put another way, to understand contemporary movements in black identity, we must pay close attention to the processes of racialization and regionalization happening among African Americans in the South.

The Black South Is as the Black South Does: Accomplishing Country Cosmopolitanism

In everyday interactions and popular culture products, black southerners, black southern culture elites, and corporate marketers operationalize a discursive epistemological strategy I call *country cosmopolitanism*.[24] Country cosmopolitanism is a best-of-both-worlds blackness that addresses the embattled notion of racial authenticity in a post-black era by hearkening back to and modernizing rural, country tropes. As a regional logic, it blends rural values and urban sensibilities to navigate—and sometimes sanitize—the post–civil rights South. In this formulation, southern rearing and residence are equated with racial authenticity, and southern signifiers stand in for the usual markings of class, gender, and sexuality distinction. Implicit in country cosmopolitanism is a normalization of the class privileges of wealthier blacks, the patriarchal privileges of black men, and the sexuality privileges of heterosexuals. Still, the strategy is also used to disrupt, usurp, and relocate the traditional boundaries and intersections of region and race. Therefore, country cosmopolitanism captures tensions between South and North, Martin and Malcolm, good and evil, real and inauthentic, masculine and feminine, Tyler and Spike, sacred and profane, Wu-Tang and OutKast, and a host of other symbolic distinctions that demarcate distinctions in black identity. While separately "country" and "cosmopolitan" seemingly signify simple polar opposites of negative and positive, stagnation and progress, I trouble these easy distinctions through respondents' appropriations and combinations of those meanings and explore these tensions and the dual processes that produce them.

Different constituencies marshal country cosmopolitanism toward convergent and contrary ends. For southerners, like the respondents in my study, a country cosmopolitan worldview facilitates the maintenance and strengthening of the boundaries of authentic racial and regional identities. For black southern culture elites, like Tyler Perry or rap duo OutKast, country cosmopolitanism is a strategy for giving voice to distinctively southern black experience. Finally, for black southern syndicates, including corporations like McDonald's and Popeyes, country cosmopolitanism is used to build an African American consumer base and foster a regional seal of approval through America's perennial marketing mascot—from Uncle Ben to Glory Foods' "Shirley"—the black American southerner. *This Ain't Chicago* foregrounds the lived experience of black southerners in its examination of the interplay of these groups' competing and overlapping uses of country cosmopolitanism.

For respondents, this country cosmopolitan, best-of-both-worlds blackness is both performed and performative, which means that it has inherent measures and markers of authenticity by which adherents might be judged. However, according to many respondents, it is also a sincere ontological articulation, and thus this book is not concerned per se with the authenticity or realness of black southerners' identity performances or the internal consistency of their identity theorizations. A strict focus on authenticity obscures the meaning-making processes that necessarily accompany such performances and the structures of power within which meaning making takes place. My respondents thought less about whether or not they were perceived as authentically southern or authentically black and more about the social outcomes of an inherent and/or accomplished southernness that operated outside of the parameters of measurable realness. Thus, I focus on how performances of southernness—accomplished, sincere, and "natural"—help black southerners erect and manage distinctions between themselves and non-southerners and articulate a distinct worldview.

While southerners may be acutely aware of the region's challenges, from poverty to under-education to racism, they go to great lengths to emphasize southern cultural superiority, even repackaging negative characteristics of the region as blessings in disguise. For instance, "If you can survive this racism in the South, you can survive racism anywhere," claimed several respondents in one form or another, signaling the perception of the South's brand of racism as distinctly worse than in other places, as well as the opportunity to prove oneself in the struggle against it. In these estimations, rather than being desperately behind other places in race relations, the South becomes a space through which one might overcome racism altogether, albeit through a historically inspired personal attitude change and not through white folks' collective "coming to Jesus." Notions such as these underscore the workings of authenticity on a discursive level, even if authenticity does not factor prominently in how people think and talk about their interpersonal interactions. Thus, although I focus on processes of meaning making, authenticity hovers over the discursive surface of social interactions, signaling broader sociopolitical trends in black identities.

This book situates regional identity, like other forms of identity, as a strategically negotiated accomplishment, one based on shared, though contested, understandings of what it means to be a black southerner. While certainly there is not an archetypal black southerner or an archetypal black South, efforts to create an authentic black southern identity and space belie this fact. I do not intend to suggest, by my use of accomplishment theories, that respondents were engaging in a crafty performance and that underneath the performative veneer a black northerner—that is, a standard or normal black person—resided. Many respondents moved quite easily between hyperbole, performance, and sincerity, which were simultaneously reinforcing. By using accomplishment, I hope to underscore a continuum of sincere black southern performances and identities and to capture the range and degree of performative investments—exaggerative signifying, measured performance, or sincerity without pretense—black southerners make in doing and being southern in public and private contexts.

Why is such deliberate effort made to erect and maintain interpersonal regional differences? Not unlike Alice Walker's assertion that "no one could wish for a more advantageous heritage" than that of southern blackness,[25] my respondents see being southern and black as a form of social and cultural capital, although they are aware of how the intersecting categories of southern and black may be as maligned as they are celebrated in popular media and interpersonal contexts. They are constantly refining their ideas about southern identity, ensuring they maintain the boundaries between themselves and non-southern others. Further, respondents recognize that their performances or southern being-in-the-world might gain them favor in interpersonal contexts, whether the prize is a job, a temporary or more permanent partner, a discount, or a tire change.

Moreover, respondents acknowledged the limits of southern identity and performance. In itself, performance does not yield an unlimited amount of social capital, as the implicit caveats in how-to manuals like *The Grits (Girls Raised in the South) Guide to Life* suggest. Performances are often limited by structural constraints, like those of race and class, and respondents pointed to those constraints often. For instance, black folks are excluded in many ways from certain southern identity performances, like the belle or the gentleman, and a lower-income woman may not have the disposable income to purchase the proper silver set to perform "up" to belle status. Identity performances also have structural implications, as they can reify or challenge existing behavioral expectations based on race, class, or in this case, regional group membership. When OutKast rapper André 3000 dons a Confederate flag belt buckle, he signifies his regional group membership by appropriating a symbol of a particular kind of white southern identity and remaking it in the image of the Dirty South. Through it, he disrupts racial and regional expectations and opens the possibility to develop a different understanding of how one might be, or do, black and southern in the New South.[26]

Yet, disruptions in the intersection of racial and regional norms and behaviors—like a black man wearing a Confederate flag in a video for an apology song dedicated to "baby mamas' mamas"—are less common in everyday life. On a micro-interactional level, the paradox is the coexistence of country-ness and cosmopolitanism, the rural and the urban. In interpersonal interactions, respondents work to accomplish and are sincerely invested in country cosmopolitanism. They use "country" as both a pejorative and a term of endearment to describe people, practices, places, and worldviews they perceive as exclusively black, rural, authentic, and, in some cases, provincial and backward. Yet, respondents' sentiments are also distinctly cosmopolitan or progressive, reflective of the forces of modernization and urbanization on black country cultures over several generations of city residence. I employ "cosmopolitanism" to highlight behaviors that anecdotally might be construed as northern or bourgie, like progressive or feminist ideas about gender equity or liberal attitudes toward sex and sexuality. Cosmopolitanism also highlights the negative consequences and outcomes of urban life on black folks, from urban alienation to urban violence. Finally, and importantly, cosmopolitanism is not always related to or emergent from urban contexts. Cosmopolitanism can highlight the shrewdness, insight, and wit typically associated with urban lived experience—characteristics that can also be rooted in country experience. That is, in their sharpness, rural folkways are not always the country, innocent, or naive behaviors we might initially think them and may in fact reflect cosmopolitan sensibilities.

The country cosmopolitan worldview draws on tropes of the rural South—like home, community, family, and food—but decenters, reconfigures, and relocates them for consumption and production in the urban South and beyond. Rural South tropes are the grounding force in this worldview, keeping black southerners centered, true to their history, and focused on what adherents argue really matters in life. Essential to this worldview is the dialectical interplay of urban and rural cultures, a characteristic of the South throughout its development that has shaped the region's material, visual, and symbolic economies. As sociologist Wanda Rushing and historians Louis Kyriakoudes and David Goldfield have argued persuasively, the intersection of rural and urban cultures and economies creates a fundamentally different urban experience that affects the way regional, racial, and spatial identities were and are formed. For African Americans, whose national identity is rooted in the region, regardless of genealogy, this explains the existence of black folks' incorporation of rural and small-town practices into their urban traditions, from New Orleans to Detroit.

As my respondents articulated it, country cosmopolitanism is more than the product of the intersection of urban and rural characteristics. Further, it is more complex than the familiar regional stereotypes of southerners as polite, hospitable, religious, family-oriented people with a penchant for barbecued pork. It is a way of both theorizing and performatively encountering the world that combines elements of black folk culture—from storytelling to signifying—to contend with, counter, and make sense of recent changes in the black sociopolitical landscape. Specifically, country cosmopolitanism calls for seemingly paradoxical approaches to race, class, and gender realities. Respondents claimed they "ain't stud'n' 'em white folks" and "white folks is harmless," while simultaneously drawing on the collective memory of Jim Crow to indict whites for continuing to perpetuate inequality and anti-black racism in structural and interpersonal contexts. They validated the elite black performance of the southern belle through debutantes, cotillions, and the unending quest for "men, money, and manicures" while acknowledging the damage these constraining norms do to men and women's relationships. In class matters, country cosmopolitanism implicitly and explicitly encourages acceptance and promotion of class difference by excluding people who are "too" country from elite social networks; however, when interregional class inequalities are the topic, "blacks up north are bourgie" and not supportive enough of black people across the class spectrum. In short, country cosmopolitanism is the theoretical validation for black southern cultural superiority relative to both whites and non-southern blacks. Yet, in its bless-your-heart way, country cosmopolitanism highlights enduring within-race tensions of class, identity, gender, and sexuality that influence the African American sociopolitical landscape.

I deploy country cosmopolitanism as a theoretical frame for understanding black southern identities in the post–civil rights context. For all of the sincerity of its espousers, country cosmopolitanism is an accomplished worldview, one bound up in already-existing performative scripts of race, class, and gender. I explore the seemingly contradictory nature of black southern performances of racial authenticity, for instance, through analyses of how black southerners play both "country" (saying "yes, sir" and "no, sir" to whites) and cosmopolitan (staring directly at whites in a restaurant or on the street without speaking), disrupting white and non-southern ideas about the performative norms of southern blackness. In examinations of gender performance, I demonstrate how black women across the class spectrum transform into humble, eyelash-batting belles, throwing about cute "country" phrases like "I reckon he ain't got the sense God gave a blade of grass" to compete for men, money, or social capital. In tandem, I show how alternative tropes of black southern womanhood challenge the legitimacy of the belle as an African American gender formulation. I also demonstrate men's investments in southern gender performances, from the country boy to the gentleman, as well as men's investments in the regional inflections of women's gender performances. Finally, I examine the workings of class difference undergirding contemporary southern identity, as southerners draw on regional differences as a proxy for traditional ideas about intraracial class differences. While I find traditional southern markers of class status, from lighter skin to church membership, at work, respondents draw on a host of social cues to establish the boundaries of proper regional and class identities. On the micro-interactional level, black southerners use country cosmopolitanism to establish seemingly innocuous, socially beneficial distinctions between themselves and others. Yet, on a structural level, country cosmopolitanism reifies existing gender and class cleavages in the African American community, but does so with a smile and down-home ease that belies its broader consequences for black politics in the post–civil rights era.

My analysis vacillates between the representations of authenticity forwarded by popular culture products, like films, and the sincerity of southerners' ruminations on their identity performances in everyday interactions. While blackness and black southernness may be carefully scripted, situationally specific performances, they are also what John L. Jackson Jr. has called "sincere,"[27] a quality distinct from notions of authenticity in that one's goal is not to achieve a predefined norm of realness. Sincerity is, rather, a *real* realness based on intentionality and interiority rather than on performance and anticipated outcome. Black southerners may therefore willingly "do" the South in mixed regional company, and unashamedly so. Whether referring to nonexistent gardens or inventing clever folk sayings and swearing such sayings have been in their families for generations, black southerners cash in on the social capital implicit in certain tropes of southern identity in exchange for privileged interactive outcomes. Rather than reading black southerners as cultural dupes mirroring representations of themselves forwarded by Tyler Perry or Popeyes, I take seriously my respondents' performances and presentations of self, endeavoring to reflect the sincerity of their sentiments as regional insiders and co-creators of regional and racial cultures.

Overview of the Book

The data presented herein are the result of five years of research, starting in 2003. In that year, I worked to build a network of respondents, beginning with members of Memphis's underground hip-hop scene who had, as demonstrated through their music, a vested interest in black southern identities in hip-hop. In my estimation, these respondents also worked to both represent Memphis and the South and to challenge negative perceptions of southerners' rap credibility. In addition to artists, I interviewed people who frequented hip-hop and soul music events, as their participation, I surmised, indicated that they, too, were interested in southern cultural expression. Beyond this network of art world participants, most of my respondents were people I met in the course of the daily round: at schools, in grocery stores, in parks, at post offices, and in a number of other every-day spaces throughout the city of Memphis and its surrounding suburbs. I also met several respondents at cultural events, including open mic sets, festivals, concerts, football games, and art showings. I talked informally with dozens of southerners who joined overheard conversations and, on some occasions, with southerners whose conversations I invited myself into, everywhere from block parties to restaurants. I generally approached people who seemed like they would not completely rebuff me, and most adhered to southern standards of politeness, even if they might have wanted to curse me and run away. Most people agreed to an interview, although I usually offered them something in return, from coffee to résumé editing services to a meal. After interviews with these respondents, I was frequently referred to family members, friends, or coworkers they thought I should interview, and I followed up on many of those suggestions.

Throughout the selection process, I attempted to garner a diverse cross-section of African Americans in Memphis who had been born and raised in the South. As such, I strived for diversity in respondents' age, class status, neighborhood, wealth and income, parental and marital status, and general perspectives on Memphis and the South. I achieved this diversity often by asking respondents general demographic questions about the people in their networks whom they had suggested I interview. While a very small percentage of primary and return migrants slipped into my sample, and I identify them as such in the text, the vast majority of the sample includes people who have lived in the South for their entire lives. Respondents represent a broad cross-section of the black population in terms of class and occupational type and status and are roughly evenly divided across gender, with women representing slightly more than half of respondents. Some respondents served as key respondents, people with whom I dis-cussed findings, shared my field notes, and solicited feedback throughout the research process. In total, I formally interviewed 106 respondents, 32 of whom served as key respondents, having allowed me to interview them multiple times over the course of the research.

Twenty-first-century Memphis, still carrying the weighty legacy of being the city that killed King and serving as the "big city" for Mississippi Delta migrants, is distinct from Atlanta, the black South's answer to the black middle-class cultural enclaves of New York, Chicago, and Los Angeles. Black southerners, and particularly black cultural elites in southern cities, draw on local histories and tropes to construct their own place-inspired brands of contemporary black southern life. I attend to these intrare-gional place distinctions with other data sources, including film, hip hop, corporate advertisement, and magazine and newspaper articles, throughout the book. Still, I refer to respondents as southerners, rather than as Memphians, because inasmuch as neighborhood and city contexts matter, region matters as well, sometimes even overshadowing city boundaries and limits. Because Memphis is neither a New South urban magnet, like Dallas, Charlotte, and Atlanta, nor a close-knit rural southern community, it is a key space in which to examine the interplay of urban and rural cultures that undergird articulations of black southern identity.

Formal interviews ranged from forty-five minutes to four hours in length and took place in people's kitchens and living rooms, at parks and coffee shops, while accompanying people on the daily round and during long waits under hair dryers at beauty salons. In exchange for their willingness and time, I fed many respondents, which was often how I convinced them to sit for a follow-up interview. I also helped with children's math homework, gave people rides, played my violin, gave advice about college, acquiesced to being introduced to single brothers and sons, and visited folks' churches. It was often through these time exchanges that I met new respondents and was able to observe dimensions of black southern cultural life, and my hometown, that I previously had not known existed.

Throughout this book, the North, or the No'f, as some respondents referred to it in playfully disparaging contexts, is a floating signifier, standing in at once for everything non-southern, everything bourgie, everything Great Migration, everything disconnected from blackness, and a great many things in between. While my respondents readily recognized the southernness of a place like Chicago, home to many of their close and distant kin and the descendants, two or more generations removed, of migrants from the Mississippi Delta, Chicago was frequently othered as No'f, often standing in for blackness gone awry. If there are cultural remnants of southernness in Chicago, respondents argued, they are the worst elements of the South's racial and regional history. In much the same way black popular and academic discourses imagine the South as fixed and unchanging, black southerners fix spaces outside of the South—spaces as varied as Los Angeles and New York and Chicago—as static, a skipping record of postindustrial urban crisis and the broken covenant between African Americans and the promised land.

Chapter 1, "Finding the Black South," considers the multitude of ways that the South has been represented by and through several publics, from academics to rappers to filmmakers. It focuses on how these varied and sometimes competing publics contributed to the production of the most recent "New South"—the South that began in the 1960s, ushered in by deindustrialization, the rapid and far-reaching social changes of the civil rights movement, African American reverse migration, and the expansion and invigoration of southern metropolises. The chapter looks at the production of regional representations in African American social memory, popular culture, and lived experiences, highlighting the connections between myths about black southern life and expressions of country cosmopolitanism. Because popular culture is more expansive than people's interpersonal interactions, I focus heavily in this chapter on how popular culture has shaped collective American understandings of southern black identities, specifically on African American theorizations of racial and regional identities.

Chapter 2, "Post-Soul Blues," moves from a broader discussion of regional and racial tropes to a specific discussion of how those tropes operate in Memphis. Situated at the north end of the Mississippi Delta, Memphis has a premium on most things country and cosmopolitan. The city is home to generations of migrants from Arkansas, Tennessee, and the Mississippi Delta, whose rural folkways transformed the physical and ideological landscape of the city over the course of the late nineteenth and early twentieth centuries. These rural roots are reflected in measures of social illness as well. Memphis has the highest urban infant mortality and poverty rate among large cities in the country. Yet, Memphis is also an international transportation hub that boasts a rapidly expanding biotechnology district and world-class hospitals. Memphis, as sociologist Wanda Rushing argues, is "neither Old South nor New South," having little of the Old South history of the Confederacy and even less of the glitzy shine of the New South. Instead, Memphis—perhaps like Birmingham, Jackson, Greenville, Raleigh, and Greensboro and the working-class black sections of places like Nashville, Atlanta, and Dallas—is a place in the geographical and temporal interstices of the failure and promise of the civil rights movement. It is therefore a key site through which to understand the relationship of black southern identities to black identities writ large.

The next three chapters examine how regional identities intersect with race, gender, and class sensibilities, respectively. Specifically, they examine how country cosmopolitanism frames and drives black southerners' race, gender, and class sensibilities and interpersonal interactions and performances.[28] I highlight how southerners who have lived continuously in the South experience their own anxieties about the changing migrant landscape around them—increased Latino migration, increased migration from black folks from "the North," and increased Caribbean and African immigration—while also shoring up the boundaries of southern culture to situate themselves as having the "best" black cultural existence in modern America.

In chapter 3, "Not Stud'n' 'em White Folks," I explore the ways in which race is experienced and theorized by black southerners, with a specific focus on their interactions with whites. Now more than a century old, W. E. B. Du Bois's observation that the color line would be the fundamental problem of the twentieth century continues to be an apropos characterization of any foreseeable southern and American future in the twenty-first century and beyond. Despite the heralding of a post-racial America, the continuing significance of race is in some cases more pronounced than ever before, especially for poorer African Americans and Latinos. Thus, while blacks overall have experienced significant gains in the post–civil rights era, moments of crisis, like the foreclosure crisis that reached its public apex in 2008, reveal the dogged persistence of institutional racism that disproportionately affects a vulnerable black middle class.

After the institutional dismantling of legalized racial discrimination, racial inequality continued and for some groups became entrenched as an inevitable fact of life. In the post–civil rights moment, race scholars have worked to document the implications of rapidly changing racial paradigms and the intersections of race and class. Whiteness studies scholars unpack and make visible the privileges and power of whiteness as an institution, thereby broadening the theoretical lens to include not only the oppression of racial and ethnic minorities but also the hegemonic privileges of whiteness.[29] Inequality scholars have developed a number of relatively infallible methods that highlight the economic and social consequences of racism.[30] Social psychologists interested in race have used various experimental designs to demonstrate that on a cognitive level, whites are at best uncomfortable with blacks and lose some executive function after interracial interaction.[31] Additionally, social psychologists have developed substantial research on racial micro-aggressions, interracial interactive slights that are particularly damaging for racial and ethnic minorities.[32] This literature argues that it is in these everyday, interpersonal, negative interactions that the seeds of racial and social stress are sown. Finally, a significant body of research chronicles African American negotiation and management of race and racism—critical race narratives of experiences of racism, coping strategies for dealing with racism, and the racial socialization of children.[33]

Cumulatively, these literatures highlight the continuing significance of race and racism and the persistence of inequality, on both structural and interpersonal levels, despite the overall economic and social gains of minorities in the post–civil rights era. This is especially the case in the South, where the stark juxtaposition of the richest and poorest black communities highlights the paradoxes of racial progress in the twenty-first century. Respondents claimed to have white folks "figured out" because of their extensive firsthand and secondhand experiences with them. Rather than fretting over the possibility of white racism, respondents accept its inevitability and structure their interactions with whites accordingly. Sensitive to the mediated South that circulates in thirdhand stories about run-ins with Mississippi state troopers, respondents "know their racists." They offered a distinctively contrarian perspective on race, race relations, and progress in the contemporary South. This position is part of a carefully crafted performative veneer, operationalized to make sense of the continued heaviness of race even in the region's most progressive spaces.

In chapter 4, "Belles, Guls, and Country Boys," I extend country cosmopolitanism to an exploration of black folks' varied performances of gender and understanding of gendered roles and behaviors. While black feminist research has thoroughly analyzed the complicated sets of controlling images, from the lady to the mammy to the bitch, that govern black women's presentations of self,[34] how these categories intersect with regional gender norms is under-theorized. More often than not, black women have to contend with systems of power that deny access not only to any positive construction of femininity but to humanity as well. While black women overall were historically excluded and continue to be excluded from categories of femininity, the institutionalized devaluation of black women's bodies in the Jim Crow South meant a unique process of gender construction and exclusion for southern black women. Nonetheless, black women strived under extraordinary circumstances to cultivate respectability and womanhood, often doing so by suppressing the most unfavorable elements of black life and encouraging cleanliness, thrift, religiosity, and birth control among the poor.[35] While white gender archetypes were erected against constructions of black gender archetypes, black folks managed to appropriate categories from which they were excluded—belle, lady, and gentleman, for instance—and participate in a racialized version of regional culture that wrested some dignity through performance.[36]

African American articulations of regional gender knowledge are important measures of the significance of intraracial regional difference. Across class, women and men respondents negotiate balances between traditional and progressive gender roles and performances, challenging their exclusion from southern gender archetypes like the belle and the gentleman and also creating quite different gender archetypes, like the southern gul and the country boy. In and through regionalized performances of masculinity and femininity, black southerners craft new, if not necessarily liberating, ways of doing gender and doing the South.

In chapter 5, "Southern Is the New Black," I explore respectability politics as they intersect in conversations about region, class, and, implicitly, native black identity. This chapter argues that country serves as a marker of class status without the pernicious baggage of traditional manifestations of intraracial class politics. Respondents drape their class biases in polite clothing, particularly in public and especially in mixed-regional company. Although southern intraracial class divisions are exacerbated by the disproportionately high value placed on skin color, hair texture, and church membership in the region, black southerners unify around the "better" version of blackness—that blackness connected to rural, and therefore humble and authentic, beginnings—to shift blame for class and community tensions, and problems, to blacks outside of the South.

While respectability politics are generally conceptualized in terms of class-based social differences, chapter 5 argues that regional differences, especially those between country folks and cosmopolites, function in tandem with and as markers of class difference for African Americans. I contend that the language of regional difference is simply a different set of clothes for the same boundaries of blackness: a "spatialized politics of cultural difference"[37] that roots authentic black identity in African American folk cultures. This, I argue, is the central accomplishment of country cosmopolitanism: a blackness that supplants the divisiveness of the traditional respectability discourse with the familiar but still problematic rhetoric of a unified community, rooted in a southern past.

Concluding the book, I detail emergent and future demographic trends in the South, and in particular in the historic old South, where the black/white paradigm is especially entrenched despite increasing diversity in the region. As the South mints new black southerners through black migration and immigration to the region, what will happen to the identity and culture chasm between rapidly expanding New South urban magnets, rural areas, and the South that is neither old nor new? I also return to a discussion about the place of the South in black identity futures. Further, the conclusion considers how country cosmopolitanism shores up the boundaries of blackness in spite of and because of an increasingly multiethnic blackness, a multiracial America, and the multiracial New South.

CHAPTER ONE

Finding the Black South

"They think we slow, backwards, always at church, always cooking, riding horses because we don't have real roads or cars, farming, saying 'yessuh' and 'yessum' to white folks, and singing and dancing all the time," said forty-four-year-old Marie, an employee of a local media affiliate. Marie described herself as a new southerner, sophisticated, and knowledgeable about world affairs. However, as she bustled about her bright red kitchen baking cookies for a function at her church, she talked about how many people from outside of the South see the region and its inhabitants as trapped in an imagined plantation past. The "they" she referred to includes anybody outside of the South, and specifically her cousins who live in Chicago, who frequently came up in our conversations. When I first met Marie (during an interview with another respondent), she was dashing off to prep her Sunday dinner on a Thursday. As many southerners do out of routine courtesy but perhaps without the fullness of meaning, Marie invited us to that dinner, after which she quickly became one of my key respondents. Whether or not she genuinely wanted us to come to dinner that Sunday, I never asked.

I was sitting in my usual spot in her South Memphis home: a tidy stool at her kitchen's movable island. As usual, the island was covered in flour, which rose and settled as she inadvertently bumped the counter space, transferring cookie dough to a baking sheet. I pointed out the irony of at least part of her assertions—specifically, the ones about southerners always being at church and always cooking—vis-à-vis her current activity. With a "humph," she looked down at her apron, around the kitchen, then down at the cookie sheet, lined with four neat rows of evenly spaced, evenly measured, soon-to-be chocolate chip cookies. As she sent the sheet clattering into the red oven, she retorted: "Well, I ain't never known nobody in Memphis, Tennessee, or anywhere else in the South for that matter to ride a horse to work."

Enduring stereotypes about the South and southerners, like these and others whom Marie and other respondents talked about at length, are the residue of the boundary work between individuals, groups, and places.

The perpetuation of stereotypes and myths about the South is essential to this boundary work. Not only do they accomplish and reify the idea of the South as a distinct place, but they also ensure that the South functions as the polar opposite to the rest of the nation. As Toni Morrison has argued persuasively about the relationship between blackness and whiteness in American culture, the South is constructed as the backdrop against which American national identity is formed and without which it cannot exist. The perpetuation of stereotypes and myths about the region are essential to the construction of the South-as-backdrop. These processes not only accomplish the South as a distinct place but also accomplish the non-South as the region's polar opposite.

Myths about the black South are carefully constructed, undergirding its mysterious pull for migrants, beyond the obvious benefits of warmer weather, a cheaper cost of living, and better employment opportunities. Corporations and cultural elites are especially invested in accomplishing the South as a sacred space, temporally fixed in a simpler moment and imbued with the highest of moral values. As the South is made and remade in the increasingly hypermediated contexts of social media and reality television, myths take on new life, becoming entrenched and more difficult to disentangle from lived experience. This mythmaking occurs in multiple contexts and over several generations, such that the idea of a place becomes rooted in national collective memory. As the nation's region, whose economic, political, and social mores have driven the national consciousness since slavery, the South has often served as a repository for national illness, quarantined, sealed off, and punished in order to maintain a national facade of progress and morality. Similarly, southern cultural products, from the blues to hip-hop, are exported as representative of America's distinct cultural gifts in international contexts. With so many investments in contorting the region in service of national identity, distinguishing the idea of the place (as country, backwards, rural, for instance) from the lived reality of a place (the South that Marie and other respondents said they live in) becomes a Sisyphean exercise.

Respondents in this study reject these negative southern stereotypes and the national weight they carry as fallacious and burdensome. When non-southerners negatively connote "country," respondents are especially incensed and quickly reframe country knowledge as, in fact, cosmopolitan. Marie, for instance, implored the figurative and omnipresent black Yankees not to let her cooking fool them. "Cooking is how the slave women killed many a master and a mistress," she often said, which made me slightly paranoid about eating as much of her food as I did.

Yet, despite their often negative connotations, southern myths are imbued with interpersonal currency, providing individuals with a virtually unending source of social and cultural capital. As I discovered throughout the course of my research, respondents readily traded or cashed in on these myths to legitimate and bolster their claims to a better blackness. For instance, although most post-soul southerners have little direct experience with the kinds and frequency of racial violence visited upon previous generations, they wax knowledgeable about incidents that happened to their parents, grandparents, and first cousins thrice removed. The often third- and fourth-hand nature of the stories accords them myth status, which therefore makes them both irrefutable and unverifiable. Yet, authenticating narratives of white terrorism is less important than understanding how such narratives function and proliferate in the post-soul black southern imagination. Narratives of white racial terror afford the storyteller social and cultural capital. Bearing witness or being proximate to egregious white racism, especially in an era of more subtle (though no less pernicious) color-blind racism, is a rite of passage for black folks. The experience of old-fashioned, overt southern white racism, the stuff of films and history, provides not only a racially authentic experience but also a site through which to claim a robust and resilient blackness.

Narratives of white racism constituted one dimension of respondents' perpetuation of southern myths in exchange for social capital. Respondents often called upon rural folkways, also second- and thirdhand, to cure colds, fix a flat tire, beat the summer heat, and cultivate urban gardens. Sometimes erupting into heated arguments and country competitions—is cod liver oil or castor oil better for this or that ailment?—discussions of rural folkways helped respondents distinguish themselves from each other as well as from their non-southern counterparts. Further, even those respondents who self-identified as atheists or who do not attend church used religious language frequently in discussions, sometimes to cross cultural boundaries but more often to erect a shared culture governed by a higher power, even if everyone is not a believer. Buddhists, Muslims, Christians, and atheists alike called or signified on a cultural Jesus to participate in a shared southern black culture. Still, such discursive moves occurred in specific and delimited contexts. Espousing a certain kind of fervent black southern religiosity could firm intraracial regional boundaries. For instance, southern black megachurches and their often notoriously conservative stance on the rights of women and LGBT communities cause rifts in black political solidarity. Finally, food and culinary metaphor was ubiquitous in respondents' narratives with ample talk of soul food and barbecues.

Respondents worked hardest to perpetuate myths about the superiority of southern cooking. Though Marie took exception to northerners' perceptions of southerners as in a perpetual state of preparing to cook, cooking, and eating, respondents and their friends, uncles, mothers, and cousins were, in fact, often cooking or eating when I encountered them. I returned the courtesy on several occasions when respondents sat for long interviews. Food-as-boundary served as an umbrella for food-related boundary work, from discussions of veganizing traditional soul food dishes to talk of "clean eating" and avoiding the consequences of a traditional soul food diet. Nuances notwithstanding, respondents frequently cited food as a distinct element of black southern identity in our initial discussions. Food, respondents argued, is the ultimate form of social capital, in that it leads to other forms of social capital, including a significant other. Collectively, these myths and respondents' appropriations of them draw on country ideologies, extricating the negative, provincial aspects of country medicine, religion, and food with a cosmopolitan spin and claim to authenticity and superiority.

Yet, beyond the usual myths perpetuated about the black South, like southern blacks being too submissive to whites, well-versed in folk cures, unreasonably beholden to religion, or cooking excessively, very little is known about the intricacies of everyday black cultural life in the South. To reconcile representations of black southern identity and the lived experience of post-soul southerners, I retrace the idea of the black South, and the South as an artifact of black collective memory, in black arts and letters and black public culture. Behind the heavy doors of the region's closed society,[1] what were the features of black cultural life? Over the course of the Great Migration, how did black southern cultures differ from the cultures of black southern diasporas rapidly proliferating in the metropolises of the West, Northeast, and Midwest? How did changes in the region ushered in by the civil rights era affect how black southerners conceptualized and expressed regional identity? Moreover, how were cultural differences and cultural change represented in popular media and academic research?

To answer these questions and locate "missing" black South(s), this chapter begins with a discussion of the place of region in African American identity. Next, I uncover the discursive black South as it has been produced and consumed by myriad publics, especially African American publics. By traversing the black South(s) popularized in the American imagination by literature, art, dance, film, music, and television, I elucidate the narratives emergent from and in the name of the black South and the function of such narratives for black identities historically and contemporarily. Finally, I show how processes of place accomplishment and regional representation inform post-soul southern identity.

Region, Race, and Native Black Identity

Like other axes of identity and difference, region and regional distinction can be difficult to measure empirically because of contested boundaries, definitions, and changes over time. Endless debates over the "real South"— what geographically and culturally counts as the South, whether the region is a "state of mind" rather than a geographically located place, and who can legitimately be called a southerner—make complicated work of locating the region in popular memory and imagination. Is Kentucky in the South? Or is Washington, D.C.? Is the South all states below the Mason-Dixon Line? States that seceded from the Union? Or states that owned slaves? Because of the "Southernization of America,"[2] is the "South" a uniquely American state of mind that exists all over the nation, beyond the geographic and historical boundaries of region? If one were to answer these questions based on the plethora of how-to guides on the market, from *A Southern Belle Primer* to *The Grits (Girls Raised in the South) Guide to Life*, southern identity is merely performative, something to be taken on and off like a set of clothes, and therefore easily achievable by anyone who can follow directions and make clearly delineated, distinctively southern choices. Further, the historical obfuscations, what Tara McPherson calls "lenticular logic," upon which white southern memory, culture, and identity are based, are increasingly being called into question.[3]

In popular media contexts and everyday life, African American southerners are less concerned with whether or not the South exists, or whether or not it is bounded on the north by the Mason-Dixon Line or, as Malcolm X suggested, by the U.S.-Canadian border. Further, unlike their white counterparts, African Americans are not generally reconciling their identities with a reconstructed history. That is, while white guilt complicates white folks' abilities to confront a troubled racial, regional, and national past that includes slavery, lynch mobs, and Jim Crow, these facts of black life and histories have been integrated into African American and diasporic black identities more broadly. Still, as a physical and geographical source of racial shame, some African Americans' relationship to the South is tenuous and rife with discomfort. Images that have come to signify racial subservience, like Aunt Jemima and Uncle Tom, give particular regional significance to flying accusations of "cooning," such as those lodged against Tyler Perry by Spike Lee or against southern hip-hop artists by their East and West Coast counterparts.

Even in interregional jest, blacks from outside of the South often characterize the region as a place where folks have yet to receive the memo about emancipation. This is especially the case in non-southerners' strategic forgetting of the South's urban centers, supplanting southern cities with the supposedly wide, easy fields of a rapidly disappearing rural landscape. Such critiques are more prominent today, as the growing success of the black South challenges the hegemony of Harlem, South Side Chicago, and Oakland as central disseminators of authentic black culture. Ultimately, while black and white southerners' qualms with the region are different, they are nonetheless similarly wrapped up in powerful discourses about identity in the post–civil rights—or as Michael Kreyling has termed it (implicitly for whites), "postsouthern"—South.[4]

In and through the idea of the South, African Americans can cultivate a native black identity, a static reference point for black culture—and the limits of authentic blackness—in the United States and beyond. This native black identity is grounded in processes of racial formation, which compel the development of shared political strategies and social practices in response to structural conditions. In response to how blackness is constructed in legal, sociopolitical, and popular media contexts, sets of performative ideals for native black identity are formed. Informed by the construction of blackness, these performances cull together historical and contemporary tropes of authentic blackness to create an authentic self that can serve as recognizable shorthand for "black American."

A host of assumptions constitute a native black identity. First, a native black identity is predicated upon the enslavement of one's ancestors in the American South, especially in the historical Black Belt that included the Arkansas and Mississippi Deltas, Louisiana, Alabama, and Georgia. Second, native blacks are distinguished by their experience of and connection to the Jim Crow South. Third, traditions of resistance, rooted in Protestantism and Old Testament religiosity, are central to native black identity. Specifically, these resistance traditions are embodied by social and collective memories of slavery and the civil rights movement. The cultural products that emerge from these collective memories and experiences, including gospel, blues, jazz, rhythm and blues, and soul, also factor prominently into a native black identity. These shared assumptions about what constitutes a native, or authentic, black American identity lead to innumerable conclusions about what black is and what black ain't, as well as about what black people do and do not do. When black folks fall out of these boxes of conclusions—by being lesbian or gay, experiencing mental illness, looking for the murdering maniac in the woods or following the

suspicious sound instead of running away like stereotypical black characters in a horror film, or playing in an indie rock band—they fall out of the
confines of native black identity. Because of the complexity of individual
identity intersections and social tastes, most African Americans must work
diligently to stay put or to jump into native blackness. This is a constraining truth even for those who are culturally closest to this native blackness:
black southerners.

Whether the performance is of native black identity, southern black
identity, or southern black identity as native black identity, negotiations
and theorizations of racial and regional identity are also deeply rooted
in African American signifying practices. As such, they are sincere in another way—as true, genuine presentations of thoughts, actions, and feelings that exist beyond the measurement boundaries of authenticity. While
respondents like Ruth Ann, who claimed, "We just do things better down
here," might explicitly reject the notion of performance, they are nonetheless aware of cultural differences that render them distinct from their
non-southern counterparts. They are, then, sure to point to something that
lends their southern presentations of self some verisimilitude, especially in
mixed company. In practice, this kind of boundary work erects a relatively
rigid dichotomy that reduces non-southern, or northern, to a monolith
category and virtually ignores the diasporic reach of the South, cultivated
over several generations of migration out of the region. Most of my respondents believe wholeheartedly in the negatively transformative power
of the city, or the North, on black identity, experience, and authenticity
and therefore invalidate their northern kin's version of blackness, even if
they are only up the road in Chicago. Respondents construct a north, or a
"No'f," to account for everywhere else but the South, even if directionally
the place in question is due west. Its geographic inaccuracy notwithstanding, this construction of a monolith North functions as an important symbolic boundary for respondents as well as for popular culture elites to draw
distinctions in worldviews and identity outcomes. I was careful to challenge my respondents' monolith rendering of the non-South and to treat
such renderings as indicative of a particular southern worldview—one that
privileges conceptions of a racial homeland, proximity to civil rights traditions, and expressions of native black identity.

Burying the South

"The South is always hot," Keith, a thirty-two-year-old high school English teacher, told me on the front porch of a soul music café in midtown

Memphis. Indeed, the July heat was bothering even me a bit (and I generally pride myself on withstanding the summer humidity from the Mississippi River). Keith, however, was not talking about the weather. He was "learning" me on the ongoing significance of the South in African American culture. He continued: "The Harlem Renaissance? Southern stories stolen from the South made to seem like they were native to Harlem Negroes' experience. Gospel, blues, jazz, funk, soul? The South. Dance? The South. [Alvin] Ailey? The South. Hip-hop? The South. Atlanta? The South."

Keith is a key respondent and a native Memphian who grew up in a predominantly black community in the shadows of Elvis Presley's palatial Graceland home and tourist hotspot. After attending a historically black college, Keith returned to his high school alma mater to teach English. I met him early on in my research on the local hip-hop scene, where he often stalked the crowd, offering up little-known and sometimes dubious southern hip-hop facts. This was not the first time I had heard Keith's lecture on the regional origins of black culture, and I often countered his arguments with Malcolm X's sentiment about the Canadian border, not the Mason-Dixon Line, being the real regional boundary for black Americans. This was the first time, however, that I witnessed Keith rehearsing his lesson in front of a non-southerner, Hasan, the lone café worker. I braced myself for his next discursive move.

I began to point out that technically, Atlanta's southernness has not been stolen or overlooked, despite some evidence to the contrary. After all, Atlanta prided itself for many decades on being in the South but not of it, being "too busy to hate," unlike the rest of its regional counterparts. Before I could launch into my usual, now half-hearted, rebuttal to "learn" Keith, Hasan, who had been not-so-inconspicuously eavesdropping as he bused, wiped, and rewiped the other two tables on the tiny porch, interrupted us. Unable to take anymore, Hasan blurted out, "Now tell me just how hip-hop came from the *South*?" Keith, who I knew had been anxiously anticipating the challenge, quickly and dramatically inhaled and proceeded to "learn" the Bedford-Stuyvesant-born Hasan with a trip through black music history, from West Africa to Atlanta crunk rapper and producer Lil' Jon. After Keith recited several field hollers that he claimed were from Mississippi's notorious Parchman Farm penitentiary, Hasan was so visibly outdone by the comedy that his shoulders shook and his eyes began to water, and when he finally let out his reserved burst of laughter at the end of Keith's lecture, Hasan fell to the ground, saucer in hand.

This exchange was one of many such exchanges I witnessed or engaged in, as southerners and non-southerners debated the South's place—and merits and credits—in African American culture. Despite the predictable heat, the South is not always hot, nor has it always been. Its co-optation during the Harlem Renaissance and Zora Neale Hurston's corpus notwithstanding, the South, as an idea, place, and product, spent most of the twentieth century being escaped from and condemned by African Americans than it spent being praised and warmly remembered. In fact, African Americans participated directly in the burying of the South, deliberately forgetting the region to shut out memories of racism and degradation and the shame of country life, greenness, and backwardness. To be "New Negroes," African Americans needed desperately to shed the vestiges of southern life, where the specter of slavery lived on in sharecropping, black codes, and Jim Crow.

The burial of the South presented a seeming dichotomy for black identity: either black folks would continue as their unreconstructed folk selves, or they would erase such selves in favor of a thoroughly modern entity absent its provincial folkness. These opposing sides have come to be epitomized by appropriations of the epistemic differences between authors Zora Neale Hurston and Richard Wright in black arts and letters.

Substantively, Wright and Hurston represented two ends of the spectrum of African American southern experience in the early twentieth-century South, and therefore their differences were far more personal and epistemological than the notion of an "intellectual debate" can encapsulate. Though Wright was critical of the state of affairs for African Americans across the country and for people of African descent globally, his personal relationship with the South rendered his critiques of the region and of black folks in the region especially caustic.[5] For Wright, the South was a source of shame and helplessness, the site of the ultimate denial of black humanity. Conversely, Hurston's free-spirited (if measured) upbringing in the all-black and relatively autonomous Eatonville focused her attentions on the power and knowledge of black folk life. As such, she was more likely to see African American life as comprising many problems, interests, and concerns, with race and racism forming just one dimension. In her 1938 essay "Art and Such," Hurston famously wrote: "Negroes love and hate and fight and play and strive and travel and have a thousand and one interests in life like other humans. When his baby cuts a new tooth, he brags as shamelessly as anyone else without once weeping over the prospect of some Klansman knocking it out if and when the child ever gets grown."[6] Here, Hurston decries the "race first" position popularized by early twentieth-century race men and women, advocating instead for an interpretation of black life that considered black humanity like all other cultural groups of human beings and not as a response to racism but rather as a complex and actualized ontology.

Conversely, Wright's narrative about his mother's response to his boyhood battle with a white child recounted in the 1937 essay "The Ethics of Living Jim Crow" directly contradicts Hurston's assertion that race and racism were not chief concerns of black folks. Wright sustained an injury requiring stitches during this childhood fight and felt that a "grave injustice" had been done him. When he recounted the story to his mother, in search of sympathy, she whipped him until he had a fever, all the while imparting to him "gems of Jim Crow wisdom." He contends that he remembers the once calming, lush space of the battle as a "symbol of fear": "From that time on, the charm of my cinder yard was gone. The green trees, the trimmed hedges, the cropped lawns grew very meaningful, became a symbol. Even today when I think of white folks, the hard, sharp outlines of white houses surrounded by trees, lawns, and hedges are present somewhere in the background of my mind. Through the years they grew into an overreaching symbol of fear."[7] For Wright, the very pastoral scenes that constituted the backdrop of black life in Hurston's South signified white racism, shame, and a hegemonic, uncritical blackness that reinforced the rules of Jim Crow through equally unkind emotional and physical violence.[8]

The dimensions of the disagreements between Hurston and Wright, and what they have come to mean for African American literature and life, have been mined at length.[9] As William J. Maxwell points out, the debate is often called up in black arts and letters to serve as "shorthand and ballast for imagined dichotomies between black rural and urban selves and cultures and the affiliated binaries of the South and North, folk and mass, all energized in the wake of twentieth-century migration."[10] That country and cosmopolitan, and all that those poles signify, could not exist simultaneously is reductive, reflecting anxieties about the place of the South in African American life and culture, first after slavery and later after Jim Crow. Still, this reduction endures in the language and performance of regional distinction employed by African Americans across regional and ethnic backgrounds. Respondents in this study challenge this dichotomy in their negotiations and integration of country and cosmopolitan worldviews.

Indeed, as Maxwell implies, the dichotomy between rural and urban that Hurston and Wright symbolize is socially constructed. However, the fact that the rural-urban dichotomy is a construction does not diminish its significance. Moreover, processes of the construction of rural and urban difference make it more difficult to disentangle from collective memory, boundary work, and racial and regional identities. Ultimately, at least in the black public sphere, Wright's urban, cosmopolitan perspectives triumphed. Modern, urban, and northern selves came to represent better black selves, while southernness signified at best an undesirable blackness and at worst a failed one. As black southern identity became more of a buried, distant memory for folks outside of the South, Wright's position became the legitimate articulation of black American identity, of black responses to racism, and of blacks' relationship to the South.

Wrightian notions of black identity were especially prominent during that critical moment of shifting identities and people between the immediate postwar period and the victories of the civil rights era. In Wright's famous introduction to Horace Cayton and St. Clair Drake's *Black Metropolis*, he makes clear this shift in black identity from the rural spaces like his native home near Natchez, Mississippi, to the urban Black Belt of Chicago. After Wright's *Black Boy*, several autobiographies situating the South as the "scene of the crime" and black southerners as "refugees" repackaged the slave narrative for postwar America.[11] As for Hurston, several forces, from her own personal misfortunes to the radicalizing tide in African American political and cultural expression, challenged the authority of her positions on the South, black identities, and the relationship between black identities and black southern, or folk, cultures. The continuous and public nature of white violence against blacks, as well as blatant racial inequality, made her stances on segregation—that blacks should remain segregated, as they could thrive in segregated spaces—and other issues seem untenable.

James Baldwin's and Ralph Ellison's critiques of Wright notwithstanding,[12] the latter's narrative of a Sartrean[13] struggle against an oppressor resonated with postwar African American publics, including southerners. When both Hurston and Wright died in 1960, Wright's escape from the South and eventual expatriation was being narrated and re-narrated in African American writers' autobiographical condemnation of the South, in sociological research on blacks in the urban North, and in an emergent form of social and racial protest that was increasingly located in urban locales, in and beyond the South. Hurston's sense of the rural folk had all but disappeared from black writing. The folk had largely vanished from national black public consciousness, as if those people no longer existed save as the subaltern oppressed disconnected from the larger freedom struggles erupting all over the nation.[14] Rurality in general, even the rural-folk-in-urban-space tropes that dominated migration narratives, had dissipated in African American arts and letters. Ultimately, the South and all its concomitant markers of backwardness were effectively buried between World War II and the major advances of the civil rights movement. Yet, after the movement, rurality, rural folks, and rural space, serving as proxies for the entire region, would return with a steadfastness and endurance fueled by cultural anxieties about the place of region and race in modern America.

The South Shall Rise Again

On the third day after Zora Neale Hurston's death on January 28, 1960, the author and her notion of the folk were resurrected. The inaugural performance of dancer and choreographer Alvin Ailey's *Revelations* was January 31, 1960, at Kaufmann Concert Hall, housed in the Ninety-Second Street Young Men's Hebrew Association in New York City, not far from the Harlem in which Hurston had spent her formative years with the "Niggerati." Even as the South was still being buried in film, literature, autobiography, sociology, and black public consciousness, *Revelations* boldly began a tradition of regional remembrance, reclamation, and accomplishment that persists in African American culture. The South's resurgence in African American social memory and public consciousness can be attributed to the reclamative powers of cultural products like *Revelations*. Reclamation processes entailed the myriad strategies black culture producers began to use in the 1960s on a national scale to resurrect staple notions of the South, and rurality and religiosity in particular. Beyond reclamation, accomplishment consisted of those culture producers' deliberate and sometimes exaggerative performances of southern identity and culture, as well as of their exaltations of the goodness, and in some cases the superiority, of their southern rearing. Through *Revelations* and other cultural products of the South's rise, Hurston's legacy and interpretations of the black cultural gifts of the folk were constructed as legitimate articulations of black identity, linking African Americans to a regional homeland and an originary set of folk cultural practices. After the successes of the civil rights movement began to lift the region's veil, opening it to the nation, the cultural products of the southern turn were able to universalize the southern experience, in effect nationalizing what had previously been seen as a geographically bound culture. Ultimately, the southern turn in black culture created a lexicon of regionalized racial tropes that have become synonymous with the black American experience writ large. Just as the nation had been southernized,[15] black America was undergoing a public, discursive, and demographic southernization. African Americans were turning South, and those who were already South took new pride in their positions as bearers of the cultural and spiritual roots of black America.

Unlike successful African American dance pieces that preceded it, including Pearl Primus's *Strange Fruit* and Talley Beatty's *Southern Landscapes*, Ailey's *Revelations* does not directly or exclusively confront and mourn white southern violence against blacks.[16] Rather, in Ailey's imagining, the South is a dynamic threshing floor for black American culture. Based on the choreographer's experiences and remembrances of his rearing in a small town in 1930s Texas, *Revelations* reclaims the southern experience, resurrecting the black South through dance, gospel music, and cultural signifying. Although Ailey spent his adolescent years in Los Angeles and his adulthood in New York, it was his southern experiences that he looked back to and from which he drew the inspiration for *Revelations*. As Thomas F. DeFrantz notes, "*Revelations* mapped rural southern spirituality onto the concert dance stage," and Ailey's memories of the South were strategically recalled and reshaped to narrate an authentic African American experience.[17] While the use of spirituals in black concert dance was not novel by the time *Revelations* debuted, Ailey's strategic use of spirituals to accomplish a distinctively southern black identity was. In a 1961 interview in *Dance and Dancers* magazine, Ailey recounted his childhood memories of the Baptist Church in Texas, which included "baptismals by tree-shrouded lakes, in a lake where an ancient alligator was supposed to have lived—the holy rollers' tambourines shrieking in the Texas night."[18] The imagery Ailey utilized, both in his choreography and in written and verbal recollections in various interviews, spoke directly to and rendered mystical a rural southern black experience. The wide popularity of Ailey's work, especially *Revelations*, and its popularity among black audiences across the country universalized the black southern experience as the black American experience. Further, as the Alvin Ailey brand has since been extended worldwide as representative of American cultural life, black southern cultural life stands in for black American life more generally. Through Ailey, generations of African American migrants from the South were compelled to contend with the buried facets of black American identity in its expressive folk form. For all of the trappings of modernity that had marked black American identity in the years since slavery, the black public sphere acknowledged a history of rurality; in effect, black America had been a country Lou Bessie, masquerading as a cosmopolitan Charmaine.[19]

While Ailey, a southerner living abroad, as it were, had to reclaim a childhood rooted in the mystery of rural southern spirituality, black folks living continuously in the South did not need to reach back so far to reclaim an abandoned identity. Indeed, for black folks living in the South between World War II and the civil rights movement, when anti-South sentiment abounded, the South was not buried or lost but the social, cultural, and geographic backdrop of a lived experience that they actively shaped. Southern rhythm and blues artists certainly sought to redefine the soundscapes of African American life as their blues predecessors had done in previous generations. They articulated a distinctly southern black experience that blended gospel and blues traditions and the sound of civil rights struggle through wa-wa guitars, rhythm sections' snapping snares, and the wails of Aretha Franklin, Otis Redding, Al Green, and a host of others. Because these artists had never buried the South, their cultural production was less an act of regional reclamation and more a reclamation of their right to speak as southerners, African Americans, and co-creators of regional and national cultures. Further, they reclaimed their right to speak as purveyors of a modern blackness that did not need to excise rurality from southern identity to be more progressive. Rejecting the notion of southerners as cultural dupes who were "singing and dancing all the time," soul artists recast southerners as instrumental in the political and cultural struggles of African American communities.

In the way Ailey's *Revelations* stood in the gap for a buried black experience and constructed a collective African American memory of the South as homeland, southern R&B artists' production of a regional brand of soul quickly began to define the general black American experience. By the 1970s, southern soul had become synonymous with the black freedom struggle, the veritable national soundtrack of hope, promise, and racial pride.[20] Its connection to the black masses, evidenced through unvarnished presentations of self and sound, rendered it a gritty, proletarian alternative to the spit and polish of Detroit's Motown. Indeed, it was the Stax sound, a product of Memphis artists' blending of the best of surrounding rural communities and a southern urban zeitgeist, that in 1972 served as the sound of black political struggle in Watts, Los Angeles.

While the Wattstax music festival is remembered today as a seminal cultural moment in the black American experience, it was the distinctly regional brand of black southern soul music—from Isaac Hayes to the Staple Singers—that served as the soundtrack of black protest, frustration, and political and existential struggle in the 1960s. Organized by Stax records to commemorate the 1965 Watts riots, Wattstax was not only a display of inter-regional racial solidarity but also the South's assertion of national, rather than regional, black importance on the heels of the gains of the "southern" civil rights movement. Documented in Mel Stuart's 1973 documentary *Wattstax*, performances of "Old Time Religion," the theme from *Shaft*, and Rufus Thomas's indomitable funky chicken, among others, coalesced to bond southern soul to black Los Angeles in sociopolitical and cultural solidarity. Soul music was the South's gift offering to urban locales beyond the region that had been besieged by police brutality, dwindling resources, and increasing violence and marginalization. Moreover, soul music combined the sounds of urban and rural struggle, from Selma and Memphis to Lowndes County and Clarksdale, as an authoritative and proven soundscape of resistance. Perennial screenings of *Wattstax* at Memphis museums solidify this bond, encouraging younger southerners into continuing their service as soul ambassadors to the rest of the country.

Like the blues artists before them, a generation of soul artists had gained recognition on national and international stages, taking over popular music. Yet, the clearest sign of the South's rise could be found in African American literature. Like Ailey and the soul artists, African American writers began to reclaim the region, penning narratives that were substantively distinct from the urban coming-of-age narratives that constituted much of the black literary landscape in the postwar era. Onita Estes-Hicks points out that beginning in the late 1960s, the African American autobiographical tradition underwent a thematic shift. A wholly evil and incorrigible South transformed into a site of productive tensions between good and evil, becoming a place remembered fondly by its black sons and daughters and a home space to be reclaimed.[21]

In and beyond autobiographical writings, black southern authors' reclamation of the South occurred most directly through a rediscovery of Zora Neale Hurston as a southern black feminist mother. Alice Walker's 1975 essay "In Search of Zora Neale Hurston" stimulated a rescue and reclamation of Hurston that then, too, became part of the broader rise of the South in African American public consciousness. Gradually dispensing with the "shame" of their southern pasts, African American writers who came of age in the South attempted to demonstrate the inherent value of that rearing and experience—including distinct life lessons gleaned only because of the region's particular racial past and present and its rich, enduring folk life—without explicitly romanticizing the region. Five years before publishing the seminal black womanist essay on her physical and figurative search for Hurston, Walker reflected on her southern rearing to discuss the gifts the black writer from the South must render to American literature. She wrote, "No one could wish for a more advantageous heritage than that bequeathed to the black writer in the South: a compassion for the earth, a trust in humanity beyond our knowledge of evil, and an abiding love of justice. We inherit a great responsibility as well, for we must give voices to centuries not only of silent bitterness and hate but also of neighborly kindness and sustaining love."[22]

Although Walker asserts that she does not "intend to romanticize southern black country life,"[23] her reclamation hints at nostalgia, which requires some element of romance, even if that romance is critical. Specifically, Walker's reflection looks back toward a generally segregated, rural black existence to embrace both the "bitterness and hate" and "neighborly kindness and sustaining love" of a black southern experiential and epistemic position. Walker and others are quite deliberate in delineating the boundaries of the South being reclaimed. Theirs is a black folk South, one in which white people exist and are undoubtedly oppressive, but their presence is relatively tangential to everyday African American cultural life— that is, a South in which, as Hurston said, black folks might have been excited about their babies' first teeth without contemplating the possible fate of those teeth as a result of white racial violence. In this literary formulation, cosmopolitanism is not rooted in living in a southern city. Instead, cosmopolitanism, within a rural context, is the ability to survive, thrive, and subvert white racism through dissemblance, tricksterism, signifying, and rural, folk wit.

In addition to reclamation work, black writers defended the region from monolithically negative representations, particularly those that had become prominent in African American public consciousness through escape-from-the-South narratives. In 1974, Addison Gayle criticized the Black Aesthetic Movement of the 1960s for what he saw as its conscious erasure of the black southern experience from black arts and letters. He implored black artists, and black writers in particular, to "reclaim the southern experience," both defending the region and challenging dominant African American constructions of the South as a space and place to which out-migrants should and/or could never return.[24]

As the southward flow of African Americans became noticeable and the region continued its slow trudge toward desegregation after *Brown v. Board of Education*, conversations about this newer, post–civil rights South were also beginning to happen in popular black media. In August 1971, *Ebony* magazine, the premier African American monthly, published a special issue on the emerging post–civil rights South, which editors called simply "The South Today." The cover of the issue features the theme in bold letters over two contrasting pictures. The top picture is a sketch of rural black slaves or sharecroppers, clad in tattered farmers' clothing and headscarves, hunched over and trudging along on what seems an endless journey. In the distance, a white male figure with raised whip appears to drive the line forward. The bottom picture, serving as a directly contrasting image, is a photograph of young men and women with Afros, peace necklaces, kente cloth, and books in hand. The cover is a pictorial depiction of the tensions in country cosmopolitanism but does not allow the viewer to imagine a scenario in which the slaves/sharecroppers and black pride youth might be one and the same. Instead, the line and movement of the slaves/sharecroppers indicates progression *from* country to cosmopolitan, from white oppression to black self-actualization. Ultimately, the cover signifies a shift, actual and symbolic, in the culture, politics, and economics of the South as a result of the Great Migration and the civil rights and Black Power movements. Southern blacks had been transformed, the cover art asserts, although they had not become New Negroes until half a century after their Harlem brethren. Through their transformation from country to cosmopolitan, the cover argues, the region had changed as well.

In his publisher's statement, John H. Johnson lays out the rationale for the issue. After asserting that "nearly all blacks in the North, Midwest, and West are only one generation from the South," Johnson contends that "with the legal maneuvering almost complete and the long-sought civil rights laws firmly on the records, many blacks are looking backward to the land of their birth. They are wondering what the South is really like today. In this issue, we are trying to tell them."[25] Although Johnson's assertion is not entirely statistically accurate, he captures a broad perception of a sizable southern diaspora that emerged under duress as blacks migrated to other regions. Further, Johnson implies both a literal and figurative birthplace; the cover's depiction of slavery conjures a common, shared origin land for all African Americans. As a medium with a national black audience, Johnson used *Ebony* to bridge the gap between the black South and African American communities in other regions, including emerging generations of people with few direct ties to the region. Specifically, the *Ebony* issue functioned to journalistically exhume the South, to put to rest rumors about whether or not the region really was a "new" South.

The *Ebony* issue paints the South in broad and middle-class strokes, challenging dominant discourses about the South like those articulated by my respondent Marie's cousins and by escape narratives like those ushered in by Richard Wright's *Black Boy*. It erects a normative, universal black South that signals a burgeoning country cosmopolitanism—a black South that is at once distinct from and better than the black urban North but nonetheless "down home." The issue theorizes the existence of the newest New South in relation to the succession of New Souths that began with Reconstruction; cites black elites from Julian Bond to Fannie Lou Hamer who implore blacks to "remigrate" and "come home"; presents articles on intellectuals, business leaders, and professionals of the South; discusses the southward migration of industry; addresses black ambivalence about the South and skepticism about the actual newness of this latest New South; and introduces the most savory of "classic" southern foods, from kidney stew to creole jambalaya. An article on the diversity of the beauty of "Southern Belles" proclaims that black southern women, "renowned for their warm, earthy, and full-bodied appearance . . . possess a charm and sophistication rarely found elsewhere."[26] The issue trades on now-familiar tropes of black southernness rooted in food, manners, and gender performances and presentations of self.

Letters to the editor regarding "The South Today," printed in the October 1971 issue of *Ebony*, were overwhelmingly positive, reflecting black migrants' continued interest in the South and black southerners' efforts to confirm that, indeed, the South had changed. Yet, precisely *how* the South had changed for African Americans, and the complicated politics of the shift, were less evident. The cultural and everyday dimensions of the post-soul South were obscured by several factors.

The first set of factors was a product of the epistemology of academic scholarship in the 1970s. Historians turned to diligently documenting the recent history of civil rights struggles in the newly opened society, and sociologists were at work making sense of the vast changes in urban America caused by migration and immigration to America's largest, and incidentally non-southern, cities.[27] Thus, overwhelmingly, historians focused on the civil rights movement, rather than on social histories of the everyday and cultural lives of African American southerners. Historians have continued to produce compelling scholarship on the civil rights movement, which frequently ends chronologically where the New South begins. Similarly, sociologists, who had followed migrating lines of African Americans north and west, focused on African American cultural life outside of the South. As such, investigations of post-soul southern black identities and experiences were largely absent from the scholarship of historians and sociologists in the years following the civil rights movement.

The second set of factors was a product of the metanarrative of the South that began to be mass-produced in the 1960s and 1970s. A veritable southern culture industrial complex worked diligently to shape the perception of the region to attract investors and reconfigure the South as the nation's region, the one most representative of American ideals on the global stage, politically, economically, and culturally. The elite political interests of a rising white "silent majority" shifted the regional strategy away from virulent racism to a relatively benign strategy designed to maintain white privilege and preserve the Old South. Middle-class and elite southerners, black and white, constructed the region as a repository for real American values, touting the dignity of working people as a selling point to attract business to the region. Together, this cultural, economic, and political strategy bolstered New South rhetoric even as historically disenfranchised populations, the poor and racial and ethnic minorities, experienced increased socioeconomic and political disadvantages over time.

Non-elite Americans also participated in the expansion of the discursive metanarrative of the South as America's region. Dave Thomas's simple, down-home burgers and fries, Cracker Barrel's authentic cooking like somebody's mama used to make, and an expanding and commodified country music genre were symptoms of the nation's anxieties about late modernity. As some rural areas and small towns were redefined and incorporated into expanding southern metropolises, and still others struggled to compete for the financial and human resources to maintain a viable economic base, Americans collectively turned to tropes of rurality to erect spaces safe from the increasingly alienating and diverse forces of a rapidly changing world.

Certainly the broadening of the South's industrial base and the expansion of the U.S. government's investment in the region, processes begun in earnest after World War II, were evidence of a materially New South, beyond the narrative and catchy slogans. However, because the region's new opportunities were not universally or evenly distributed, increased prosperity for all was short-lived. The economic realities of the deindustrializing urban North, uneven gains in the South, and new manifestations of the old racial order, though, only fueled the production of an alternative, mythical South. New South boosterism in the 1980s situated the region's troubled history as an asset, emphasized interracial cooperation, and highlighted the shared cultural histories of blacks and whites through food, family, and religion. The emergence of black political power in the urban South, coupled with the expansion of black wealth in the region, corroborated this new characterization of the region.

In service of this New South narrative, which said nothing of the South's still disproportionately lower spending on education or its enduring poverty or high levels of incarceration, elite southerners across race and ethnic boundaries attributed the region's success to natural and historical characteristics. Better weather and the beauty of natural landscapes, the narrative went, produced more pleasant people and congenial conditions for interracial progress. Coming from a broadly agrarian past, southerners were hardworking and honest, which made factory relocation to the region a natural match between employer and employee base. Interracial honesty and forthrightness, rather than the unspoken racism of the urban North meant better race relations. Southern mores and culture were distinctly American, reflective of the enduring American spirit in spite of homogenization and globalization.

In black public consciousness, a different set of narratives, forwarded by black cultural elites, emerged. These narratives served specific racial and regional authenticity and identity goals. First, the South's natural landscapes and place as the ancestral landing ground of most black Americans during slavery made it African Americans' closest connection to the earth, to Africa, and to a legitimate notion of *home*. These landscapes, from the Mississippi River to the red clay earth of the Carolina piedmont to the piney woods of Texas, keep black folks across class rooted, protected, and connected. As African Americans returned south to a black American homeland, emergent regional differences, questions about authentic black identities, and increasing income and wealth gaps served as the backdrop for a grand mythologizing of the black South. Despite and because of critical questions about the complexities of class, gender, race, and southern identity in the post–civil rights era, middle-class black Americans were especially invested in flattening intraracial distinctions.

Second, by contrasting urban and rural landscapes and situating the latter as a refuge from the former, the ills of urban life, including poverty and the hubris brought on by success in the big city, were effectively contained. Black southerners' tireless work, both remunerative work and emotional and moral labor for their communities, was held up as the missing communal piece in black progress. While "making a way out of no way" or "a dollar out of fifteen cents" are mantras of struggle across region and race, the black South discursively claimed a premium on triumph through struggle, with the civil rights movement as its key and unsurpassable precedent. Finally, black southern cultural norms of Christian religiosity, politeness, close family connections, and soulful dispositions were held in stark contrast to a post–civil rights generation of black folks increasingly disconnected from normative race, region, religion, and gender norms: femininity and masculinity, Jesus, family, singing and dancing, and community and racial responsibility.

These narratives about black southernness vis-à-vis other forms of blackness are now as ubiquitous as narratives about white southern girls in sundresses sipping sweet tea. Although they are contested, evidenced by, if nothing else, broad and loud African American objections to Tyler Perry's representations of black folks, these narratives nonetheless form a powerful discursive fabric that complicates attempts to research and represent the diversity of black folks' lived experiences in and of the South. I turn now to a discussion of how hegemonic narratives of the black South are articulated and maintained in films about the black South, as well as how alternative representations of the South (that both challenge and affirm these narratives) have emerged as black southerners make sense of shifting regional and racial boundaries and identities.

Reel Southern Blackness

The black South that emerged in the post-soul moment is a product of tensions between boomers and hip hoppers; natives, returners, and newcomers; country-ness and cosmopolitanism; and the mediated South and the lived experience of the South. Amid these tensions, however, a dominant vision of the South as a better space for African Americans emerged. Nowhere was this vision more prevalent than in a series of films that focused on the black South, beginning with Julie Dash's 1991 *Daughters of the Dust*.[28]

Expanding the boundaries of the South as text to the film medium, black South film sought to reckon with modernity, urban disinvestment, and the contradictions of the post–civil rights era through (re)imaginings of tropes of the rural South. While Dash's *Daughters* sought to think through a forgotten South like the literature of the "southern turn" in the 1970s, by the late 1990s, black South film turned decidedly toward not only reclaiming the South but also asserting an authentic and better blackness. *Down in the Delta* (1998), directed by Maya Angelou, *Tyler Perry's Madea's Family Reunion* (2006), *Tyler Perry's Meet the Browns* (2008), and Malcolm D. Lee's *Welcome Home Roscoe Jenkins* (2008) situate the South as the optimal regenerative space for African Americans disconnected from their roots, alienated by the urban condition, or victimized by underemployment and poverty. These films collectively articulate a different, and in some cases better, more authentic blackness, drawing on black southern tropes like family, history, feminine power, and the land/earth and community to make their claims.

To establish this better blackness, many of these films actively juxtapose modern, urban life, embodied most often by Chicago's South Side, with good, if anachronistic, rural blackness, usually epitomized by a maternal home on sprawling and lush land. *Down in the Delta* and *Meet the Browns* in particular both take a dysfunctional black family from a dysfunctional South Side Chicago ghetto to re-center them—providing them spiritual healing, closure, and lessons in morals and the importance of family and community—in and through the rural South.

A year after Theodore Witcher's *Love Jones* presented a buppie Chicago of jazz and spoken word lounges, record stores, lake shots, steppers' sets, and elevated and Amtrak trains, *Down in the Delta* presented a different kind of Chicago, one of sterile housing projects, rampant drug use and dealing, poverty, and violence. Yet *Down in the Delta* is not a critique of urban disinvestment and structural racism. Instead, the film utilizes Chicago to critique the entire Great Migration project, and the non-South and urban life more generally. The protagonists are the Sinclairs, a product of the Great Migration to Chicago from the Mississippi Delta after World War II. The matriarch, Rosa Lynn, left the South after the death of her husband and spent her working years in Chicago as a domestic laborer, presumably in white homes. Her adult daughter, Loretta, played by Alfre Woodard, is unemployed and the single parent of two children. She frequently abuses alcohol and drugs to cope with the abandonment of the children's father, her daughter's autism, and her ineffectualness as a parent and adult. Loretta's son, Thomas, a preteen, serves in tandem with Rosa Lynn as a maternal figure. He cares for his younger sister and earns money for the household, which he hides from Loretta lest it be used to purchase drugs, by snapping pictures of Chicago tourists with his instant camera. In their cramped Chicago apartment, daughter Tracy, beyond her toddler years, screams almost incessantly from her crib and drinks from a bottle, which Loretta fills with soda to quiet her. Thomas and Rosa Lynn encourage Loretta to apply for a cashier position at a neighborhood grocery store, but the interview ends abruptly when Loretta cannot perform simple arithmetic calculations. Discouraged, Loretta goes on a drug and alcohol binge, and when Rosa Lynn finds her, she decides to send the family to the Delta for the summer to stay with her brother, Earl.

Over the course of their Greyhound bus trip to and through the South, the landscape changes from cacophonous urban poverty to quiet rural bliss, an immediate juxtaposition of North and South that obscures the black middle class in the urban North and the prevalence of southern black poverty. The juxtaposition is also embodied by polar character differences. While Rosa Lynn has moved to Chicago, lives in a veritable urban war zone, and has a daughter incapable of improving the life chances of her fatherless children, her brother, Earl Sinclair, is a picture of personal and material success—a success the film implicitly and explicitly ascribes to his uninterrupted connection to the South. Earl lives in the family home, once the plantation big house of the white Sinclairs, who owned his ancestors. His family is intact, as he lives with and cares for his wife, Annie (played by Esther Rolle), who has Alzheimer's disease. He owns a restaurant famous for the various instantiations of chicken on its menu. Earl does well enough with concoctions like horseradish cilantro chicken to employ an in-home care helper, Zenia, played by Texas native Loretta Devine, to assist with Annie. Earl's son, Will, played by Wesley Snipes, is a successful lawyer living in Atlanta with his wife and two sons. Will, we learn, functions as both similar to and the opposite of his cousin Loretta. While Will has the material success and stability that Loretta lacks, the film situates Will as just as disconnected from family history as Loretta and her children.

Although Loretta's adjustment to the Delta is not without hiccups—the lack of readily available beer and the notion of hard work in the restaurant trouble Loretta initially—she comes to appreciate a life that seems a world away from the South Side of Chicago. After the summer, she, Thomas, and Tracy make a permanent move to the South and even convince Rosa Lynn to visit from Chicago, which she has not done since migrating there. At the close of the film, Tracy's screaming, once her primary form of communication, has been replaced by verbal language, as she has learned to say and wave "bye-bye" in proper context. Thomas, though challenged by what he characterizes as the relative difficulty of the schooling in the Delta, expresses appreciation that the teachers do not yell and that he does not have to carry a weapon to go to school. Loretta has gainful employment as manager of the restaurant, which Earl has offered her because of her new-found work ethic. Further, while intimate relationships seemed impossible in Chicago, Loretta has a burgeoning friendship with Zenia and even has potential heterosexual relationship prospects.

Down in the Delta situates family, community togetherness, and history as especially important for black southerners, and implicitly for non-southerners who may, too, need to come down to the Delta to be healed of their urban ills. Within the main exegesis of the film, a separate narrative about a family candelabra, which Rosa Lynn pawns to buy the family's bus tickets to the Delta, tells the history of the Sinclairs, from slavery to freedom. The candelabra had been used to purchase Nathan Sinclair, which separated him from his wife and children, and was later stolen by his son Jesse Sinclair during the chaos of the Civil War. The candelabra, called Nathan, has been passed from eldest child to eldest child and is a symbol of the family's connection to each other and to its history. As the eldest, Rosa Lynn took Nathan with her when she left for Chicago, where it served as a male presence in the absence of her husband. However, the film argues that the rightful place of Nathan, and therefore the rightful place of the Sinclairs, is in the geographic, rather than the diasporic, South, at the family home in the Delta.

The film goes beyond just indicting the urban North. Through the character of Will, the film condemns post–civil rights generation black middle classes and New South southern cities, like Atlanta and Charlotte. Will, troubled by the emptiness of middle-class life and questioning the broader purpose of his work as an attorney, represents disconnection from family, urban alienation, and alienation from a proper racial identity. The subtext is that were Will engaging in the kind of social justice work he is eventually inspired to do by film's end, he would know the purpose of his labor. Will and his family do not visit the Delta often, and Earl has to cajole him to come for his mother's birthday. When they do visit, their outsiders' status, both as urban and bourgeois, is evident. Will, hurt that his mother does not actively recognize him, is ambivalent and reluctant to engage with her.

Will's wife, Monica, played by Anne-Marie Johnson, reaches toward Annie, who shrinks back with fear in her face. Invited to sit down on the porch, Monica opts to stand instead, a sign of regional disrespect almost as blasphemous as not speaking to a person after looking him or her in the eye. After a minor shoving match between Thomas and her sons, Monica blurts out to Will, "See, I told you we didn't belong here!" Her exclamation is both about their status as bourgeois and about their status as city dwellers. The film situates them, and Will in particular, as having abandoned the responsibilities of family and community for meaningless personal gain, like "fifty cable channels." Like Loretta, Will learns the importance of family and community, spending quality time with his cousin, overcoming his feelings toward his mother and her illness, and putting his lawyer skills to good, purposeful use in the community's rally to bounce back after the chicken plant closes. Thus, the film argues, even a big city lawyer with a normative middle-class life can find value, redemption, and even purpose in the Delta.

Down in the Delta received mixed reviews from critics, but undoubtedly the narrative reflected sentiments in the broader black public consciousness, especially as journalists took increasing notice of return migration trends in the 1990s. The film stands in somewhat stark contrast to anthropologist Carol Stack's *Call to Home*, an ethnographic investigation of African American return migration to communities in the Carolinas. Stack's research, which ignited anew social scientific examinations of the demographic features of return migration,[29] focuses on what might be conceptualized as typical rural southern communities—relatively impoverished places, devastated by unemployment and deindustrialization, in which caring for family members in need is more complex than the easy nurturing Earl offers his wife, Annie, his niece, Loretta, and his great-niece, Tracy.

Whereas Stack's respondents must invest emotional and physical labor in the maintenance of family and community property, the Sinclair property is kempt, having been brought back to its original glory after falling into disrepair under the white Sinclairs' care. While *Down in the Delta*'s South stands in as a proxy for middle-class life, Stack's respondents largely leave middle-class, metropolitan lives in the urban North to navigate and contribute to a poor community they left behind. When the exogenous forces of deindustrialization—the town's chief employer, the chicken plant, announced plans to close—threaten *Down in the Delta*'s fictional Delta town, Loretta and Will work together to pitch an action plan to the community. The community meeting, led by Loretta, ends with chants of "We can do it," a personal responsibility discourse challenging myriad factory towns, southern and not, to collectively resist the powers of capital through old-fashioned American folk ingenuity, a cosmopolitan outwitting of big capitalists.

Down in the Delta's narrative is replayed in more elaborate and sometimes more complex fashion by two key films made ten years later. In the first, *Tyler Perry's Meet the Browns*, single mother of three Brenda Brown, played by Angela Bassett, escapes the violence and disadvantage of the South Side of Chicago and heads to rural Georgia for her estranged father's funeral. There she finds not only family and belonging but also wealth, in the form of a house, and a man, in the form of hometown boy Harry, played by former NBA star Rick Fox. Men, too, are redeemed by a connection with the rural South. In Malcolm D. Lee's *Welcome Home Roscoe Jenkins*, the title protagonist's priorities are awry. Host of a successful talk show, Roscoe is engaged to shallow *Survivor* winner Bianca. Like *Down in the Delta*'s Will, Roscoe has not been home in years, returning reluctantly for his parents' golden wedding anniversary celebration. For the Sinclairs, the South is a source of uplift from moral and financial impoverishment. The small Georgia town that forms the setting for *Welcome Home Roscoe Jenkins*, on the other hand, is a source of "beat down," sometimes quite literally, for protagonist Roscoe. However, this is in the spirit of necessary and familial tough love. Ultimately, the ego-beating Roscoe sustains cleanses him of the city ways that have rendered him rootless and arrogant. His focus shifts from what the film situates as the empty and alienating goals of individual success to the more laudable goals of humility, family, and community building. Although Roscoe returns to Los Angeles, he leaves the South with a renewed sense of what is "really important," dumps the self-centered Bianca, and rides off into the sunset with childhood crush, prom queen, and southern belle Lucinda.

Filmic representations of the black South in the decades around the turn of the century largely continued trends established in African American literature beginning in the 1960s. Yet, alternative imaginings of the black South emerged. For instance, *Jason's Lyric* (1994), *ATL* (2006), and *Hustle & Flow* (2005), set in Houston, Atlanta, and Memphis, respectively, present a complicated urban, rather than rural, South that is not so different from the metropolises roundly critiqued by *Down in the Delta* and *Meet the Browns*. Further, the 2009 film *Mississippi Damned*, based on the true stories of black Mississippians, presents a family and small-town South that is toxic rather than healing. Beyond film, southern hip-hop music and culture presents an alternative black South that straddles the boundaries of the best and worst of racial and regional cultures. These alternative narratives notwithstanding, the South found in popular discourse is one that reinforces the dichotomies of urban and rural, cosmopolitan and country, and obscures the workings of intraracial class differences.

Wright's Revenge

Like Hurston's "happy darkies," tropes of the new black South are highly contested. African American literary scholar Madhu Dubey has argued persuasively that reclamation of southern distinctiveness since the 1960s arose in tandem with major political and economic changes that thrust the region definitively into the modern era. She further contends that rapid modernization in the region spurred swelling interest in reclaiming that which made the region culturally distinct—rurality, "rootedness," and localized, face-to-face interaction untouched by globalizing forces.[30] Seemingly strange bedfellows maintain these tropes of southern distinction. On the one hand, conservative and/or racist white elites interested in maintaining the racial status quo promote a rural nationalism that hearkens back to a "South that wasn't there."[31] On the other hand, African American elites, literary cultural elites in Dubey's analysis, reclaim the rural South to make sense of, erase, or as Hazel Carby famously framed it, "discursively displace" the urban crises of non-southern metropolises.[32]

These arguments extend easily to the black South films discussed above. Not only do films like *Down in the Delta* and *Meet the Browns* actively displace urban crises, but they also disconnect such crises from broader structural forces, rendering underemployment, drug abuse, and violence the outcomes of the loss of normative family values through migration. Dubey situates such representations of the South as aimed at maintaining and rearticulating a neoconservative politics that justifies institutional racism and intraracial class hierarchies. Political scientist Adolph Reed made a similar argument in an April 1996 edition of the *Village Voice*, contending that the proliferation of nostalgia for the South—"in every major newspaper and excuse for a news magazine at the supermarket checkout line, in the classroom, in the local bar, across the dinner table, in cultural criticism, in foundation boardrooms and policy papers, on the talk show circuit"—is particularly problematic for the achievement of gender, sexuality, and class equity in black communities.[33] He locates what he calls black nostalgia for a segregated past in the class and age anxiety of black baby boomer elites, arguing that nostalgia for pre-desegregation black life reinforces the middle-class, paternalist, and patriarchal norms of the segregated black community. In segregated communities, intraracial distinctions—family background, class, place of residence, political affiliation—facilitated privileged African Americans' abilities to police and control working-class and poor African Americans. Certainly, segregated black communities existed all over the country, and black folks' nostalgia for a segregated past might not necessarily equate to a longing for a segregated southern or rural past. Research consistently demonstrates that African Americans prefer to live in communities where at least half of the other families are African American. Still, it is in and through the American South—because of larger black-to-white population proportions and consequently higher numbers of distinct black communities, cheaper costs of living, and concentrated black political power—that what Reed calls the "dangerous dreams" of a pre–civil rights South might be contemporaneously realized. Essentially, for Reed, Dubey, and other critics of the turn South, middle-class black and white southerners alike are active and complicit in maintaining interracial inequities, as well as interracial and intraracial class inequities, by hearkening back to the social order of a seemingly less complicated rural past.

While these critiques highlight the ways in which power—white racial power, black middle-class/elite power—is operating in otherwise innocuous if nostalgic remembrances and representations of the South, they miss the ways in which individual actors challenge and harness this power to erect individual distinctions, represent their own marginalized life experiences, and lay claim to authentic, or perhaps more accurately, sincere, existences.

The turn South has persisted over the past two decades in literature, black film, and hip-hop music, adopting more sophisticated forms of articulation. Still, popular culture representations of the black South are distinct from black southerners' everyday articulations of regional distinction, which are inherently more muted and nuanced than a Tyler Perry film. While respondents in this study were open to criticizing southern regional culture, including Tyler Perry films, they moved quickly, and often performatively, to position the South as better than other places, and consequently southern blackness as better than other manifestations of blackness. Respondents clearly shared the underdog spirit inherent in much of southern identity—that is, because the South is often maligned as backward, southerners often respond by glorifying the very traits that others find problematic—but supplemented their analyses with proof of the region's superiority. However, this desire to performatively privilege a black southern existence belies ongoing interracial and intraracial tensions that black southerners may be unwilling or unable to reconcile. Further, the privileging of southern blackness over and against a specifically northern blackness sometimes implicates class-inflected tensions stemming from personal experiences.

Reclaiming the (New) Black South

The newest black South enters contemporary black popular consciousness by way of southern hip-hop, black southern film, chicken sandwich commercials, and documentaries of bus trips through the South by African American public intellectuals.[34] Processes of primary and return migration undoubtedly contribute significantly to increased positive—and sometimes positively propagandistic—attention to the region. Newcomers to the South, who constitute a significant portion of the pattern of "reverse migration," bring with them positive collective memories of the region made possible by a host of cultural artifacts and post-soul cultural products. Cultural artifacts—from the guttural sounds of Muddy Waters, to the writings of Alice Walker, to Alvin Ailey's *Revelations*—lend themselves to a set of historical memories that are critically reflective on the black southern experience.

Post-soul cultural products, from film to theater, hip-hop to television, build upon, reinforce, and sometimes engender these historical memories. Through these products, African Americans who have never lived in the South have ready access to shared memories of the region in much the same way that contemporary African Americans have a shared memory of the experience of slavery.[35]

Certainly, negative collective memories of the region—those immortalized by file footage of brutality during the civil rights movement, documentaries like *Eyes on the Prize*, and films like John Singleton's *Rosewood*—abound. Yet, through efforts to reclaim a native home space, positive collective memories, coupled with narratives of the region's progress along racial lines, outweigh these negative collective memories for many African Americans, especially younger generations. While new migrants and return migrants may be motivated by cultural artifacts, cultural products, and personal, family memories—a grandmother, cousin, or uncle from "down south"—such motivations are often underscored by black southerners' personal and performative desires to claim and articulate a black experience both distinct from and better than that of African Americans in large urban centers outside of the region.

African American reclamation of the South, particularly beginning in the 1960s, signaled a shift on the terrain of regional identity. Whereas regional identity had long been reserved exclusively for whites, black reclamation of the South signaled to African American and white publics that regional distinctions not only existed for black folks but were moreover essential to black American lived experiences. Despite those features of being black in America that transcended space, place, and time, southern transplants claimed the right to speak as different kinds of black folks, reared and raised according to different, and in this case southern, ways of knowing and being. As such, an explosion of cultural products that attested to that difference, from literature to music to film, has emerged and challenged the marginalization of southern blackness. As the socioeconomic differences between regions decreased overall, these cultural differences—as lived, performed, produced, and consumed—increased, expanding into a profitable culture industry that features products from reality television to tourist attractions.

For folks who lived continuously in the region, the South did not require reclamation. Although these reclamation efforts by southern transplants were central in shifting popular discourse about the South, as was the growing publicity around the "southern" civil rights movement, southerners in the South set about the work of accomplishing the South. To be sure, southerners recognized themselves as regionally distinct before this moment, particularly in their travels outside of the region and in constant contact with visitors from "the North." Still, the growing sense of pride attached to southern identity ensured that those distinctions would be highlighted, accentuated, and marked as clear boundary lines in black American identity.

Regional accomplishment is sophisticated boundary work that facilitates within-race distinctions between individuals and groups. In the landscape of modern black regional identity, distinction is accomplished through the dichotomous juxtaposition of "the South" and "the North," rural and urban, good and evil, authentic and invalid, Old South and New

South. Specifically, central to this accomplishment is the achievement of a productive tension between "country" (a simple, commonsense approach to life imbued with the historical wisdom of working the land) and "cosmopolitan" or "citified" (a sharp and sophisticated approach that indicates shrewdness rather than naïveté). Through these juxtapositions and tensions, southerners forward their distinctive worldview, continue to excavate the buried South, and work to control the representation of black southern identity, and by extension black identity writ large, in the public sphere.

Beyond the accomplishment of a better identity that constitutes a best-of-both-worlds blackness, black southerners and cultural productions about the black South work to accomplish the South as the authentic home space for African Americans. By situating the South as a racial homeland— a more geographically and cognitively accessible homeland—these discourses engender a less laborious racial solidarity. This solidarity, in turn, protects the normative center of black American identity—Christianity, heteronormativity, and middle-class status. Even as within-race class differentials in the South outpace those in other parts of the country, wealthier black southerners can point to their southern residence as a marker of linked fate. Ultimately, ideas operationalized in service of regional accomplishment may legitimate or obscure within-race inequality, both masking and aggravating class tensions between African Americans.

CHAPTER TWO

Post-Soul Blues

In April 2011, the Memphis Grizzlies, the city's NBA team, won its first playoff game in franchise history. The Grizzlies, whose "all heart, grit, and grind" mantra was as much the story of the team as the story of the city, went on to beat the top-seeded powerhouse San Antonio Spurs in six games in the first round of the Western Conference. After game 6, power forward Zach Randolph responded to a reporter's query about why Memphis loved him so much. "It's a blue-collar town; I'm a blue-collar player," he said. "Ain't nothin' been given easy to me, and ain't nothin' been given easy to this town."[1]

The next month, with the Mississippi River at historic levels, President Barack Obama visited Memphis to deliver the commencement speech to Booker T. Washington High School, which had been selected for the distinction from among some 400 schools in the president's controversial Race to the Top competition. Under the leadership of principal Alicia Coleman-Kiner, the South Memphis school had significantly improved its graduation rate over the previous five years. This improvement occurred despite the challenges of disproportionate poverty and the closure and demolition of Cleaborn Homes, the largest housing project in the city and home to a number of Booker T. Washington students, through a Hope VI initiative. In addition to historic flooding, a historic NBA post-season, and a historic visit from the president, the city of Memphis and Shelby County were embroiled in a historic and contested attempt to consolidate the largely white county and largely black city schools. Memphis, however, is accustomed to managing historic moments and versed in the co-occurrence of tragedy and triumph that constitutes a blues existence in a blue-collar town. Thus, while the excitement of the moment was evident in extra niceties in the grocery store, animated conversations between complete strangers who might not ordinarily talk to one another about the possibility of change in the city, and flurries of tweets and Facebook posts of place pride, in the wide lens of the city's history, these were ordinary times.

For instance, a yellow fever epidemic that began in 1878 quite literally wiped out the city, which gave up its charter and existed only as a taxing

60

district of Shelby County until 1893. The city's population was overwhelmingly rural, engaging in direct agricultural and agricultural support labor in service of the city's powerful stake in the production and distribution of cotton. Like other southern cities, Memphis made little investment in improving the human capital and potential of its residents. Further, despite its growing black population, it rigidly adhered to a biracial system that disadvantaged the city's black and poor white residents.

The tragedy of the yellow fever epidemic brought a young Ida B. Wells from Holly Springs, Mississippi, to Memphis in search of work to support her younger siblings after her parents' death. Her work exposing the inequality of the biracial system and its most egregious manifestation—lynching—ensured her vilification by whites but ignited a tradition of protest and struggle in the city. Though Memphis was undoubtedly a country town, coming alive only to serve as the economic engine of cotton distribution season, communications studies scholar Jacqueline Jones Royster has argued that Memphis's lyceum circuit had a radicalizing effect on Wells.[2] Indeed, the lyceum was a distinctly cosmopolitan black political presence that pulled openly at the limits of supposedly disengaged country-ness.

As labor historian Michael Honey has demonstrated, many black and working-class Memphians were invested in labor struggles in the interwar and postwar periods that were intimately intertwined with civil rights struggles.[3] Thus, the sanitation workers' strike that brought Martin Luther King Jr. to Memphis in 1968 was part of the long history of nothing coming easy to the city or to its most marginalized constituents. In the blues tradition of the coexistence of good and evil, tragedy and triumph, the existential and material promise offered by King's fateful visit could not be realized without the tragedy of his assassination. Eventually, the sanitation workers won important concessions and rights that were a beacon for labor struggles nationally. Many respondents in this study contended that since the assassination of King, the city has been in a holding pattern of sorts, mired in sadness about the as yet unrealized promises of the civil rights movement and the lack of race and class resolution after King's death. Because many respondents were born or came of age after the civil rights movement, they carry with them this sadness, even as they recognize the ways in which the city has changed and continues to triumph.

Most respondents were teenagers or young adults when the city elected its first African American mayor, Willie W. Herenton, in 1991; when it opened the National Civil Rights Museum and the Pyramid; and when Beale Street was finally transformed from urban renewal wasteland into redeveloped tourist play space. Yet, while many of their parents "battled the plantation mentality" as they organized in labor and civil rights struggles,[4] many of my respondents spoke of battling and surviving "the plantation," a reference to working at the "SuperHub" of now-hegemonic shipping corporation FedEx, housed at the Memphis International Airport. For these post-soul respondents, Memphis is, as rapper Daralik argues, "the city of blues and booze and bad news / gangland feuds and throwaway twenty-twos," but also home to "fly girls raised on cornbread and butter."[5] Like their early twentieth-century and soul predecessors, respondents balance the challenges ("gangland feuds") and benefits ("fly girls") of a distinctively southern black urban life.

Despite a relatively high poverty rate, African American outcomes have improved overall in the city as education, wealth, and income increased. Still, after the 2008 economic downturn, poverty rates went up, as did the percentage of vacant homes. White and black middle-class flight to suburban communities, and in particular to DeSoto County, Mississippi, contributed to an increase in racial residential segregation. The infant mortality rate continues to be the highest among America's sixty largest cities. Like in most places, African Americans have been disproportionately affected by recession, as middle-class African Americans lost hard-won wealth accumulated over the past thirty years.[6] In 2009, the city of Memphis and Shelby County filed civil suit against Wells Fargo Bank for unfairly targeting at-risk African American homeowners and contributing significantly to foreclosures in black communities, which adversely affected African American wealth. In 2012, the city and Wells Fargo entered into a settlement agreement that may eventually contribute to community restitution, but the long-term implications of the confluence of factors that led to black middle-class wealth decline are not yet clear. While good and evil are often balanced and coexistent in the blues tradition, for many respondents, the city and its black residents in particular are in a goodness deficit.

This chapter considers the ways in which Memphis, a Soul City haunted by plantation patterns of exploitation and resistance, stands at the geographical and epistemological center of a *post-soul blues*. I use blues and its descendant form hip-hop as the language through which to understand contemporary black life in Memphis specifically and in the South more generally. Aesthetically and culturally, post-soul blues is the musical and bodily lexicon of black southern life in the post–civil rights era. Politically, this post-soul blues is a set of performative narratives utilized to navigate the contemporary contradictions of the South and racial progress. Tensions between country and cosmopolitan are embedded in and played out through post-soul blues.

I focus on the inheritors of soul and civil rights traditions in Memphis, the hip-hop generation, demonstrating how Memphis and the South signal important shifts and continuities in black American and regional identities and cultures. In what follows, I show how post-soul Memphians' relationships with the social and historical memory of Beale Street as a site of black cultural production, as well as their endeavors to create and continue Memphis's black musical and political traditions, reflect their conceptualizations of lived experiences and identities in the post–civil rights era. I move back and forth between the narratives of respondents and relevant themes and accounts from popular culture, including film, music, and television, which function to speak for and to black southern-ers. I also document how the narratives of a "grit and grind" Memphis and a best-of-both-worlds South are utilized by some black public intellectuals in service of a broader, purportedly authentically black political agenda wedded to traditional narratives of black communities and organizing. Ex-amining such narratives, this chapter continues the discussion of country cosmopolitanism, demonstrating how respondents' operationalization of the region's political and cultural legacies figures into their articulations and conceptualizations of regional and racial identities.

Urban Hustles, Southern Flows

Midtown Memphis might be what urban sociologist Richard Lloyd de-scribes as neo-bohemia, an amalgamation of the alternative—independent coffee shops and record stores, artists and artisans, and society's general fringe.[7] However, because the city's Midtown community, which spans nearly ten square miles, has a sizable African American population, Mid-town is a neo-soul bohemia where tensions of class, race, and art are flanked by a sprawling medical district to the west, the cultural economy of Soulsville to the south, the ravages of urban infant mortality and envi-ronmental racism to the north, and the wealth of East Memphis. Although I took the city and its surrounding suburbs, as well as the metanarratives circulating about city and region, as my field site, Midtown was often the physical starting point for my inquiries about cultural production, black identity, and southern identity. I spent the initial years of my research in hip-hop clubs, at art showings, at artist gatherings, and at various other arts events talking with local artists about their craft, their networks, and their perspectives on racial and regional identity.

Certainly, Midtown was a meeting place for the city's bohemian cultural elite, but it also symbolized for some respondents Memphis's possibility for diversity and interest convergence across racial, ethnic, class, and sexual orientation boundaries. For most respondents, however, Midtown was a reminder of the city's continued marginalization of predominantly African American communities, including Graceland's Whitehaven; Frayser, whose namesake high school made national news in 2011 for having nearly 100 pregnancies in the school within one school year; Orange Mound, the nation's first African American–constructed neighborhood, plagued by an uptick in drug-related violence and criminal activity in the 1980s; and Hickory Hill, disparagingly called Hickory Hood, which has battled the vestiges of urban disinvestment since the turn of the twenty-first century.

Regardless of one's perspective on Midtown, it offered the most numerous, varied, and reasonably priced venues for the performance and exhibition of art in the city in the late 1990s and into the next decade. As such, it was the place in which young African Americans, particularly those espousing some brand of black consciousness, converged to exchange ideas and art. While key venues were located in South Memphis and downtown, Midtown served as the epicenter of black arts communities in Memphis. On the rap scene, The Spot, located in the medical district and wedged between a medical school parking lot and a barbershop, was a key place for live rap music.

Before 2004, the rap scene in Memphis comprised a set of loosely organized rappers, deejays, and fans, many of whom had been moving in and out of the scene since its origins in the late 1980s. Some artists, like Three 6 Mafia and 8-Ball and MJG, had achieved national success with a signature Memphis sound: one that blended soul samples and a post-soul interpretation of Memphis's typical high-hat sound, which has been transformed in the post-soul era into the accented eighth-note snare. Still others, from Gangsta Boo to Project Pat to Skinny Pimp, occasionally rose to the national surface but were ongoing powerful regional players and representatives of Memphis hip-hop. These artists were the ultimate artistic articulation of country cosmopolitanism. They were southern and gangsta, where southern equaled country and gangsta equaled the cosmopolitan violence and street shrewdness thought to exist only in the "real" cities of the urban North, Midwest, and West.

Beginning in 2004, the local hip-hop scene underwent a more thorough organization, in which divides between southern gangsta rap and southern rappers who might have been more readily identified as conscious or alternative rappers were slowly bridged. Rap shows became more frequent, artists shared production tips and leads, and fans came to expect, sometimes beyond reason, an ongoing underground hip-hop scene that showcased the do-it-yourself ingenuity, style diversity, and rap prowess of Memphis. Although shows eventually became less frequent as rappers, producers, and musicians worked to balance the art with family and fiscal responsibilities, the organizational resurgence of the scene inspired the increased visibility of a host of musical artists in the city.

A key player in this organizational resurgence and subsequent rise in the proliferation of the post-soul music scene was the Iron Mic Coalition, a collective of rappers distinctly outside of the southern gangsta rap tradition but simultaneously operating with the same place-based and artistic inspirations. "901 Area Code" is from the collective's 2005 debut album, *The 1st Edition*, which features ruminations on everything from race and class inequality to the scrumptiousness of various preparations of chicken. The music for "901 Area Code" consists of a slowed-down sample of a wailing Gladys Knight, a break-beat with concomitant Memphis high-hat, pioneering Memphis rapper 8-Ball's scratched and sampled voice saying, "Memphis, Tenn, that's my muthafuckin stompin' ground," and another male voice answering 8-Ball saying, "Real Memphis." Over these elements, rapper Daralik gives a lyrical introduction to Memphis, articulating its simultaneously urban and cosmopolitan ("gangland feuds and throwaway twenty-twos") and rural and southern ("fly girls raised on cornbread and butter") existence. At live performances of "901 Area Code," women audience members (myself included) would raise their plastic cups and say the lyrics on cue for the gendered, hunger-inducing shout-out.

The intersection of urban and rural cultures that influences contemporary hip-hop and soul scenes in Memphis reflects the country cosmopolitanism of Memphians and other southerners in urban contexts working to reconcile a southern, and therefore rural-inspired, and urban existence. Further, Daralik's characterization of Memphis as the city of blues and booze and bad news points to the still unresolved blues—economic, social, and political—of the post-soul generations in Memphis. In addition to the existential blues of the lived experience of blackness in America, this blues includes disproportionate infant mortality, chronic illness, and violence. As in other urban contexts, hip-hop has become the creative space through which youth theorize the social world, their lives, and their futures. Yet, contrary to other urban contexts, Memphis hip-hop is explicit about its indebtedness to history, including civil rights and music traditions, and the infusion of rural sensibilities into urban cultures. Surrounded physically and epistemologically by the legacy of soul music and civil rights history, artists marshal these cultural artifacts to accomplish a distinctively black and southern urban identity.

While a host of local factors supported the Memphis hip-hop scene's resurgence around the turn of the century, the previous decade of southern rap's rising tide in national contexts also contributed to the energy behind southern rap on local scenes across the South. As Roni Sarig carefully demonstrates in *Third Coast*, by 2004, southern rap had become a national and global phenomenon, much to the chagrin of East and West Coast stalwarts. Several southern acts, largely based in the region's urban places, worked to carve out a space in hip-hop and black identity politics to reconcile the paradoxes of urban and rural cultures and the promises and failures of the civil rights movement in the post-soul South. In Atlanta, OutKast and Goodie Mob resurrected a southern funk sound that centered the South's funk, playa, and Cadillac cultures. In Memphis, 8-Ball and MJG perfected southern gangsterism, and Triple 6 Mafia/Three 6 Mafia generated a high-energy buck sound that later evolved into the internationally renowned crunk sound popularized by Atlanta's Lil' Jon. In New Orleans, Master P's No Limit and later Cash Money Records not only brought traditional New Orleans club music, bounce, folk songs, and chants into the mainstream but also ushered in a new era in rap entrepreneurism. In Florida, and Miami in particular, the booty/bass sound of 2 Live Crew had paved the way for Slip-N-Slide Records, of which Trick Daddy and Trina were the pied pipers. In Houston, Geto Boys and UGK ushered in a distinctly black Texas sound that drew on funk and soul as its soundtrack. Finally, in Virginia, Timbaland, Missy Elliot, and the Neptunes forwarded a futuristic southern sound that capitalized on soul samples as well as experimented with new sound, cadences, and production techniques that would solidify southern rap's place on the national hip-hop stage. In less than a decade, southern rap emerged from relative obscurity to international phenomenon, with established New York–based record labels opening regional headquarters to capitalize on the southern sound and moreover on the broader public's desire to consume it.

This was no small feat. Because of the commonality of some black cultural tropes, like call-and-response and some cadences and rhythm patterns, hip-hop on the East and West Coasts had incorporated racial traditions into the music that southerners implicitly and explicitly claimed as regional property. Thus, southern rappers undertook a successful accomplishment campaign, accentuating their musical and cultural differences from dominant rap as well as asserting a place within the confines of the rap tradition. Houston's Geto Boys had achieved national acclaim with "Mind Playing Tricks on Me," which featured an Isaac Hayes sample to introduce a southern gangsta rap narrative of urban angst in 1991. With

OutKast's release of *Southernplayalisticadillacmuzik*, which debuted at #3 on Billboard's R&B and hip-hop chart in May 1994, southern hip-hop gained increasingly mainstream attention for its distinctive sound and southern, or country, take on urban life. In 1995, Goodie Mob's soulful "Soul Food," which featured CeeLo Green's distinctive voice on the chorus, was balanced with the group's "Dirty South," a southern morality tale about urban neighborhoods, drug dealing, violence, and survival. Reprising a longtime underground and club hit for a broader audience, Three 6 Mafia, the progenitors of crunk, released "Tear da Club Up '97," featuring the group chants and mosh pit buck jumping that came to define crunk music and southern hip-hop more generally.

While some southern rappers articulated a regionalized version of black urban life, others capitalized on the spatial distinction provided by rural cultures to give hip-hop an alternative home, relocating it from high-rise urban housing projects to poorer, medium-sized communities in deltas and piney woods. For instance, Bowling Green, Kentucky's Nappy Roots' video for "Awnaw," from their 2002 debut album, *Watermelon, Chicken & Gritz*, features many group members donning overalls and straw hats, wide shots of wooden and metal shotgun houses, tractors and other farm equipment, big rig trucks and pickups, and cornfields. They then combine these general symbols of southernness writ large with a new southern blackness of rims and candy-painted Chevrolets. The video for their follow-up single, "Po' Folks," features black and white working-class Kentuckians' narratives about the "down-home country" of Kentucky. Both singles broke into the Billboard Hot 100 and into the top 20 of Billboard's R&B and hip-hop chart that year, narrating a different version of urban life and black experiences of marginalization and poverty. The success of these narratives is partly attributable to their rejection of a shiny, inauthentic progress in favor of a commitment to the American folk—working class, country, and rural or small-town.

Similarly, David Banner's first major label and solo release, *Mississippi: The Album*, debuted at #1 on Billboard's R&B and hip-hop chart and at #9 on the Billboard 200. While Banner is not entirely the country boy the Nappy Roots present, the difference is in place experience—Bowling Green, Kentucky, versus Jackson, Mississippi. The title song's chorus declares that Mississippi is a place "where the boys still pimpin' them hos / Cadillacs still ridin' on vogues / where my soul still don't feel free / where a flag means more than me."[8] Banner's chorus both signifies an urban, cosmopolitan experience, including pimping and Cadillacs with rims, and a country, rural one, with references to the Confederate flag conjuring images of slavery and sharecropping. Further, Banner utilizes the idea of Mississippi as a signifier of both a rural and urban Dirty South, mining the intersections of these spaces in his ruminations on racism, pimping, and poverty.

Even artists from outside of the South worked to accomplish a regional identity rooted in the intersection of urban and rural cultures in the South. Afrocentric R&B and rap group Arrested Development, which gained popularity in the early 1990s with a string of feel-good, introspective hits, including "People Everyday" and "Mr. Wendal," is probably most famous for its hit "Tennessee." Although the group's fame largely came from their time producing, collaborating, and recording in Atlanta, group founder Speech is a Milwaukee native with southern roots. He spent time between his Milwaukee birthplace and his grandmother's home in Ripley, Tennessee, an hour's drive northeast of Memphis. "Tennessee," a personal reflection that linked a positive black identity to Africa via the South, won the group a Grammy Award for Best Rap Performance by a Duo or Group in 1993 and undoubtedly contributed to their win for Best New Artist that same year.

The black-and-white video for "Tennessee," shot in Georgia despite the song's title and subject matter, features the group outside of a solitary, isolated, and therefore presumably rural shack interspersed with shots of rural landscapes and southern railroad lines. The song's chorus—"take me to another place / take me to another land / make me forget all that hurts me / let me understand Your plan"—imagines the state of Tennessee, and by extension the South more generally, as a spiritual and historically rich refuge, where one can commune with God and the ancestors, "walk the roads [his or her] forefathers walked," and "climb the trees [his or her] forefathers hung from."[9] As represented by the song, the South is literally "another land," one in which time is fixed, ancestral ghosts are abundant, and a connection to history is unavoidable. "Tennessee" is widely acclaimed as a divergence from the gangsta rap sounds, styling, and subject matter that dominated radio airwaves and video play in the early 1990s. Yet, while those in the group might be remembered generally as "conscious" artists, Arrested Development's alternative and introspective blackness was rooted in the physical and spiritual South that situated country folk knowledge as both cosmopolitan and an antidote to the ills of urban life.

Not all southern artists fix the South as temporally past and spatially rural. Indeed, most southern artists work to exploit the dissonant simultaneity of past and present, rural and urban, to distinguish themselves from the North and West. Southern women artists, in particular, offer alternative versions of southern identity that often challenge the sometimes static nature of male artists' narratives. For instance, although Erykah Badu is typically thought of as an R&B or neo-soul artist, her connections to hip-hop and self-proclaimed B-girl status situate her more squarely in a broader hip-hop tradition. As such, she offers a blues woman's episte-mology that centers black women's experiential knowledge that is at once universal and rooted in southern traditions. The video for her inaugural popular single, "On & On," features Badu's blending of filmic interpreta-tions of both *Gone with the Wind* and *The Color Purple*, which signal her race, gender, and regional allegiances. Yet, Badu does not always so de-liberately inhabit recognizable tropes of southernness, lending her work a broader appeal to black identities beyond the South. Thus Badu, along with other southern women artists like Missy Elliot, Trina, and Beyoncé, forwards various versions of southern black identity that are shifting and complex, adding nuance to the accomplishment of regional identity in hip-hop and R&B.

Certainly, southern hip-hop is place-oriented, in that it often represents a particular state, city, or neighborhood like Kentucky, Atlanta, or Mem-phis's Orange Mound. Yet, by constantly signifying on one another's lyrics, musical styles, and common southern tropes, from "country" and "nappy" to "vogues" and "dubs," southern rappers established the South as a uni-fied place with urban/cosmopolitan hustles and rural/country/south-ern flows. As country and cosmopolitan are effectively integrated into a distinctly southern black artistic worldview, place differences—between Kentucky and Mississippi, between Atlanta, Houston, and Memphis—are subsumed under the South's regional umbrella. The South, as an idea and geographically bound entity, then, serves as an overarching space and place through which country cosmopolitanism is articulated.

Representing the Black South

The successes and prominence of southern rap and its accomplished narrative of urban-rural intersections extended beyond the airwaves and video spins to film. Southern hip-hop offered an alternative historiogra-phy of the genre, in particular the music element of the genre, that situ-ated the South, and not the Bronx, as its true spatial and epistemological origin. Further, film presented different, regionally inflected versions of the black American experience. Through these films, southern locales, de-spite their place-to-place differences, become a unified stand-in for black American identity. Like the southern turn in literature and culture that began in the 1960s, these films not only offer an alternative to hegemonic representations of blackness but also situate southern blackness as a better or *the* better version of blackness.

Three films in particular—*Hustle & Flow* (2005), *Idlewild* (2006), and *ATL* (2006)—accomplish a distinctive regional and racial reality, situating the post-soul blues, hip-hop, as an organic product of that regional distinction. I read these films in their historical order, with *Idlewild*, set in 1930s Georgia, as the retrospective anticipation of the contemporary Atlanta and Memphis of *ATL* and *Hustle & Flow*, respectively. Together, these films offer an alternative representation of black American life that hint at a different kind of racial blues, a southern black blues, born of the paradoxes of black success and black oppression in the post-soul era.

Idlewild opens with alternating stills and moving shots of the southern black middle class—babies, women, men, young girls and boys—and institutional artifacts of the black community, including barbershops and churches. Accompanying the film's opening is classic big band music laced with trumpet solos performed by Arturo Sandoval and interrupted by hip-hop scratches. This temporal incongruence characterizes the entirety of the film, as hip-hop and big band jazz, rural and urban, and modernity and history collide as clock hands turn backward and forward at high speeds, eighth notes dance on sheet music, and a rooster engraved on a whiskey flask becomes animated and offers advice to one of the main characters, appropriately called Rooster. Further, these co-occurring characteristics signify southern hip-hop's spanning of past and present, rural and urban.

The film follows the two main characters, Percival and Rooster, played by hip-hop and Grammy Award–winning duo OutKast (André 3000 and Big Boi), both of whom were also co-producers and music supervisors. The major arc of the film leads to a moment that becomes pivotal in both of their lives. Percival, a mortician's son, is a quiet, "eccentric" pianist, engulfed more in his music than in the social world. He is a throwback to rural morality, a simple gentleman who falls into an ill-fated romance with a woman who blows into the town of Idlewild, posing as a famous singer. Rooster, introduced to the bootlegging and number-running businesses as a child, performs in a juke joint, aptly named "Church," and spends his time after work bedding women from Church while his suspicious wife and numerous children await his return. After Rooster witnesses a double murder, the diegesis barrels forth through bootlegging, Church performances, and a blossoming romance toward a climactic gun fight, an accidental shooting, an attempted suicide, and a resolute exodus of Percival from Idlewild on a train to Chicago to start a new life after tragedy.

Self-consciously writing a history for southern hip-hop music and culture and southern urban culture, *Idlewild* effectively addresses a significant temporal gap in understanding the black South in the context of the
Great Migration. With an especial use of historical effects and context in
the film's cinematography and plot, *Idlewild* provides a window into the
urban South after the waves of African American migration from the South
to the North. As such, it narrates a cultural history largely absent from
scholarly treatments of black cultural production and identities, offering
the South, and a rural-urban South in particular, as the epistemological
home of hip-hop.

While a number of black films set in the 1930s South imagined the South
as "the scene of the crime" and the North as a space of freedom, or conceptualized the South as a rural haven and the North as a space of violence and
loss of some vital cultural essence, *Idlewild* presents a southern town—not
quite the big city, but beyond agricultural subsistence and not mired in the
poverty associated with rural existence in the South. As a fictional southern
town, Idlewild is a representation of the urbanized spaces to which many
African American migrants moved as they exited rural towns on their way
to the urban North. It exists in a liminal space between the idyllic spaces
that dotted black-cast films of the early twentieth century and northern
urban centers.

Essentially, the town reflects the intersection of urban and rural cultures that continues to characterize most southern cities. While the di-
alogue in three places makes reference to the bright lights of northern
urban centers—Chicago, New York, and Harlem in particular—as places
where the characters could start anew and effectively maximize their creative talents, Idlewild is not necessarily a hindering space. The life circumstances in which the characters find themselves—an overbearing
father stifling Percival's creative desires beyond taking over the family
mortuary business, singer Sally Shelly's desires to further her career in
the big city and travel the world—necessitate a new beginning in a new
place. That is, despite the fact that some of the characters leave the South,
it is obvious that a complex and different African American life continues
in the region.

A temporal fast-forward from *Idlewild*, the Antwone Fisher–penned
ATL, billed as "a new American story," offers a southern alternative to the
hegemonic 'hood films of the 1990s and continues, although not as strategically and deliberately, a conversation about the cultural contributions of
the South to the contours of black American identity. The film is the narrative of four friends preparing to graduate from high school and confronting

pivotal moments in their lives. It tells a coming-of-age story that has all of the urban trappings of 1990s 'hood films—drug dealers, guns, cars, violence—but these signifiers of black-urban-ness are operationalized differently in this, a deliberately southern, black film. The main character, Rashad, played by Atlanta native and rapper Tip "T. I." Harris, narrates the opening of the film and declares simply, "Down south, we grew up quick," while the sampled voice of Ray Charles sings "Georgia." The opening credits feature a number of still and action shots, including time-lapsed shots of the bustling Atlanta freeway and skyline, cotton plants and Confederate flags, barbershops and churches, and a young Coretta Scott and Martin Luther King Jr. A heavy bass break-beat drops and the voice of Atlanta rapper Ludacris picks up the speed of the easygoing "Georgia" sample. The key shifts from a mellow major key to a relatively ominous minor key with string and piano chords and timpani marking the beginning of each bar. Yet, as the hook reoccurs, the key returns to major. The alternating major and minor keys in the song, as well as the simultaneous signifying on contemporary and historical musical moments—contemporary hip-hop and Ray Charles's bluesy, country voice—are illustrative of the film's attempt to present a decidedly urban story mediated through southern/country culture and to engage in the production of a southern post-soul aesthetic. In the way Charles's "Georgia" frames contemporary hip-hop verses, southern sensibility frames, and drives, this urban narrative.

The film begins as the foursome prepare for Skate Wars, an annual competition at the skating rink, which serves as the social center of the lives of the black, predominantly working-class youth in the city. Ant, the protagonist's younger brother, is unfocused in school and quickly distracted by the lure of making fast money working for the neighborhood drug dealer, played by OutKast's Antwan Patton. As Rashad and his crew prepare for the competition, Rashad manages a romantic interest with dubious class credentials, his younger brother's troubles, and his uncle's working-class angst and parental ambivalence.

ATL asserts its new American story through its central settings and character outcomes. First, by situating Martin Luther King Jr. Drive's Cascade skating rink as a central space of black youth leisure and cultural production in the film, *ATL* decenters the housing projects, street corners, and basketball courts synonymous with black urban identity in popular and academic contexts for locales outside of the South. *ATL* replaces common tropes of black urban identity with synchronized skating, complex choreography, and southern hip-hop. Second, in places where the narrative might overlap with familiar representations of black working-class and urban poor life, the film offers alternative outcomes—outcomes that implicitly occur only down south. For instance, while Ant's drug-dealing aspirations eventuate in his being shot by the drug dealer, *ATL* rejects the normative 'hood film ending where innocent victims die. Instead, Ant is only wounded. He straightens up in school, stops smart-mouthing the teacher, and seems to have a promising future. Upon graduation, the four friends also have relatively positive outcomes: one becomes assistant manager at a fast-food restaurant; another opens a shop where he makes gold, silver, and platinum teeth for customers; the smart friend enrolls in an Ivy League institution; and the protagonist draws comics for the local newspaper. While the endings for the foursome, particularly the opening of a gold teeth shop, may not all meet normative standards, they highlight the range of possibilities of post–civil rights black youth while keeping enduring challenges, like drugs and violence, in clear view.

While southern hip-hop is a key element in *ATL*, it takes center stage in Craig Brewer's 2005 film, *Hustle & Flow*, the first released of the three films discussed in this section. The film offers perhaps the most deliberate accomplishment of the South as the center and historical referent of black American identity, positioning the South as the home of hip-hop in no uncertain terms. As the soul sounds of the Bo-Keys, of Stax and Hi Records fame, play in the score, Brewer has Shelby, portrayed by Nashville native D. J. Qualls, say the following between drags on a marijuana joint: "The thing is—and I believe this, man—rap is coming back home to the South. Because, this, *this* is where it all began. Heavy percussion, repetitive hooks, sexually suggestive lyrics, man it's all blues, brother! 'Back Door Man' to 'Back That Ass Up,' it's all about pain and pussy . . . and making music, man, with simple tools, by any means necessary. You got to get what you got to say out. Because you've got to! Every man has the right—the goddamned right—to contribute a verse!"

Here, the connection between hip-hop and blues is made plain, and the South is privileged as the place "where it all began." In *Hustle & Flow*, Memphis serves as both the setting and inspiration for a story about pimps, hos, hip-hop, and redemption. The film begins with the protagonist-pimp D-Jay, played by Terrence Dashun Howard, waxing philosophical to one of his sex workers, Nola, in his rusty blue-with-a-purple-hood-and-front-quarter-panels Chevrolet Caprice Classic as the two work the track in a grit and grind part of downtown Memphis socially distant from the shiny FedEx Forum in which the Grizzlies play. The opening sequences in the film have the audience ride along with Nola and D-Jay down various main throughways in the city—six-lane streets lined with various chain stores, local shops, fast-food joints—to the twang of a rock-and-roll electric guitar. The soundtrack, filled with old blues cuts, new sounds by premium Memphis soul band the Bo-Keys, and contemporary southern hip-hop songs, aurally signals a post-soul blues. The narrative follows D-Jay's hustles, which include pimping and selling drugs, and his rap flows as he struggles to have his voice heard and represent an authentic Memphis. The film ambles toward a climax the audience is prompted to anticipate in the first scene of the film—a Fourth of July party at which Skinny Black, an underground Memphis rapper turned successful hypermedia rapper, played by Atlanta rapper Ludacris, will be in attendance. *Hustle & Flow* is the story of what one character calls the "simple [cultural] tools" of hip-hop production in a blue-collar town, highlighting the trials of an underground rapper trying to complete a demo tape, from equipment mishaps to noisy neighbors interfering with recording. Although the film ends with the protagonist being arrested and jailed for assaulting Skinny Black, he enters the local jail with a hit song on radio, street credibility with his incarcerated counterparts and the jail guards, and buzz around the city.

Although the gold-toothed, pressed-and-curled protagonist-pimp is a relatively unlikeable character—after one of the sex workers challenges his authority, he puts her, drawers of her clothes, and her infant son out of the house in the early hours of the morning—he embodies the blues tradition and compels audiences to champion him as an underdog. His strivings to survive, make ends meet, and better himself in difficult circumstances reflect the city's tradition, as well as the southern and American tradition, of triumphing over such circumstances. Ultimately, it is hip-hop, rooted in blues and soul traditions, that saves each of the main characters from his or her ontological and material rut, highlighting the redemptive power of a hip-hop that has returned to the South.

Hip-hop and soul artists and consumers in Memphis see themselves as both aligned with and at the forefront of black social and political culture, drawing on the city's history of civil rights organizing and musical cultures to legitimate their claims to a "better" blackness. At the center of such claims is the intersection of urban and rural cultures and conditions. Yet, while respondents in this study often imagined this intersection as good and productive, they also sometimes acknowledged that the intersection can combine the worst of urban and rural contexts. Southern violence, poverty, and oppressive gender relations undergird a good portion of southern hip-hop narrative, and in the case of D-Jay, the post-soul blues yields an angry, anxious pimp capable of engaging in and rationalizing troubling degrees of manipulation, violence, and heartlessness. Still, across gender and class, respondents rallied around the grittiness that is the Dirty South, even as they seek out the polish of an urban cosmopolitanism that will ensure that even if nothing is given easy, the struggle is worthwhile.

Beale Street Blues

Contemporary hip-hop and soul cultures in Memphis undoubtedly have their performative roots in the collectively remembered African American space of Beale Street, a key geographical and spatial intersection of urban and rural cultures in Memphis. Once hailed the "Harlem of the South" and "black America's main street," Beale Street was a bustling black place from Reconstruction through World War II, complete with blues, juke joints, churches, jazz, gambling, and politics and deemed a site of authentic black cultural production by persons from and outside of the black community. Falling into disrepair in the postwar era and targeted by urban renewal efforts, Beale Street's initially slow decline was quickly realized through these efforts after the assassination of King. The once vibrant space went largely unused for a number of years. Recent gentrification and downtown revitalization efforts in Memphis, similar to those occurring in neighborhoods and midsized city downtowns across America, have rectified the emptiness and disuse of the space.[10] However, most respondents contended that physical markers of Beale Street's connection to black southern cultural production, save for four-foot stone and slate historic markers, have been removed in the redevelopment process. Rather than black America's main street, Beale Street has become, they claimed, a Main Street, America, complete with generic tourist spaces, from bars and restaurants to knick-knack shops, differentiated only by the particularity of its commodified "fantasy city"[11] theme: barbecue, Elvis, music, and soul.

Yet, the social construction of Beale, based on its historicity, coupled with the phenomenology of Beale as a black place in collective memory, persists as an active element in black lived experience in Memphis, despite the demise and eventual destruction of what respondents conceptualized as an authentic Beale—the Beale where black juke joints and black Baptist churches faced one another—that began over a century ago. There are post-soul manifestations of that Beale, including the various street performers who attempt to recreate a separate cultural space physically outside of what some respondents deemed cookie-cutter blues clubs. Yet, in each instance, the incompatibility of such post-soul manifestations of that Beale with the contemporary presentation of Beale as a sanitized tourist draw effectively excludes these productions from dominating present-day Beale.

One instance of the incongruity of that "authentic" Beale and the contemporary Beale occurred in respondents' perceptions and recollection of the Beale Street Flippers.[12] While "flipping" in modern national contexts usually conjures up the buying, fixing up, and selling of properties, flipping was part of the bodily lexicon of black youth, particularly boys, who came of age in post–civil rights Memphis. While flipping is commonly associated with low-income African Americans, it occurred across class groups, as my lower-middle-class neighborhood was frequently a site where boys and girls proved their acrobatic prowess and garnered respect. At the center of my street was a cove, situated on a slight incline. If a set of backflips, turns, or twists down the flat street that intersected with the cove had not clearly yielded the best performer, the cove, with its incline, was the final decider.

The group of young men who came to be known as the Beale Street Flippers emerged from now-demolished Cleaborn Homes, a short spatial distance from Beale Street but a long social distance from the tourist space that Beale Street was becoming in the 1980s. Reanimating the street performer tradition of Beale, the Flippers, made up of a group of friends and relatives, began with small black audiences who either validated them as the best or acknowledged their talent but who nevertheless favored someone or some group from their neighborhoods. From the late 1980s through the mid-1990s, the Beale Street Flippers became an integral element of the experience of Beale for black Memphis residents, a way in which black Memphians could literally take over the space of Beale Street without police aggression or reprisal. However, as tourists—both those from out of town and whites from Memphis and surrounding areas—came to make up the majority of the Flippers' audiences and as downtown Memphis shifted more definitively into a sanitized urban entertainment destination, the Flippers took their show on the road, performing with the Harlem Globetrotters and at various festivals and NBA opening and halftime shows across the country.

Respondents saw what might have otherwise simply been a natural expansion of talent into bigger markets as caused by white discomfort with living, breathing black performers who were not relatively nonthreatening older blues men on Beale Street. To be sure, the Flippers' black masculinity, southern accents, and disciplined but powerful and moving bodies disrupted Beale Street developers' desires to create a interracial but definitively middle-class space for the enjoyment of a Beale distant from its progeny—post-soul blackness, youth cultures, and hip-hop. Yet, as the

Flippers' business savvy has increased over the years and they have packaged themselves and been accepted as a key link between Beale's past and present, they have become an institutionalized presence, whether or not they are physically performing on Beale, in the Beale Street space.

Still, respondents were skeptical, citing police harassment, token representation, and a general feeling of being unwelcome on Beale. Whether their perceptions are verifiable fact or not, other evidence of the absence of contemporary blacks on Beale seems to speak to their narratives. While hip-hop is the natural outgrowth of blues, jazz, and soul music traditions in Memphis, there is no dedicated hip-hop club on Beale Street. Though promoters and entrepreneurs have attempted to establish one over the years, a broad contention on the part of developers, and of the white and green interests they represent, is that a hip-hop club on Beale would bring violence and would change the nature of the street. In short, hip-hop is squarely outside of the experience of Beale that developers want to offer to its largely white tourist clientele.

Blackness exists on Beale Street, then, as historically fixed or otherwise nonthreatening, such as in the "No black. No white. Just blues." slogan that dots the Beale landscape on T-shirts and buttons. James, a thirty-two-year-old barber who has "been through with Beale Street" since he "was 'bout 20 years old," summed up many respondents' sentiments about the slogan. When we met in the early 2000s, James was cutting hair out of a storefront shop in North Memphis flanked by a hot wing place and an independent tire shop. "It ain't no black, all right. Ain't no real blues either. But it is some white folks down there. Plenty of 'em." James, who grew up near the North Memphis neighborhood of New Chicago, further contended, like many respondents, that police presence on Beale Street is designed to discourage certain kinds of black patrons—"niggas who gon' act a fool," James said— but simultaneously alienates many African American residents.

Despite the physical absence of Beale's post-soul legacy in the street's landscape, the social memory of Beale operates on the street's spatial periphery, or "off Beale," as it is frequently called. Hip-hop and R&B shows, while rarely taking place at venues on Beale, are often held in spaces in close proximity to Beale Street and, more significantly, in close proximity to the historical production of black Memphis music, including Sun, Stax, and Hi Records. This spatial proximity to historical places of black music production is both a historical consequence and deliberate endeavor. The use of spaces for the recording, production, and performance of music is often passed from musician to musician so that spaces of historical consequence maintain the same utility even if ownership changes.

Thus, beyond the lingering manifestations of de jure segregation and the historical location of music spaces, Memphis hip-hoppers deliberately choose to inhabit spaces in close proximity to the original production of soul music, sometimes competing for access to those spaces when spaces in other predominantly black areas of town are open and available for use for a comparable fee. Further, this spatial proximity arises out of an active association of contemporary Memphis music production with historical Memphis music production, as well as from a concerted attempt to recreate music spaces in order to authenticate and legitimate contemporary hip-hop production and performance. Thus, the centrality of Beale as the locus of black music, with soul studios located just to the east and south, is essential to the southerners' claiming of their "right to contribute a verse" to the cultural and political landscape of black expression.

"Livin' the Legacy"

Whether they wanted to be or not, post-soul generation black Memphians have been socialized into living the legacy of civil rights and soul music. Trips to the National Civil Rights Museum, rituals on free Tuesday afternoons and certainly for the King holiday, hold black Memphians responsible for the legacy of civil rights. Further, this socialization implores black Memphians to strive to challenge the increasingly complex structural inequalities of race and class in the post–civil rights era. More recently, trips to the Stax Museum of American Soul have become a part of this socialization and education. In addition to the museum, Stax has a music academy and charter school where children learn to play and live the legacy. Outside of these more formal agents of socialization into the history and musical legacy of the city, the soul classics FM radio station that is conspicuously heavy on Memphis music for a corporately owned and operated network and the local AM African American station, WDIA, socialize black Memphians into a possessive investment in the city's political and cultural history. Jermaine, a hip-hop producer who played trumpet in his high school marching band, articulated this connection to the legacy of Memphis music in contemporary hip-hop: "It's like, when I write, I hear the connection to Memphis soul, and that's why I'm always sampling on Al Green, you know . . . his voice, [sings] 'yea!' and that band's back there thumping, you can feel the Memphis, the soul, the South *pulsating*. [Taps on the table in rhythm.] It's like [Al Green] and the others saw all of this coming, you know? And they left us the tools to create a new sound through their old—well, not old, you know, timeless—sound."

Jermaine, who attends the local historically black college, deliberately demonstrates his connection and homage to Memphis soul in each of his beats, as he frequently samples southern soul music in his work. Like other respondents, he described housecleaning mornings with blues and soul music as the soundtrack for mopping and baseboard scrubbing. Antoine, a deejay for another local group, has the same sort of intentional relationship to soul music. I asked him how he thinks about Memphis soul music in the beats that he produces. "I'm totally conscious of the legacy. You know, it's like the hardships of the city throughout the years brings out the worst in you and puts you in the worst situations to bring out the *best* things you can do. Takes tragedy to make soul; takes getting let down. It's kinda hard to find your soul if you haven't had it hard. So, if I feel the same hardships that they did, the sound that gets produced is the same sound." When I asked him about the hardships he was referring to, both his and those of the women and men who produced Memphis's soul music in the 1960s and 1970s, he returned with, "You're from Memphis, right?" Many respondents assumed I knew precisely what they meant when they talked about "how crazy" Memphis or the South is, "all the race issues," "how corrupt things are," and "how hard it is growing up" or how hard it is "just being in Memphis" or in the South. In these contexts, living the legacy was not equated with feelings of triumph over struggle but rather with living in the shadow of a legacy of hate, branded upon the city as the site of King's assassination and ongoing racial discrimination.

Once respondents became comfortable with the idea that I was from Memphis and accorded me a measured insider status, I frequently pushed them to explain what they meant as if I were not from Memphis. For the few respondents who were not from the South or had spent most of their lives outside of the South, black Memphians were defeated by a southern racial history of slavery, Jim Crow, and civil rights. Hasan told me: "I mean, I lived in Brooklyn. Bed-Stuy. There's police brutality [in Brooklyn] and all of that. All of the problems you have in a city where there's a bunch of people of color. But these people here are so beat down [. . .] so beat down by the history. It's like, all of the black folks here walking 'round like they still depressed about [the assassination of] King. Like they responsible or something." Ruth Ann, who lived in a predominantly black neighborhood before moving to the suburban Germantown as a teenager, also boiled the issue down to black/white racial interactions—after some prodding.

Here, things are so black/white. It's crushing. When you go out in public places where there are whites and black people, it's like a war. I mean, you can't even get a latte without them just staring at you. For me, it's like in the everyday interactions—the grocery store, the Starbucks, the gas station—that I feel like, "Wow, Jim Crow." [. . .] It's like, "Segregation isn't legal anymore, but we still don't want you coons in our store, or our space or whatever, so we just gon' look at you and make you feel dark." Uncomfortable, like, out of place.

Even Kiara, who is from Mississippi, argued that Memphis's racial history affects the way people, especially black people, experience the city. Raised in Jackson, which respondents often referred to as a smaller Memphis, Kiara is familiar with the black/white racial paradigm. When I encountered her donning an airbrushed "I Heart Jackson" T-shirt at a neo-soul show, she was defending the shirt's assertions from a couple of flirty neo-soul scene regulars, who insisted she had to have the shirt airbrushed because no one would screen-print such a thing. Coming north to Memphis to pursue a college degree, Kiara defends Jackson from naysayers by highlighting Memphis's own unresolved blues tensions. In an interview with her a few weeks after her T-shirt defense, she asserted:

KIARA: And y'all [Memphians] make fun of us [people from Mississippi] for being country and like we got it the worst. Jackson ain't nothing like this.

ZANDRIA: Why do you say that?

KIARA: Because, black people are all angry all the time here. I was down at the [National Civil Rights] museum and that woman was down there with her signs accosting people.[13] And I know the story and all that, but there's so much tension centered on that one thing. And the tension kinda radiates out to other things, so then you turn on the news and see brothas and sistas committing all sorts of crime [and it's] like, this is a city that's still got some serious problems. Unfinished business.

Still, whether respondents saw living the legacy as repressive, promising, or mandatory, they generally expressed a sense of responsibility for tending to this "unfinished business" of the civil rights movement through the use of soul music, the teaching of soul histories, and everyday service and struggle. Don, whom I first met at a service project for unhoused men in the North Memphis community, framed his service work as a continuation of the legacy of King and of "all the people who struggled to make this city a better place," a theme frequently echoed among respondents involved in all sorts of labor. "We responsible for each other," he said. "I'm responsible for you; you responsible for me. That's the lesson of [Martin Luther King Jr.] that these white folks just ain't got. They ain't responsible for us as human beings. You know what I'm saying, we *are* responsible for ourselves on a *personal* level. But we s'posed to look out for each other, too, like as spiritual brothers and sisters. White folks don't see us that way, like as their God-kin. But that's okay. That's why I'm here every week."

Don is indeed dedicated to the work he does, sometimes getting off from his third shift at a technology corporation and heading straight to the service site. When he was furloughed from work in late 2008, he continued to serve, using savings to purchase toiletries and other items for the clients. Raised in an Orange Mound church and growing up in South Memphis, Don's grandmother was instrumental in teaching him the significance of service as part of his community kinship. Many respondents, like Don, saw whatever service they engaged in, formally or informally, as rooted in a spiritual kinship. Yet, they also saw this as race work for which they were responsible, lest "[Martin Luther King Jr.] would have died for nothing." Whether respondents wholeheartedly link their social responsibility to King's assassination or operationalize it as a familiar and powerful trope to justify their work is unclear. However, just as artists, entrepreneurs, and culture producers operate on the peripheries of Beale Street, respondents argued that they operate at the margins of service to speak for people shooed unceremoniously from the center.

From City to Region

While living the legacy is a place-specific phenomenon, many Memphians use "Memphis" and the "South" interchangeably, a function of the South's otherness as well as of the ongoing desire to highlight distinctly southern black identities and experiences as separate from non-southern black identities and experiences. To move from city to region, respondents first looked to the rural South, and to the Mississippi Delta in particular. Brian, a single father whom I met as he deftly maneuvered two toddlers into swings at a North Memphis park, was eager to draw the connections between the physical and social landscape of Memphis and his great-grandmother's home on the outskirts of Greenville, Mississippi. "You know, it's bigger than the city of Memphis [. . .]. Memphis is a Delta place, always has been. A southern place. [. . .] All of us here is from the Delta in some kind of way. We all have these Delta tendencies. It's so country here. Especially the old black neighborhoods, like in North Memphis. You go down Hollywood [Street] and the storefronts all look like

Delta storefronts. You can't tell if you in Mississippi or Memphis except for the paved, four-lane [roads]."

In Brian's estimation, "Delta" functioned as shorthand for the rural South, as it often does in popular, literary, and scholarly contexts. He talked at length about similarities between Memphis and the Delta, from music styles, worship practices, and criteria for starting a fight to facial features and architecture. Brian's contention collapses the diversity of the rural South by situating the seventeen-county Mississippi Delta between the Yazoo and Mississippi Rivers as the quintessential South. Nevertheless, respondents often used this shorthand to unify communities as diverse as small black towns in the Tennessee piney woods to communities in rural Georgia and the Louisiana bayous. In this way, "Delta" stands in for a rural southern experience that is unique to black southerners regardless of their location in the region. Southern cities serve as the urban counterparts to this universal rural community.

Because black communities were often built hastily to accommodate expanding populations as people migrated from rural areas in search of work, these communities do continue to resemble their architectural forebears in the Mississippi Delta. Other respondents talked about Memphis in language similar to Brian's, describing the city as a "country town." Not only did being a Delta country town—or as it is sometimes called, the biggest city in North Mississippi—make Memphis distinct from Chicago, but in respondents' estimations, it also distinguished it from newer South destinations like Atlanta and Dallas. Indeed, Memphis's position as the first major urban stop out of the Mississippi Delta influenced its character, as rural populations migrated to and settled in the city for much of the late nineteenth and early twentieth centuries.

Respondents also situated the city as more authentically southern, and in some cases more authentically black, in a post–civil rights context. Brenda, a single mother of two and a paralegal, told me over the blast of competing speakers blaring both reggae and soul music at Memphis's annual festival Africa in April that "it don't get more southern than Memphis and still be a city. When people don't like it here, that's why." Brenda, who attended college in Boston briefly before returning to Memphis and settling in a then-integrated Hickory Hill, has family in Sunflower County that she ensures her children see every summer and each holiday. As we navigated the brightly colored booths selling white and yellow shea butters, incense, knockoff purses, handcrafted earrings, and paintings, I asked her to say more about what she meant about Memphis being on the precipice of non-urban southernness.

BRENDA: Well, after Memphis, you got the Delta, and ain't nothing but country down there. There's Jackson, [Mississippi,] but it's 'bout deserted. And New Orleans is a different kind of South.

ZANDRIA: What about in Georgia, like Atlanta, or Florida or the Carolinas?

BRENDA: What? That ain't no South. Or no real South no way. What kinda music come outta there? What they done sung? Hell, don't we got the most churches here? A church make you South and black! We win on that! And look at all these black folks 'round here! We win on that, too!

For Brenda, the soul tradition and contributions to American culture, black Christian religiosity, and a relatively high number of black people rendered Memphis an authentic southern and black place.

Several respondents, including most key respondents, drew on quantitative logics to calculate regional and racial authenticity. Though Memphis, like urban areas across the nation and the South especially, has a growing Latino population, it straddles two different New Souths: the New South of urban magnets and growth centers, like Dallas, Charlotte, and Atlanta, and the enduring Old South of Louisiana, Mississippi, and Alabama, where black/white racial patterns are particularly entrenched. Memphis's position in the middle, respondents contended, makes it the best representative of native black identity. Jayla, a twenty-eight-year-old human resources professional whom I met on one of several trips to area beauty salons, talked at length about black identity, drawing on her experiences in Atlanta during college as well as on her intermittent visits with uncles and aunts in the Mississippi Delta. Newly married to her Trinidadian husband, whom she met in Atlanta, she drew a contrast that many respondents without much contact with West Indian populations made as well:

There are lots of ways to be black these days. I didn't [. . .] think about that before I met [my husband] and his people. But there's like this main way to be black: like you gotta be a Christian and go to church, you gotta live in a black neighborhood, you can't talk white but you can't have a foreign accent, and that's what you see on TV, too. [In Memphis] you don't really have a lot of different kind of black folks mixing in the culture, and the [Latinos] we do have are like separate and not mixing either, or they're with the white folks if they can be. So it's like this is where real black folks are.

Highlighting the usual tropes of blackness that are particularly pronounced in the South, like religiosity, Jayla contended that the overwhelming presence of "regular" black folks, as opposed to "different" ones, constitutes an authentic blackness and southernness. In a follow-up interview with her several months later, I asked Jayla in passing how her husband was adjusting to Memphis since their move from Atlanta. She recounted with excitement her efforts to socialize him into the "real" South.

> Oh, I took him to the Civil Rights Museum, to Stax, places I had never been before, too, like [the Rock & Soul Museum] and had him listening to Rufus [Thomas] records. And [begins laughing uncontrollably] I took him down to Mississippi where my uncle and 'em live and had them giving him the Mississippi treatment: popping chicken heads, scary stories about lynchings and the Klan and everything. He's been *hazed*. I was down there [in Atlanta] with him and his people eating all they food and listening to they stories. He didn't know nothing about the South except for them Atlanta folks. I said, "Naw, Boo, here's some real South, some real black folks for ya."

In addition to hazing her new spouse, Jayla attempted to thoroughly expose her husband to "real" southern and black culture, effectively inauthenticating both Atlanta as a southern space and Trinidadian as a black ethnicity. When pressed, she admitted that she had not, herself, popped chicken heads or spent much time with her uncles in the Delta at all but had them play along with her husband's initiation. To his mortification, they had eagerly obliged.

The southernness that she and her uncles showed her husband was certainly a deliberate achievement, an accomplishment garnered through at least some exaggeration of the lived experience of southern rural cultures. Still, this accomplishment required some strategic displacement of a modern Memphis. After all, Jayla and her husband live in one of the most racially and ethnically diverse neighborhoods in the city—where there are few, if any, vulnerable chickens in the yard.

From Region to Race

In 2008, the fortieth anniversary of Martin Luther King Jr.'s assassination was commemorated in Memphis with a number of events, including a race conference, gospel concerts, a march, and events at Mason Temple, where King gave his last speech, and at the National Civil Rights Museum, on the site of the Lorraine Motel, where he was shot. Much was made by some of the absence of presidential candidate Barack Obama from the commemoration, as other presidential candidates had journeyed to Memphis to demonstrate their commitment to civil rights. Among those present at the various celebrations throughout the city were journalist Tavis Smiley and Princeton University professors Cornel West and Eddie Glaude Jr. At a concert in downtown Memphis in July of that year, at which Smiley was present, the journalist was given the microphone to inform the audience of "something special" that he, West, Georgetown professor Michael Eric Dyson, Glaude, and others would be doing in the city in the coming months.

From the balcony, I peered over the rail as Smiley and West left their seats down front and headed to the stage. As Smiley took the microphone, the woman behind me whispered loudly to her companion, "Now, what the hell you think they doing?" Her comment inspired giggles, rumblings, and "um-hmm"s throughout our section of the balcony, which in turn spurred someone farther back to question West's wardrobe. The full-scale laughing and violent stifling of snickering that followed were quickly halted, ironically, by a "shush" from Person Zero.

I convinced this person, Ms. Doris, to do an interview with me to compensate me for what I told her I was sure was spittle from her "shush" on the back of my neck. In her early fifties, she asked me a series of questions about the research, and several times asked if I was a journalist. We stood in a narrow side lobby of the downtown concert space until I convinced her that I was not a reporter and would keep her statements anonymous. After she acquiesced and gave me her contact information, she relaxed and began to explain. She said, half to me and half to herself, "You know, you just have to wonder when some big shots say they coming to do 'something special.' They aren't going to build a shelter or donate any money or anything. They're here to take something." I did not get to ask her what she meant then, as facility employees eager to close the building ushered us out. I noted her comment, not so much for its content but for the sense of ominousness with which she had said it.

When we sat down for an interview a few months later, she told me about the work her South Memphis church does with several local HIV/AIDS outreach organizations. She cares for her grandmother, who lives with her in a subdivision of bungalow-style houses near the city's southern limits. She described herself as in the trenches working on some of the city's most complex social problems, and she again expressed resentment of what she sees as lip service to these issues. I asked her to say more. She replied, "People come here and get what they can get, and it does no one here any good. I'm not even talking about white people. I'm talking about our people. It makes them look good to come here and hang with the po' ol' country bumpkins. It's the history of this place that they want to be a part of. Not making it better for the people that are here now."

Attending an elementary school in the Orange Mound community when King was assassinated, Ms. Doris recounted hazy remembrances of watching news reports at a neighbor's house. The sentiments she shared were even more pronounced among younger respondents, who often feel that focus on the civil rights era does little to address the continuing significance and new manifestations of race and racism. She maintained that the "something special" would not be of use to black Memphians.

I called Ms. Doris in May of the following year, when audiences were introduced to this "something special" on African American cable channel TV One: the documentary *Stand*. After some cajoling, she agreed to watch the documentary. To decrease the likelihood that she would change the channel, I offered to make the seventeen-mile trek to her house with some cookies and bring her some crushed ice, her grandmother's favorite. After proclaiming that she did not want to trouble me, she quickly agreed.

We—Ms. Doris, her grandmother, and her son, visiting from New Orleans—crowded around Ms. Doris's twenty-inch television set on her kitchen table. Smiley introduced viewers to his "soul patrol": his assistant, Raymond Ross; Eddie Glaude, Cornel West, and Michael Eric Dyson; West's brother, songwriter Cliff West; gospel artist BeBe Winans; actor Wren T. Brown; comedian and writer Dick Gregory; and two high school students from Memphis, cousins Daron Boyce and Robert Smith, whose grandmother Ms. Doris insisted she knew. Their purpose, Smiley told us, was to recapture an age when black men stood for something as well as to understand, in the wake of the fortieth anniversary of the King assassination and a historic presidential election, what it means to stand for something in contemporary America.

In the documentary, Memphis serves as the soul patrol's rendezvous point, as well as a beginning and ending point from which the crew could reflect. Shuttling back and forth between Memphis and Nashville, which together stood in for the civil rights South at large, the soul patrol stood reflectively on the balcony where King was shot; listened intently and in some instances tearfully to a performance by the Fisk Jubilee Singers; and went "back" to church, including Mason Temple, where King delivered his final speech, and St. Andrew A.M.E. Church in South Memphis. During the documentary, Ms. Doris received a number of phone calls from church members instructing her to turn the television on channel 67 if she had not already.

Stand delivered a normative, male-centered reading of contemporary black politics that questioned Obama's racial authenticity through an operationalization of regional politics: a southern strategy in black, as it were. Civil rights, community organizing, working-class black folks, King, churches, historically black colleges, and gospel music served as the rallying imagery of this strategy, effectively highlighting an imagined distance between the Yankee Obama and the struggles of the civil rights movement and everyday working people. Afterward, Ms. Doris's church members rang her cell and house phone, and I helped her field calls. When things were settled and most of the cookies were eaten, I asked Ms. Doris if she thought her suppositions from our interview the prior winter had been confirmed. "Now what did we get out of that?" she asked me. "Just what did we get out of that?"

Ms. Doris was not the only respondent to question the equality of the relationship between the public intellectuals featured in *Stand* and the broader Memphis community. Her sentiments highlight an enduring feature of the post-soul blues. As one of OutKast's songs says, "The whole world loves it when you sing the blues."[14] That is, in the post–civil rights context, stories about infant mortality, scores of pregnant girls at a Memphis high school, disproportionately high rates of HIV infection, flooding—in short, the blues—abound. Across age and generational differences, black southerners widely accuse race leaders and public intellectuals, such as Jesse Jackson and Al Sharpton, as well as non-southerners, of being unnecessarily outraged at white folks' behavior and not outraged enough about everyday and institutional injustices black folks experience.

Marcus, a street hustler who sells bootlegged DVDs, among other things, said that black folks outside of the South do not really care about what is going on in the South. After encountering Marcus selling his wares all along the city's western corridor, from outside of an African American mall south of Graceland to a North Memphis barbershop I frequented, I asked him to sit for an interview with me. In our first interview, he reiterated a refrain of his that had become immensely popular in the barbershop, as customers and barbers alike imitated Marcus's fervor: "Kanyé [West] say *George Bush* don't care about black people? Hell, black people don't care about black people!" I was eager to hear what was behind the popular refrain, and Marcus told me that black folks are focusing on the wrong things and are "getting up in arms" about things designed to "get them on television":

Okay, like that thing that happened in Louisiana with the dudes and the nooses [the Jena Six case].[15] Yeah, they probably whipped that white boy. Yeah, the jail sentence or whatever might have been unfair, but that happens every day, everywhere, to black folks everywhere. You can't really focus on what they do, because they gon' do what they gon' do to you.

Plus, ain't nobody came down to 201 [Poplar, the address of the county court and jailhouse] and protested for me and all the other niggas when the folks [police] got us hemmed up on some unfair shit. I guess it's 'cause there wasn't no nooses or nothing like that. Next time I get hemmed up on some bullshit, I'm gon' have my white partner burn a cross outside my apartment. Then Jesse 'nem will come get *me* out of jail.

Marcus reported being the victim of police brutality and receiving unfairly long jail sentences for relatively minor misdemeanor infractions. He argued that folks like Al Sharpton come to the South only when "it's something about rights" and "being up in white folks' faces to get some of that government money." I continued to see him in the usual places, and I asked him for a second interview several months later to follow up on our discussions. I met him at his tiny efficiency, which smelled of incense and the salty seasonings of ramen noodle packages, to give him a ride to our interview spot at a South Memphis park. On the uncomfortable stone benches, we half-watched the end of a three-on-three tournament on which he had bet. Commenting on the burgeoning basketball skills of his three-year-old son, he told me reflectively:

> My baby, my first baby, he . . . he . . . you know, he died, you know. He was six months. My sister baby died, my cousin baby died, and this other girl stay down the street, her baby died. This was when I was in [a North Memphis neighborhood]. All of them, they babies was born early. They all live over there by [a chemical plant], too. Where is the good Reverend Doctor Al and Jesse then, to protest [the chemical plant]? The white folks can hang a Confederate flag and [nooses] all through [that neighborhood] if don't no more of our babies die like that.

Memphis's infant mortality rate continues to be the highest urban infant mortality rate in the nation, and Marcus attributed the particular cases of infant death with which he was familiar, including the death of his six-month-old son, to a chemical plant in a North Memphis community. Explicit in his statement is a critique of black leadership's failure to respond to enduring crises in the African American community, such as mass incarceration and infant mortality. Yet, implicit in his statement is an intraracial class critique, one in which Sharpton and Jackson pretend to engage the poor to serve their middle-class interests. While he might think Kanyé West's critique of former President Bush is sound, Marcus might argue that Bush's not caring about black people is to be expected; after all, as he contended, white folks "gon' do what they gon' do to you."

Efforts like *Stand*, for respondents, fall in line with what they see as opportunist appropriations of the South, its history, and the legacy of the civil rights movement. Academics, too, identify a veritable civil rights industrial complex from which some black public figures benefit by association. In a June 5, 2009, CNN online commentary, political scientist Harris-Lacewell offered an analysis of Smiley's documentary that was quickly circulated around the black intellectual blog circuit, sparking what are now ongoing and cyclical conversations about what constitutes productive and respectful critique of a black president and about the role of black public intellectuals vis-à-vis a black president. Harris-Lacewell argued that *Stand* "yearned for an imagined racial past . . . [which] by their accounting . . . had better music, more charismatic leaders and a more-involved black church."[16] At its core, Harris-Lacewell's critique highlights the inherent contradictions and willful rewriting of history that make possible and problematic the claims of *Stand*.

Rather than being unique in its articulation of black politics and black communities, *Stand* is emblematic of the appropriation of the South and of sanitized memories of the civil rights era in service of racial authenticity. Perhaps much more blasphemous than appropriating the legacy of King, Smiley's soul patrol appropriated an imagined legacy of the black South—a better blackness—that centralized control of black institutions in the hands of a few male leaders and community activists and subjugated women, LGBT communities, and other undesirables to helper roles, or excised them completely from the narrative. *Stand* ultimately takes the usual class politics—middle-class anxieties about the ability to keep the race "on message" when poor black people are out supposedly buying their children Michael Jordan tennis shoes—and shrouds them in the legacy of the civil rights movement. However, it goes a step further, taking an all-male bus trip through the South to persuade audiences to look toward a better blackness for sociopolitical inspiration and historical rootedness.

There is certainly a difference between everyday southerners' situation of black southern identities as authentically black and the appropriation of those identities as authentically black to promote a political agenda that obscures the diversity of black communities in national contexts. Yet, for better or for worse, representations of southern experience are most often rooted in traditional southern cultural tropes: working-class folk, spiritual, connected and close-knit, downtrodden yet triumphant. Nevertheless, in practice, a completely folk life, or even a folk-inspired life, is not possible for many respondents. They therefore deploy tropes of the folk, or

country-ness, in tandem with a distinctly cosmopolitan post-soul life, laying claim to racial authenticity in ways accessible only through southern
experience.

Memphis: Home of the Post-Soul Blues

Memphis's location at the temporal, geographical, and spatial intersections of civil rights and post–civil rights, soul and post-soul, and Old
South and New South render it both similar to and distinct from many
places in the South. The city is distinctive for what sociologist Wanda
Rushing has highlighted as its confluence of paradoxes of power, place,
and identity. Despite its booming industries, including transportation
and biotechnology, the city's continued underinvestment in education
coupled with the persistence of poverty among a substantial portion
of African Americans and Latinos root Memphis firmly in familiar Old
South power dynamics.

Respondents frequently cited what some call "a negative energy" from
Memphians about the city, where people are down on the city and locate
their personal blues in the city and its inhabitants. Some respondents retorted, "Only in Memphis" or "That's Memphis for you" in response to any
negative publicity about the city in local or national media, from being
designated the fattest and ugliest city on various lists to being featured on
the A&E channel's real crime show *The First 48*. While locals in a number
of places are down on their neighborhoods and hometowns, respondents
contended that Memphians' overall hatred of the place was especially pronounced. Even generally upbeat respondents recounted to me moments in
which a fellow Memphian's negativity about the city changed their mood.
To counter these negative narratives, a number of campaigns, including
the "I Love Memphis" public art project and the *I Love Memphis* blog, have
sought to capture voices of hopeful city residents and balance the blues fog
of history and inequality that hangs over the bluff.

Still, tales of woe are the stuff of any good blues narrative and as such
are requisite elements of the city's accomplishment of place. Certainly, as
I demonstrated above, outsiders hijack the city's blues narrative to demarcate the political boundaries of authentic blackness and to lend credence
to their own epistemological positions. Locals, too, draw on the blues narrative to authenticate themselves as southerners, as the folk, and as au-
thorized to speak on inequality. From Millington, Tennessee, native Justin
Timberlake to the shirts sold in Beale Street shops that declare, "No black.
No white. Just blues," blues and soul histories serve as simple covers for

the enduring inequality that disproportionately affects the city's African American population.

Despite its appropriation by others, blues in its various forms, including funk, soul, neo-soul, and hip-hop, remains the language through which southern black identity is articulated in the post-soul era. Through hip-hop, black southerners have fashioned a post-soul blues that blends the country, rural, and folk knowledge passed down through generations with cosmopolitan critical analyses of the realities of race and class in the city. Cognizant of the presence of the blues as a cultural and structural fact of blackness in Memphis, respondents contended that the adversity not only makes them stronger but renders them better southerners and better black folks as well.

Respondents claimed that much of Memphis's blues and blues authenticity is attributable to its enduring rural character and proximity to the Mississippi Delta. Though Memphis might be a "Delta place," it is not, in fact, the Delta. Black Memphians are glad of that, some more openly than others. Yet, patterns of poverty and structures of interracial interaction similar to that of the Delta undergird the post-soul black experience in Memphis, even for the middle classes. Cosmopolitan ideologies do not always neatly address the persistence of the country Old South of racism, strict gender norms, whispered politics of respectability, and a seemingly unending struggle for equality.

CHAPTER THREE

Not Stud'n' 'em White Folks

I was at a city government public service facility that, like many local and state government service offices, employs predominantly African American women. Black women make up a growing segment of the black middle class across the country, but particularly in the South. As employees of city government's service sector, the four women at this particular facility, behind their respective panes of glass, interact with a cross-section of city residents and face the challenges of their race, perceived class, and gender statuses as they work as agents of local government. I have used this particular branch of this government service facility each year for three years and remember and recognize the women employed there, as they do me. During this visit, I found that the office had moved to a new space in the same shopping plaza, a space far nicer and roomier than their previous location. There are even chairs in the facility's waiting area now. Previously, customers stood in far-too-close proximity and anguish waiting for their number to be called. In those tight spaces, all of the rules of southern decorum and public politeness were tested to their fragile limits.

The office was empty save for a woman rustling papers in one of the new chairs, and I did not have to pull a number. I walked up to the middle window, and after exchanging catch-up pleasantries, I commented about the new space. "This sure is an upgrade from where y'all were," I said to Ms. Jefferies, who was busily typing away and frowning at her computer screen. She is a stocky woman with a cropped haircut as no-nonsense as her varied facial expressions. As her coworkers nodded, bowed their heads, waved their hands up to God, and muttered "amen," Ms. Jefferies widened her eyes and slammed her hands down on the counter in front of her, leaned forward, and shouted through the plexiglass, without pushing the intercom button:

MS. JEFFERIES: Oh, honey, that is an understatement! An understatement, I tell you. That other office was horrid. They had us in there, chil', we was all so sick, Ora [gesturing to a coworker] suing the city for what they done to our health. There wasn't room to do your own work without touching the other person, and when we tell 'em about it, they say, here are some gloves to keep down germs. Some damned gloves? Then they had the bathroom about five feet from the break room where we ate! Where we ate! That means there was just shit and whatever else you got to do in the bathroom right across from where we ate! And the germs, we was in way too close proximity!

ZANDRIA: Well, so y'all complained or what?

MS. JEFFERIES: Hell yes, we complained, but them white folks don't care. Because it's us up in here [vigorously rubbing the back of her hand to signify that "us" means "black people"]. Well, there was that one little white girl that work with us, but hell, she may as well been black, she was from the wrong side of the tracks, honey, and she had a nigga child and a nigga baby daddy and had them ol' nigga hairdos all the time. I'm telling you, you can't trust white folks to do right nowhere, no how, when money's involved . . . and when doing right by colored folks is involved. Especially these good ol' Dixie boys 'round here.

ZANDRIA: So how did you get this new place?

MS. JEFFERIES: Honey, we started shutting this office down. We told them. We told them white folks, but they wouldn't listen. I said, we can't work under these conditions and we are not going to. So we shutting the office down. The office supposed to be open 8 to 5? We'd shut it down on lunch, or we'd shut it down at the other peak time, from 3:30 P.M. on, when folks getting off work. Then when the white folks called the other white folks complaining this office wasn't open, because you know this is like the center of the city so lots of people come here rather than going to the offices further out, oh look, they bought us a bigger, nicer space, but it was with they teeth gritted the whole damned time. I tell you these white folks ain't no good nowhere.

Ora, her colleague who had been "mmm-hmmm"ing the entire time, interjected and playfully chided her: "Aw, Ms. Jefferies, nowhere?" she said with a laugh that anticipated a rise out of her longtime coworker. "Yes, I repeat," said Ms. Jefferies, cutting her eyes to her right toward Ora, "no*where*. 'Cept maybe in heaven. And they cheated to get in there. Anything else I can do for you today, Ms. Robinson?"

I met Ms. Jefferies, who has been working for the city for seventeen years, at her home not far from the office a few months later. Like I have known her to do in the office, she spoke loudly and clearly. She smoked, as my mother would say, like a chimney as she told me about the developments on the job since I had come in the previous fall. The new office was just one small step forward, as she and other coworkers were putting together a petition for a number of other concessions, from a raise to updated software that would decrease time-per-customer by two minutes. The experiences of Ms. Jefferies and her coworkers undoubtedly mirror the experiences of disadvantaged service workers across industries, and their ability to resist and win some conciliations for their working conditions is rooted in activist and civil rights traditions. Yet, in the South, these experiences are particularly racialized as indicative of the continued manifestation of Old South racism, whose prominent features include whites intent on not treating blacks fairly or equally and middlemen blacks who are granted some political and economic power in exchange for managing the black working classes.

I asked Ms. Jefferies how these new negotiations were going, and she sighed and cocked her head to the side, half looking at me, half looking off. "You know, I have been praying a lot about how it's gon' go, praying for the white folks to find some act-right in them, somewhere. But you know, I told my sister the other day, I'm gon' stop praying for these white folks. A white woman supervisor came into our location the other day and talked so crazy to us that Jesus must've glued my mouth shut and the Holy Spirit must've bound up my fists. After I felt my pressure rise up, I said, you know what? I can't be stud'n' 'em. I can't be stud'n' 'em white folks."

Ms. Jefferies's sentiments are representative of those of many folks I talked with, especially working-class and lower-middle-class thirty- and forty-somethings. "Not stud'n' 'em white folks," at the very least, means supplanting emotional reactions to everyday racialized injustice, whether a slight in service during a restaurant visit or a blatantly discriminatory employment outcome, with indifference. Many respondents indicated that they are neither surprised nor regretful when "good" white folks go bad, nor do they demonstrate or express gratefulness or surprise when "bad" white folks do good. Belying this indifference are sincere attempts to reconcile the continuation of Old South racism with the race and class promises of the New South. That is, as Ms. Jefferies told me, "that 'the South done changed' mess done got in all our blood, even mine, because it *has* changed. But it's still the same some kinda way."

Everyday racial realities in the contemporary urban South counter hegemonic discourses about African American experiences in the region, even as they signify and affirm complex racial pasts that seep into the present and threaten the future in distinctly post–civil rights ways. That is, as much as southerners might want to say that things have not changed, new forms of Jim Crow must be acknowledged, stealthy products of what sociologist and race scholar Eduardo Bonilla-Silva has called "racism without racists." While the South has come to represent an invidious, torturous racism that fundamentally and systematically denies black humanity, it has also come to embody a racial paradise, one in which black political and economic power trumps forms of racism for which the South is most infamous. Respondents reject hegemonic constructions of the region's racial landscape although they cannot exist outside of the influence of such constructions. Still, their conceptualizations of race and racial interactions are informed by the intersection of three factors.

First, they are informed by intergenerational collective memories of "Old South" racism, tied to specific people and specific places but not necessarily to the entire region. Most respondents talked about a pivotal experience of racism that they experienced firsthand or, more often, that they had heard about second- or thirdhand from kin and community members. Second, respondents' theorizations of race and region are informed by the specter and spectacle of Old South racism: the ongoing metanarrative that recurs in conversations with non-southerners about their fears of the region, in civil rights–era films and documentaries, in conversations about "the N-word," in debates over Confederate commemorations, and in the iconography of the Old South. Third, respondents' impressions and assertions are informed by black racial realities and contradictions of the New South, including unprecedented wealth for some and continued impoverishment for others. Together these elements—collective memory, the specter and spectacle of Old South racism, and the growing intraracial class divide in the region—shape black southerners' approach to race, racism, and racial interaction. Black southerners claim to have "figured out" white folks because of this region-based experiential and epistemological position, gained over generations of close proximity to whites. Such claims bolster black southerners' assertions of a better blackness, in that, as Ms. Jefferies's coworker Ora told me in the office that day, they "don't get all worked up over race like [non-southern blacks] because we already know the score." As such, these claims draw on the commonsense wit of country-ness and the healthy, but not overpowering, skepticism of cosmopolitanism.

Yet, the boundary work inherent in these claims yields a carefully crafted performative veneer that functions in two ways. First, these claims are part of the process by which respondents make sense of continuing instances of white racism and prejudice, institutional and interpersonal, in a supposedly new South that has transcended its history of racial oppression. By casting all whites as racist a priori and dismissing instances of white racism as expected, respondents mask the true and continuing significance of race in their everyday interactions. Essentially, to resolve tensions in their epistemological position—knowing white folks but being surprised and even shocked by whites' behaviors—respondents, at least outwardly, do not "study them white folks."

Although my respondents, like Ms. Jefferies, are generally racially sure, a phrase Keith used to describe when he knows he has been discriminated against on the basis of race, there is an uncertainty in their assuredness that characterizes the changing contours of race. While vestiges of Jim Crow are certainly visible and evident, the region is profoundly different for older respondents who grew up in the segregated South. As Marie once said during one of our kitchen island cook-and-chats, "Sometimes it's hard to trust your gut on these white folks. Sometimes the signal's confusing." For younger respondents who did not directly experience legal Jim Crow— although many of them have certainly experienced "new" Jim Crow in interpersonal and structural contexts—the "gut" to which Marie referred is almost wholly constructed from collective memory, metanarratives about the South, and extensive analyses, by themselves or with friends, of negative interracial experiences.

In this chapter, I explore the interplay of the specter of Old South racism and New South black realities in interracial interactions in the contemporary South. Respondents pass down and draw on regionally ingrained folk wisdom about whites and white racism and situate this knowledge as key to knowing precisely how to best engage whites. Like Brooklyn native and rapper Mos Def advises, southerners simultaneously "keep white folks out their faces, in their prayers, and in their crosshairs."[1] While black southerners are often constructed as "country" in the pejorative sense vis-à-vis race relations—submissiveness, eyes lowered, jumping off the sidewalk to let white people pass—respondents fundamentally repudiated this idea. For most respondents, a "country" approach to racism is one of clever wit, strategic subversion, and dissemblance. Cosmopolitanism enters the picture when they refuse to operate as tricksters in the shadows. Respondents often confront and out racists and perceived racism rather than suffer in silence. Yet, cosmopolitanism can also take on a more problematic form. In an effort to move beyond race in a post-racial era and give whites "the benefit of the doubt," some respondents count themselves as progressive, and in their estimations cosmopolitan sophisticates, when they eschew discussions of race and inequality. In turn, they construct others who talk about race openly as country, backward, and race card players always on the lookout for The Man and the Klan.

Both manifestations of country cosmopolitan views on race—black tricksterism that emerges from the shadows to indict whites for their racial biases and a color-blind blackness that is wholly silent about race—underlie the deceptively simple racial calculations that black southerners make to navigate the complex racial terrain in the modern South. The simplicity of these calculations is the accomplishment ruse: that is, while contemporary black southerners may have intimate folk knowledge of whites, firsthand and inherited, and may draw on this knowledge to anticipate, explain, or ignore white racism, the unfulfilled promises of the New South engender a hidden disappointment when whites misbehave—even if black folks expect them to do so.[2] I draw on contemporary race paradigms and collective memories of the South to contextualize the country cosmopolitan racial logic inherent in respondents' everyday negotiations of race. Respondents often engage in complex labor to make interracial interactions appear effortless and harmless. For many of my respondents, appearing unfazed by negative interracial interactions is an integral part of being "better black folks," although the appearance belies deep racial wounds, both real and fictive.

On the Continuing Significance of Race

Race continues to be as integral to American social structures in the "post-racial" era as it was when the U.S. Constitution counted individual enslaved African Americans as three-fifths of a human being. Today, blacks are still more likely to be discriminated against in every social institution, from housing to employment to health care. Blacks die earlier and have more chronic illnesses, are more likely to be offered more expensive credit even when they are well qualified, are less likely to have stable wealth, and are more likely to be incarcerated and for longer periods of time than their white counterparts for similar crimes. Further, these outcomes cannot be explained away by differences in class status between blacks and whites. Even when class is held constant, middle-class blacks fare worse on most measures than their middle-class white counterparts. Thus, while the intersection of race with other sites of oppression, including gender and class, yields different manifestations of inequality, differential access to opportunity and privilege is a consistent feature of the experiences of people of color in the United States. Continued and intractable structural discrimination is the long-term effect of the entrenchment of racialization processes. Even when people's attitudes about race, equality, and social justice become more progressive, because race is indelibly inscribed onto social institutions, undoing structural discrimination is seemingly impossible.

Few African Americans would be surprised by the outcomes of academic research on race, and many share experiences of race and racism similar to those highlighted in research on black folks' self-reports of racism. Several scenes of American racism are now so familiar to African Americans that they have become a part of the metanarrative of interracial interaction in "post-racial" America. There is the elevator scene, in which a white woman tenses, clutches her purse, and/or moves as far away as spatially possible when left alone on the elevator with a black man, regardless of the latter's appearance or dress; the street scene, where whites cross the street when blacks approach or where blacks are passed up by an available taxi; the retail shopping scene, where blacks are followed and/or routinely ignored; and the restaurant scene, where blacks receive subpar service and/or are routinely ignored, leading to the chicken-or-the-egg conundrum of black folks' tipping practices.[3]

These narratives are part of African Americans' collective experiences of racism, so much so that they are regular fodder for black comedians and serve as points of reference in everyday conversations about racial experiences. High-profile blacks' experiences of racism—Danny Glover's inability to get a cab in 1999, the denial of Oprah Winfrey's entrance into a high-end boutique in Paris in 2005, and the 2009 arrest of Harvard professor Henry Louis Gates Jr. in his home—also become part of this collective experience of racism. Similarly, regular black folks' experiences, whether in an elevator or restaurant, or the more disturbing incidents, such as the police killings of Sean Bell, Oscar Grant, Tarika Wilson, and Jonathan Ferrell are sobering reminders of the impact of race on everyday life, particularly in confrontations with powerful agents of government structures.[4]

The simultaneously fluid and fixed nature of race, charges of reverse racism, and denial of continued racial inequality—all fixtures of the post-racial age of Obama—make difficult work of navigating the realities of race in modern America. As both cultural anthropologist John L. Jackson Jr. and journalist Touré point out, it is increasingly difficult to locate racial discrimination with certainty, leading to what Jackson calls "racial paranoia."[5] Jackson argues that African Americans draw on "tools that allow us to see past what [whites] say, or even do, into their very hearts," to determine whether or not they are racist.[6] This is particularly true for black southerners, whose historically intimate interpersonal contact with whites requires a sophisticated system of negotiation and has resulted in both enduring theories of white folks' behaviors and a propensity (to claim) not to study them.

In everyday interactions, racial paranoia works in tandem with Bonilla-Silva's notion of racism without racists. That is, not only might blacks be unsure if a particular interpersonal interaction was, in fact, racially motivated, but they also might be unsure if a particular structural outcome—an interest rate on a home or a car—was racially motivated. In the absence of the familiar racist of our collective American memories, it is increasingly difficult for most people to disentangle the structural web of institutional racism to point to a culprit. In fact, in our supposedly post-racial era, even crimes clearly motivated by racial hatred, from the dragging death of James Byrd Jr. in Jasper, Texas, in 1998 to the 2011 beating and murder of James Craig Anderson in Jackson, Mississippi, are divorced from the larger structural and power contexts in which they occur. Instead, they are reduced to the random behaviors of wayward extremists who do not represent the nation's broader sociopolitical moment.

White denial of more covert forms of racism, coupled with the wholesale dismissal of racially motivated hate crimes as outliers, creates a schizophrenic racial culture in which reason and logic are all but eliminated. Yet, whether markers of racism are present, ubiquitous, absent, or in question, black folks continue to function as metaphysicians of sorts, predicting and anticipating white behavior to protect themselves from harm as well as to defend themselves when harm is inevitable. It is in this climate that respondents, armed with country lessons, collective memories, and genuine, cosmopolitan desires for racial progress, theorize and make sense of interracial interactions in the New South.

Racism Happens

Respondents in this study, especially those of the post-soul generations, largely saw themselves as "not fretting" over race. In conversations about their perceptions of race and racism, the overarching narrative was surprisingly consistent across age and class groups: "White folks are racist." "That's just how it is." "You can't fret about it." Respondents could always point to an embodied culprit, a real-life perpetrator of racism, even in structural contexts. They refused the notion of paranoia, taking comfort in what they saw as a known quantity—white racism. Alelia, a thirty-four-year-old assistant manager at a department store in a suburban mall, went to a predominantly white high school in the suburban community in which she still lives and works. For our first interview, I offered to bring her a catfish plate—two fried catfish fillets, spaghetti, slaw, hush puppies, and two slices of white bread in a Styrofoam takeout container—from a fund-raiser another respondent was doing for her family reunion. We met in Midtown, which is as far from South Memphis as I could drive without winding up with soggy catfish and warm slaw. Between our bites, Alelia told me a number of stories about innocent black people being stopped and searched for stolen merchandise by store personnel and security. Despite confronting racism since she was a small child as one of the few blacks in her community and school, she expressed discomfort with witnessing or personally experiencing racial discrimination. As she summed up another story, she laughed uncomfortably and said quickly:

> But you know it's gonna happen. [The department store] is just that kind of store. Especially in [the mall in which she works]. Once they see you didn't actually take anything and they let you go, you just call right up to corporate and get yourself a fifty-dollar gift card. I tell my friends to come in here and look suspicious. I promise you can get those new shoes. The funny thing is, they don't even try to train [the security people and store personnel] not to profile people. You'd think they'd see the relationship between all of these complaints and the fifty-dollar gift cards. But they don't.

When I asked her to talk about what she meant by "looking suspicious," she detailed how she tells her friends to conform to prevailing notions of black women as loud, entitled, and underserving and encourages her friends with children to bring them along for added effect. She noted that not all or even most of the security guards and store personnel are white, but "they may as well be white, and you can count on them to act white." I asked her if she thought a fifty-dollar gift card—particularly one from the culprit institution—was enough to compensate for the public humiliation of being accused of something one did not do. She responded without looking up from her catfish plate: "Of course not. But you may as well get something. It's *gonna happen*. I wish I could get fifty dollars every time somebody discriminated against me. Like a ticket for parking in a no-parking zone? Fifty dollars for misdemeanor discrimination." She slapped her free hand on the wooden picnic table and with the other deftly combined a bit of catfish, a piece of white bread, and some cole slaw.

Alelia's experiences and sentiments are not uncommon. She and others repeatedly contended that interpersonal, and even structural, discrimination "will happen" and emphasized the importance of having a strategy at hand to deal with it, such as calling a company's regional or national corporate headquarters for compensation. However, she dismissed the psychological consequences of discrimination as unworthy of consideration because they, like discrimination, will happen, so she maintained black folks should get something for the trouble. I asked Christopher, a stocky twenty-eight-year-old with a desktop publishing business, if he prepares himself for experiences of discrimination when he goes out into the world. He said, "There is no way you can really prepare yourself. You still feel, like, assaulted every time something happens . . . but you don't go into a situation all paranoid and stuff, like, 'I know some white person's gon' do something to me today.' You know something could happen, and if there are white people involved, it probably will, but you just don't think about it. You can't. It'd drive you crazy."

Christopher saw his sentiments as rooted in the country ways of his parents and grandparents. Both of his parents are Mississippi Delta natives who migrated to Memphis in the 1980s shortly after he was born. They have close ties to their home county, and Christopher, like many black urbanites, southern and not, spent many summers and holidays in the Delta. An avid golfer, he met me for our second interview at Memphis's historically black golf course in the southwest part of town, built for the city's black residents in the 1940s. I asked him what he knew about his mother and father's experiences coming up in Mississippi, and it took the entire course to scratch the surface. He told me stories about his parents, his grandparents, both sets of which were still alive and still married, and his great-grandmothers:

My father and mother came up in a time where black folks could and would just go missing. Or, where they would have to leave before they met some nasty fate. And we're not talking about the Klan. They say there never was the Klan. It was just regularly clothed people who might be the local grocer—they might play with their kids or something, but they could just as well participate in making someone go missing if they got out of line. So, they developed a natural, like, protective suspicion. And they couldn't think about it all the time, or it would kill them. So, for me, I have that protective suspicion, too. I think they are better prepared for things than I am, though. From years of dealing with white folks, they know the best thing to do, no matter what I tell them. When I have children, I'm going to teach them like they taught me: "White folks can't stop you, but they'll sure try. Leave them in your rearview mirror." My mother still says that to me.

Christopher's approach to race matters emerged not only from his parents' country sensibilities but also from his own cosmopolitan spin on their teachings. He contended that, fundamentally, his parents' assessments are right, but that the temporal and spatial difference matters for how he and his future progeny will have to negotiate interracial interactions with whites. "I have to work with white people," he said. "My parents had their own [land] and did not have to deal with whites as much as some of the sharecroppers. But I have to work with white folks. And they're not all bad, you know, I'm progressive. And I know I have to work hard for mine. But like Mama said, some of them will try to stop you, so I've had to leave quite a few of them in the rearview."

For Christopher, the city requires an entirely different set of racial norms, although these norms are still informed by country epistemologies. By describing himself as progressive in the context of his declaration that white folks are not "all bad," Christopher rejected the implicit country idea that all whites are bad until they prove otherwise. For Christopher and other respondents with similar narratives, theirs is a "softer" approach to race that allows them to interact with and work with whites without giving off their true racial feelings. Still, there was ambivalence among respondents about whether or not one should or could have honest conversations about race or share their true racial feelings with whites. Jayla, who tortured her new husband with chicken killings, told me how her childhood friend reacted to her decision to cut her long, relaxed hair and wear her naturally textured hair.

> Now keep in mind, I went to school with this white girl from elementary all the way through high school, and we went to [college in Atlanta]. I've been to her house, she's been to mine, all of that. I told her basically that I was tired of wearing my white girl hair and was going to wear my own natural hair. I said I was tired of "European beauty standards," you know, I'm in college around all of the Black Power people, learning different things. She was shocked. She said, "So my friend is gonna be nappy-headed now?" I couldn't believe she had said that. I thought I could share that with her, but obviously, I couldn't without her making fun of me. I didn't say anything else like that to her, you know, nothing that had to do with race. She just couldn't understand. We eventually weren't good friends like that anymore.

Jayla's tone of voice, including a slight shakiness within it, indicated that she was obviously hurt by this exchange, despite how she might have downplayed its significance in the rest of that interview and in subsequent interactions we had. Yet, Jayla's was not the only narrative of sharing gone terribly wrong. I asked her how this incident has affected the way she thinks about racial interactions. She looked up to the ceiling of her kitchen, as if searching for how to frame her answer, then she looked squarely at me. "You know, my mother would tell me not to trust her, and I would be guarded about other white folks, you know, like I would smile in their face, never tell them what I was really thinking about anything, you know, standard stuff. But we had been friends. And that was actually the first time I had said something racial in nature to her. And that's how she acted. I told my mother what happened, and she said, 'I'm sorry, baby. But what I tell ya?' She said it just like that."

Jayla's mother's admonishment is not unlike that of many black southerners, particularly older black southerners. Although my mother worked diligently to raise my sister and me without a priori judgments about white folks' motives and behaviors, she also saw it as her duty to objectively inform us about the interracial and cross-class mores and norms, from preparing us not to be invited to our white counterparts' birthday parties to describing to us how our friendships with whites would change as we entered high school. Although she never said, "What I tell ya?," she could have on any number of occasions when we learned the hard way that her racial logic was right.

Such sentiments about how to relate to whites have even been immortalized in black popular culture, most notably by Aaron McGruder's character Robert Freeman, voiced by actor John Witherspoon, in the cartoon version of the syndicated comic strip *The Boondocks*. In the series, like in the comic strip, Robert Freeman, or Granddad, is a southerner who migrated north. The pretext for the strip and the show is that Granddad has moved with his young grandsons, for whom he is sole guardian, from a poor neighborhood on Chicago's South Side to a predominantly white suburb, the fictional Woodcrest. On the first episode of the show, Huey Freeman, the level-headed, if nationalist, grandson, is dreaming about telling a group of white people a number of truths, which amount to somewhat widely held sentiments among African Americans that are generally not known to whites, at a garden party in their new neighborhood. Stepping to the microphone and requesting that the attendees pardon his interruption, the dream Huey declares, "Jesus was black, Ronald Reagan was the devil, and the government is lying about 9/11." The previously peaceful gathering immediately erupts into chaos as the white neighbors begin to riot, beating each other and setting things on fire. Huey is abruptly awakened from this dream by a slap from Granddad, who says accusingly, "Having that dream where you made the white people riot, weren't you?" When Huey protests that he was only telling the truth, Granddad scolds him. "How many times has I told you you bet' not even *dream* about telling white folks the truth!" He continues, "You better learn how to lie like me. I'm gonna find me a white man and lie to him right now." While Granddad's narrative has comic effect—after all, it is presumably the middle of night when he is going to find a white man to lie to—it is reflective of the narratives about whites, racial truths, and, implicitly, interracial interactions, echoed by several respondents, across age. While this approach to whites—deliberately deceiving them—may seem extreme and also country, it is also cosmopolitan in its cleverness and agentic tricksterism. Jayla's mother's "What I tell ya?" was akin to Granddad's dream-interrupting slap. Rooted in the cultures of dissembling and signifying integral to black folks' survival in slavery and the Jim Crow South, half-truth-telling and outright lying continue to serve as cornerstones for how black folks approach interacting with their white counterparts, perhaps especially in the South.

Progress and Denial

Racial and regional requirements of dissembling and signifying notwithstanding, most respondents attempted to, at least nominally, ascribe to the "too busy to hate" rhetoric of the New South and conceptualized themselves as equally responsible as whites for moving interracial conversations forward. Despite the palpable racial animus in the city, as evidenced by critical issues like the merger of the city and county schools, there is a recognizable hint of progressive interracial cosmopolitanism, especially among the middle classes, that necessitates a tacit abandonment of Old South racial mores. Thus, most respondents, across age and class, claimed to give every white person the "benefit of the doubt," a sort of "innocent until proven guilty" position on whites and racism. This willingness to give whites the benefit of the doubt is reflective of attempts to shed a "Granddad" kind of country-ness, one that is rooted in an always already present distrust of whites and perhaps some inherent anger and bitterness.

Most respondents attempted to keep white folks "out their faces" and "in their prayers" or simply did not study white folks at all. Still others strove to adhere to the notion that at least when it came to younger white southerners, the South, indeed, had become more progressive. Michael, a lanky thirty-seven-year-old from Memphis who works as a financial analyst for a private firm, contended for much of our first interview session, which was conducted over a Labor Day barbecue, that he did not think about race "in that way" on a daily or even weekly basis. A graduate of a historically black institution, Michael recognizes race, racial/cultural difference, and racial inequality but has not experienced the "Jim Crow" inequality for which the South is infamous. He and his wife, LaShaun, live in a well-to-do former suburb of Memphis that has been gradually incorporated into the city limits over the past decade where the median household income is almost twice that of the city. He swatted flies hovering over his barbecue spaghetti and talked at length about his racial neutrality: "You know, I give everyone the benefit of the doubt when it comes to whether or not they are a racist. I know that some whites, especially in Memphis, are brainwashed by racism and that they simply can't help it, but there are those who were just raised different, and in either case, I'm completely okay until something goes wrong. But I'm also not really looking for something to go wrong. I'm just trying to do my job, do my work, pick up my kids from school, get my dry cleaning, minding my business, you know."

While Michael gestured toward what some respondents saw as Memphis's worse racism, he contended that Memphis's racial climate does not structure how he goes about his everyday life. Many respondents who are younger and employed in professions where they regularly interact with whites, as superiors or as subordinates, were more likely to see themselves as giving everyone the benefit of the doubt but acknowledged in varying degrees the probability that they would experience some level of racism, racial discrimination, or racial resentment, as one respondent called it, as they go about their everyday lives.

Throughout our interview session, LaShaun was buzzing about, clearing plates, assisting Michael on the grill, and pouring beverages, and she paused several times during his monologue to give him a "Negro, please" look—a universal look of skepticism. A teacher at a predominantly white elementary school in the county, she remained verbally silent, even when Michael, unable to ignore her body language any longer, blurted louder than perhaps he intended, "What?" in response to one of her looks. I followed up with an interview with her several weeks later, and she problematized Michael's experiences with racism as very different from how he let on at the barbecue:

LASHAUN: If I had a nickel for every time that man came home and relayed to me a situation from work or wherever that was clearly a matter of race, but that he took as a matter of something else—"just people" he says, "that's just people, Shaun"—I could quit teaching little white children the FOIL method and sit at home.

ZANDRIA: Why do you think he might think those situations are not race related?

LASHAUN: Because he's racially naive. But I don't understand why [. . .] He grew up here just like I did, spent summers with Grandma in Mississippi and all of that. He ought to know these white folks better than that. I think it's playing golf with his coworkers. He thinks if you play golf together and listen to old school hip-hop together then it's all good.

For LaShaun, Michael's racial naïveté was inexplicable, given that she assumed that he, and by extension other black southerners, should be so keenly aware of race that spotting racist situations would be second nature. She also saw Michael's denial or refusal to see race as willful.

It's like he buys into the hype. He gets on me for being "doom and gloom," like things haven't changed. I mean, yes, they have changed from, like, our parents' time. There aren't the colored water fountains. But you feel like there's [a colored water fountain]. We all feel it. Even if you aren't one of those people that thinks about "The Man" and racism all day. You could be as oblivious as you want to about white folks, but you feel it. I think [Michael] just, like, denies that feeling. If he feels it, you know, I think he just goes, "Naw, it can't be like that."

LaShaun bears the brunt of Michael's experiences of racism, as he shares them with her frequently. They are upsetting to her, as she described on several occasions, as is Michael's naïveté. She contended that if he would only recognize and accept that racism will happen, particularly in his industry, he would be able to better navigate his everyday experiences of racial discrimination and undermining in the workplace.

While LaShaun chides Michael for denying the feeling of racism, it is exactly this denial, regardless of the form it takes, that has allowed respondents to claim epistemological superiority over non-southern blacks. In denying or rejecting the feeling, they contended, they are overcoming the feeling, not letting the debilitating effects of discrimination take hold. Still, in this denial, willful or unintentional, remnants of those deleterious effects always seep through the porous surfaces of country cosmopolitanism.

It is then—at least for conceptualizations of race—that black southerners' performative, signifying, and hyperbolic accomplishment of country cosmopolitanism emerges. Witness these statements from a cross-section of respondents, all made in nondirected conversation—that is, in conversations in which I had not asked a question to prompt a response.

> MS. JEFFERIES: I don't care if they don't want me in the neighborhood. I got a right to be there. [My neighbors] don't have to like me. Stay out of my way, and I'll stay out of your'n, and we'll get along just fine. Long as you don't burn no cross in my yard.

> RUTH ANN: I know they promoted her because she white, and you know what? *I don't care.* She ain't gon' have nothing but trouble on her hands when she get up there and can't do the work because she ain't been trained. Who wants all that trouble?

> JERMAINE: Oh, you want to give me bad service? Well, bring it on. It's a war. I started putting my money on the table. This is your 20 percent. Every slight, every empty glass in need of a refill, every fake smile, I'm taking something away.

In each of these statements is an accomplishment of racial discrimination or mistreatment as unimportant or, in Jermaine's case, as a war in which the respondent has the upper hand. Unfriendly neighbors, being passed over for a promotion, or not receiving decent service at a restaurant are clearly undesirable interracial interactions, but these respondents and others minimized the negative interaction to emphasize their agency. Whether or not these statements reflected their true feelings about their respective situations is less important than the fact that they were adamant about these statements *as* truth, as sincere representations of their feelings, or of the way they should feel, about interpersonal and structural experiences of discrimination.

Picking Out a Racist in a Crowd

I received a phone call from LaShaun around the Christmas holiday later that same year, and she invited my daughter and me to come over for a small gathering. She encouraged me to arrive early and make "extra certain" that I brought my recorder. "You have just got to hear what Mr. Happy Race has to say," she said with a knowing air. When I arrived, unsure what LaShaun had told Michael about my visit, I was greeted at the door by their two daughters, four and six, who hastily spoke and just as quickly grabbed my daughter and darted off to a playroom.

Michael was over the stove tasting and re-tasting some sauce and welcomed a break from agonizing over what was missing from it, and LaShaun gave me a big grin from the kitchen table. After exchanging pleasantries and catching up, she demanded that Michael tell me what had been happening at work. Michael sighed and dutifully obliged:

MICHAEL: We [he and his white coworker] were on this new project, and I was amped about it 'cause it was going great, we were working well together, you know. I put in a lot of work to this thing, though, working at home and whatnot. And we golfed a lot, had drinks a lot, really working this thing. And *LaShaun* told me . . . [He pauses.]

LASHAUN: Uh-huh, don't stop now! LaShaun told you what?

MICHAEL: She told me that that guy was no good.

LASHAUN: And what else? Tell her what I said spe*ci*fically.

MICHAEL: We had him over for dinner a few times, and after the first time, she said he had a sneaky, racist look in his eye. [LaShaun nods.] I said, "You can't look in someone's eye and know they're a racist, plus we've been working good together." I thought we were going to present our results together. I come to find out that he had been submitting them to the boss as his. His alone, you know. Man, when I found out, I kind of confronted him like, and said, you know, "Hey man, why did you do that?" He said he didn't know why I was upset because I was black and I was going to get promoted anyway because I was black. You know, not because I did all of this work. He told me, "I need this, Mike. You'll be fine." And I felt silly. I felt like Pollyanna or somebody with her bubble just burst.

In LaShaun's calculation, all it took was one look, one interaction, one dinner, and she had already predicted Michael's racial fate on the project. LaShaun drew on much the same racial logic that Dave Chappelle attributes to black folks in "Jury Duty," a sketch from the second season of *Chappelle's Show* that recreates voir dire for several high-profile cases. Playing a potential juror for the O. J. Simpson trial, Chappelle declares that "Furman" is a racist name and that, "as a nigga that says 'nigga' a lot," he could conclude that Furman "says 'nigga' all the time" and that he was "probably a racist." Out of curiosity and because I was attempting to remain professional, I asked her to describe the look in Michael's coworker's eye.

I don't know. I can't say exactly, you know, or do it for you because I don't have a racist look in my eye. But I do know one when I see one. I know. And if you think about it, you know, too. Like an old sheriff or something in one of those *Rosewood*-type movies, just not acting racist. Sneaky like. He was just too good to be true. [Raising her voice.] He was white, wasn't he? What else is there to it? He was white, and he wasn't as good or swift as Michael, so he was going to use him to get ahead.

LaShaun's inability to describe or pinpoint the look or feeling is in line with the difficulty of pinpointing racism in this contemporary political context. However, she took the math a step further and simplified it. His whiteness a priori meant, for her, that something was not right about him; the "sneaky, racist look in his eye" solidified that claim. His characterization as racist was set once LaShaun determined that he was not as "swift as Michael."

Many respondents shared LaShaun's methodology. In addition to the "racist eye," which was by far the most commonly reported way that black folks ascertained who was racist, folks in various occupations, from fast-food worker to dental assistant to lawyer, pinned racist white folks down on walking like a racist, speaking (or not speaking) to them like a racist, and even eating like a racist. Brianna, nineteen, a tiny woman with a piercing glare who said she generally does not have problems with whites and has a number of good white friends, described herself as a closet white girl because of her love of country music. Still, she said that she knew her boss at a chain retail store in a suburban mall was going to be a racist when this woman arrived at the company orientation: "Everything about her said 'racist,' down to the way she walked. I just knew she was going to be a pistol." When I asked Brianna just what "everything" was and what about her boss's walk said "racist," she replied matter-of-factly:

I mean, she just looked at us like she hated us. The chairs we were sitting in was like this close together [she gestures with her hands a space a few inches wide], and she just moved and waddled all between them, bumping into us, talking to us about all the things that would happen to us if we stole stuff. She had this walk. Like she was bigger than the world. But it wasn't like she was confident or anything. It wasn't an "I'm the shit" walk. It was like she was scared of us and wanted to walk all over us. And she tried to, too. I ended up complaining to the district manager because she thought we were her slaves . . . I wrote that in the complaint, too.

Brianna, who grew up in an African American community between Midtown and East Memphis, said that though she had not experienced racism before the incident at the job, she knew what to look for. Her parents and grandparents had described for her in detail experiences of racial discrimination in workplaces, public spaces, and other interpersonal contexts. Brianna was eventually promoted to manager of her location. Her manager, incidentally, was transferred shortly after her complaint to the district manager, although Brianna was not sure whether she requested a transfer or was transferred by the company. Brianna insisted that she tried to warn the other young women about her, "to watch [their] backs and count and recount [their] drawers," but that many of those who began working at the company around the same time she did were sabotaged by the manager with the racist walk.

Even outside of the workplace, where respondents may be more likely to view superiors as racist, people marked everyday exchanges, such as speaking, as racist. Although greeting strangers is one of the main differences that folks highlight between the South and other regions, with southerners supposedly greeting everyone they meet on the street, this is, of course, like many tropes of the South, a carefully accomplished distinction that does not always happen in everyday southern life, particularly interracially. Robert, twenty-seven, a construction worker with a local home building company, admitted to being especially ruffled when white folks do not speak to him, particularly when he speaks first. He said, "My mama taught me to speak to people when you're passing them on the street, or if you're somewhere else and you're in a position to make eye contact and speaking is appropriate at that time. I'll be walking down the street, and I've learned now to make sure that I make eye contact, and sometimes I even smile. If I go through all of that, and you look me in the eye, or even if you don't look me in the eye, and you don't speak, you are clearly racist."

Robert described the careful racial, regional, and gendered behavior he undertakes to navigate everyday interactions. He is tall and a fitness enthusiast, but he is aware of how his body might be read by whites and said he adjusts accordingly. Although he grew up in an African American community in southwest Memphis, Robert said he quickly learned to navigate interracial interaction when he turned eighteen and moved away from home to a new apartment community being built east of Hickory Hill near the suburban Germantown. He cited the manners his father and grandmother taught him as essential to his success. Further, he highlighted the importance of southern greeting norms, contending that if a white person does not properly acknowledge him after he has taken all of the proper and mannerable steps, then he or she is racist. I suggested that perhaps the people he is encountering just happen not to be from the South and do not know the customs. He was nearly exasperated with my offerings of alternative explanations: "Oh, come on. Even if you aren't from here, even if you're uncomfortable with speaking, you know the rules, and you do it regardless. No, I'm sure these folks are racist. If you don't speak where everybody speaks, you're a racist. I mean, I guess you could be sexist, too, like, you could be scared of me because I'm a black man, but that's why I smile sometimes, just to give them that extra comfort like I'm not trying to rob them or ask them for spare change. And they still don't speak."

Robert is unnerved by white people who do not speak, given that he has done it "their way" and "the mannerable way" to no avail. Yet, sometimes the southern implicit requirement to speak has left other respondents wishing white folks would not even bother. Steven, a self-described starving artist and painter who recently graduated from the local art college, is just as ruffled by white people speaking to him as Robert is when white people do not return a greeting. Steven spent his early childhood in Atlanta and then lived in Detroit with his father for six years until he was fifteen, when his father, tired of Steven's repeated insubordination, sent him to Memphis to live with his paternal grandmother. Now twenty-four, Steven told me he is far calmer than he was in his preteen and early adolescent years, when he was running with the "street niggas" and trying to make some extra cash. For our interview, I fed him and another starving artist, Raymond, who tagged along with him. Like several respondents, Steven equated what he reads as white folks' phoniness with racism.

> See, you're walking, and you're minding your business. And I don't necessarily speak to white folks on the street. I speak to all the black folks, but not necessarily the white folks unless I'm feeling especially "kumbaya," like if I got paid for a piece or something. But boy, they see me, looking like a hippie, and they're just a-speaking, "Hi! Howareya!" [He widens his eyes and leans in close to Raymond for dramatic effect.] And I'm like, "Hi, white person. Don't use me to fill your I-spoke-to-a-black-person-so-I'm-not-racist quota." They still racist. Anytime a white person speaks to you with that much enthusiasm, they are a racist. They probably just called somebody a nigger on their job and are trying to atone for it.

Like many respondents, Steven highlighted southern greeting mores as phony in general, and especially across race. Steven also acknowledged that his presentation of self—wild locs, nerd glasses, and holey hipster jeans for our first interview—encourages whites to speak to him. Raymond, twenty-six and still working his way through school, concurred.

RAYMOND: Exactly. Especially around [Midtown]. I'm on my skateboard the other day, and a white woman stops me and says, "Hi, how are you? I'm Jenny," or whatever she said her name was. "Did you know that some nonprofits are trying to get the city to build some skate parks?" She was an older white lady, too, like she was in her fifties or something. I told her, "Yeah, I heard about that." And she commenced to wanting to have a conversation, like I was her best black friend. She said she hadn't seen many of "us" skating. The very next day . . . or maybe it was a few days after that . . . I saw her again at [a Midtown café]. She was sitting with a guy, and I spoke to her. She acted like she didn't know me. I reminded her of who I was, that she'd seen me outside of [a local college] and stopped me while I was skating and all of that. She was like, "Oh, I'm sorry, I don't remember." It was the same woman. She had the same voice, same hair, same white woman shoes and everything.

ZANDRIA: What do you think was up with that?

RAYMOND: I'm telling you she was R-A-C-I-S-T. Or maybe she was just an opportunist, or maybe somebody dared her to talk to a black person. She was all "let me speak to this black guy" one day, and the next, she's all like "I don't know this black guy at all; why in the world is he speaking to me?"

STEVEN: Come on, man. There could have been anything going on; that could have been her boyfriend and she didn't want to acknowledge the conversation in front of him.

RAYMOND: Well, explain to me this. [Long pause.] Why was she *eating* racist?

ZANDRIA AND STEVEN: What?

RAYMOND: She was tearing that food up, just ripping into that bagel with her teeth, like she was taking out all her pent-up racist anger on it.

After demonstrating the woman's eating style on some of the cornbread that accompanied our meal—and making a mess—Raymond resumed "regular," non-racist, eating. Regardless of the circumstances that precipitated her not speaking the day after initiating the conversation with Raymond, he interpreted the woman's ignorance, feigned or not, as racist.

Although many of these and similar declarations were in jest, like Raymond's, there was a hint of sincerity in their expression, such that most people wanted to prove to me, and to any skeptics, that their calculations, however lacking in empirical replicability, were accurate. Many respondents, however, offered no proof, as it were, for their assertions, citing their southern rearing as credibility enough. As Ms. Jefferies said to me several times, in different iterations, "If you's raised in the South and don't know that you can't trust these white folks and that they ain't up to no good, then you ain't got the sense God gave two dead fleas on a horse's ass and you may as well just get yo' tap dancing shoes out and start cooning for them because that's exactly what you gon' be doing."

In the New South, racism is both specter and reality, and in most calculations, white racism is lurking just below the surface of everyday interactions and behaviors. Most respondents situated the assumption of white racism as the first and natural defense against white racism on micro and macro levels. While many respondents articulated this defense in jest, continuing interpersonal prejudice and racial micro-aggressions almost always genuinely disturbed them, as evidenced in LaShaun's raised voice, Jayla's consternation, and Alelia's expressions of dismay. In their recounting of these experiences to me, the emotion with which they described how the experiences made them feel did not indicate that they could easily dismiss them as inconsequential, even if they could claim not to study white folks.

Passing the Test on White Folks

Whether race is a specter or reality, some black folks ain't "stud'n' 'em white folks," regardless of the circumstances. For a few days I followed Ms. Mae, a seventy-six-year-old woman who does in-home nursing care and also works in a nursing home part-time, going with her from home to home as well as to her job at the nursing home, tucked away in a formerly white and now predominantly black and Latino neighborhood behind a long-empty lot of a former used car dealership. Ms. Mae is extraordinarily spry, telling me that she eats only what she grows—she has a sprawling vegetable garden in her rolling backyard in southwest Memphis—or what someone catches for her. She told me about a number of racial skirmishes, which she said are just part of black life in the "New Old South." She said that she's a good person, so no matter what clients do, she is going to do her job. She has been engaged in nursing care since she was in her early twenties, working for whites and blacks over the years.

Although her daughters, fifty-four and forty, both lawyers living in Atlanta, have encouraged her to leave the profession over the years, she insisted that she enjoys the work, although she does not always enjoy the clients. I asked her to estimate how many clients she has had over the years that she would call "racist."

Oh, I done had plenty of racist ones, so I don't really think about it. That's who they are, bless they heart. But this new one [patient], she takes the cake with her meanness. She's ninety-four, and she's a feisty heifer, she can get around pretty good, but she's got Old Timer's [Alzheimer's] and needs constant watching 'lessen she'll be down the street. But whether or not she's having an Old Timer's episode or she normal, I'm always some kind of black Sal, some kind of nigger, colored, whatever she want to say. And she don't want me to touch her. When I need to bathe her, she be just a-hollering. I smile at her and say, "Come on Ms. Jamison," and sometimes I calls her out her name, too. Not a mean name, no, never a mean name. But I call her Ms. Scarlett or Ms. Mary or something. She say, "Don't you touch me with your filthy black hands!" and shake a finger at me like this here [shaking her index finger at me], and I told her that I was gon' care for her like I'm being paid to do whether she like it or not. I told her she wasn't gon' be neglected on my watch, no matter what she said.

Mae is determined to simply do her job and come home and insisted that she likes to care for people and that this is what she is called to do. She invited me to come with her to meet Ms. Jamison as she worked her shift from 2:00 P.M. to 6:00 P.M. on a Wednesday afternoon while Ms. Jamison's daughter ran errands. Ms. Jamison was indeed feisty and began barking orders with a remarkably strong voice as soon as we entered the house. When she realized I was there, she rose up a bit in her chair and leaned forward, squinting.

MS. JAMISON: Well, what is this you've got here with you, Mae?
MS. MAE: Why, this is a young lady that is doing some graduate work. She's in school. She's working on her PhD, and she's interviewing me.
MS. JAMISON: [. . .] I still say y'all aren't really suited for higher thinking.
MS. MAE: Well, just like my daughters are lawyers, she's going to have her PhD, and you still gon' be sitting right there in that chair.
MS. JAMISON: Oh, hush it, Mae, you ain't raised no lawyers, no you did not. And what that gal want to talk to you for anyhow? Your black self don't know nothing. [Laughs.]
MS. MAE: Is that so? Well, I know it's time for your bath, and boy I know you ain't gon' like that none too much. So, I guess my black self does know something, huh?

I was unsure of what to make of this exchange and did not know whether Ms. Jamison was serious or not. I was slightly bothered by it but have encountered my share of Ms. Jamisons, so I was not altogether shocked. I quickly realized that Ms. Mae seemed unmoved and matter-of-factly continued her work. Ms. Jamison sat back and was tight-lipped for the rest of my time there, which Ms. Mae told me after we left was very unusual for her, save for when she is experiencing an episode of dementia. When she is not as well behaved, Ms. Mae said Ms. Jamison will bite, spit, kick, and fight. I asked her, like I am sure her daughters have on a number of occasions, why she stays, especially when this woman is particularly difficult relative to her other clients. She responded: "I figured God done put me there with that woman in order to give her one more chance to get into heaven before she makes that long walk. You know we always have to save white folks from themselves. I know God wants me to get Him some more souls for heaven. You can't really think too much about what they're saying or doing. They'll be taken care of in the great hereafter. Or they'll burn up in it. One or the other."

That black folks, and black southerners in particular, should "save white folks from themselves" is not a new idea, but it was certainly a rare one among respondents. Further, in this instance, Ms. Mae shrouded her work with Ms. Jamison in religious rhetoric that gives her labor a higher purpose, one that her daughters, and in some ways I, cannot understand. She also used the religious language to give responsibility for the punishment of Ms. Jamison over to a higher power. Ms. Mae described herself as having been "feisty about race" when she was younger, having participated in labor union organizing during the civil rights movement, but said she thinks less about things, and in particular white people, changing now. "I figure we about done made all the progress we gon' make on that front," she said about race relations in the South, adding, "We [blacks] have to do for ourselves with what we've got, even though it ain't enough." Like Ms. Jefferies, but for different reasons, Ms. Mae marshals the power of prayer and spirituality to heal what Ms. Jefferies calls "wicked white folks."

Although nearly forty years Ms. Mae's junior, Keisha, a singer on the neo-soul scene, expressed sentiments similar to Ms. Mae's, although she objected to saving white people from themselves. Still, like Ms. Mae, she argued that trying to understand white people—or, as Ms. Mae would say, "[thinking] too much about what they're saying or doing"—is futile. She said she thinks of them like "scenery," like a "tree or a parked car." From a small Arkansas town just across the Mississippi River where the racial line dividing the black and white sides of town is physical and cognitive, Keisha said she was taught to ignore whites unless communicating with them was absolutely necessary. Over time, they faded from her primary view and were relegated to the periphery, an epistemological position that did not change when she moved to Memphis to finish high school at fifteen. She told me on the way to a rehearsal and sound check for a show the next day, "Girl, I don't be thinking about these white folks. You can't. It will make you insane. You just have to give that over to God and keep stepping." This interview, our second, occurred shortly after the Jena Six controversy. She told me that nothing that white people do, including hanging nooses from a tree, surprises her. "I don't know why all those folks went down there [to Jena, Louisiana] to protest like they were shocked or outraged or something. If a white person hangs a noose, or calls you a nigger, or checks your e-mail while you're away from your desk at work, you cannot let those things faze you. They are trying to get under your skin and get you off your game so you'll be so busy thinking about their next move that you don't make any of your own."

Because Keisha talked quickly, I initially misunderstood "checks your e-mail." Later, when it came up again in our conversation, it made sense to me, and I asked her to explain before I started with more questions. She told me how her coworkers attempted to "terrorize" her during her stint at a literacy nonprofit in Pittsburgh: "I heard they had run off two other black women. They would literally be at my desk checking my e-mails when I would go to lunch or to the bathroom. They were trying to terrorize me because I was doing well, bringing in all the grant money. They would move things on my desk, all of that. But I didn't get worked up about that. They didn't know me. I'm from the South. I know white people. White people do not bother me at all. You can't get me off my game that easily." What Keisha described is clearly a hostile work environment, and the events she detailed could happen with any combination of people, regardless of race, gender, or sexuality. Still, Keisha saw the coworkers' behavior as racialized because they were white and had driven away two previous black female employees. She implied that the black women had been run off because they had not been from the South and therefore had not properly handled their experiences at the nonprofit. I asked her what being from the South had to do with navigating a hostile work environment. She continued, "Black people up north get uptight about white folks . . . and they scare easy. We don't. We come from people that can take a lot of stuff from white folks and overcome and are still great and still keep it moving. [My coworkers] weren't about to get me spooked with some petty mess like that. I would just keep on smiling. I think they thought I was crazy after a while. . . . They [management] even offered me a raise and promotion to stay. I bet they don't do another black woman like that."

Keisha attributed her triumph at the nonprofit to her southern rearing, and also to the collective memory of black southerners' struggles. Her account speaks to the sense of superiority she felt not only in not becoming flustered by what she saw as the pettiness perpetrated by whites but also in not being forced out like the non-southern black women. For Keisha, black southerners, and perhaps black southern women specifically, are best able to navigate white racism. Still, when I suggested that after a while such experiences might take a significant social and psychological toll, she dismissed that idea outright: "I'm not weak like that." Other respondents shared what seems a steel will against white racism, a determination not to be deterred—and, if necessary, to find a white person to lie to immediately.

As a researcher, I had a difficult time reconciling the "not stud'n' 'em white folks" sentiment with what I saw as respondents' complex vulnerabilities. Because most respondents worked with and interacted with white folks, even when they did not actively choose the latter, I saw them, like most racial and ethnic minorities, as susceptible to racial micro-aggressions. Because of the nature of race relations in Memphis—which comprises both an "in your face" racism that outsiders usually attribute exclusively to the South and a subtle racism that is more difficult to pinpoint empirically—I saw them as particularly vulnerable and yet also particularly in denial about that vulnerability.

I also had trouble reconciling their sentiments with existing scholarship about the long-term effects of racial stress on African Americans, despite the fact that this scholarship does not explicitly focus on region as a factor that might produce different outcomes. Respondents' approaches to racism combined rural wit and collective memory with two articulations of cosmopolitanism: the shrewdness to recognize and manage racism and the progressiveness to give white folks "the benefit of the doubt." To "not study" white folks was the ultimate demonstration of having transcended a troubled racial past, particularly in the South, and most especially in the city that killed King. Some respondents mobilized this ability to distinguish themselves from non-southern blacks and to claim a superior epistemological position, one that was not vulnerable and supposedly did not require emotion management. Rather than declare that "this racism is killing [them] inside," as a character in a *Chappelle's Show* skit did, they decentered what they constructed as inconsequential instances of racism as peripheral and insignificant. Yet, this accomplishment required considerable work that seemed to delegitimize typical responses to racism. That is, there seemed to be little room in the country cosmopolitan position on race to experience the ramifications of racial stress, anger, sadness, or any response that would take one off his or her game.

New South Theory, Old South Methods

The New South rhetoric encourages southerners, across race, to bracket slavery, Jim Crow, and the civil rights movement as temporary troubles from which the region emerged better and triumphant. Beyond the gains of the civil rights movement that legally dismantled Jim Crow and sought to redress past discrimination at the federal level, a number of key changes mark the region's racial progress. The emergence of black political power in major metropolitan areas beginning in the 1970s, including black mayors and increased black representation on municipal councils, signaled an unprecedented kind of black power, albeit a power firmly entrenched in traditionally white systems. The expansion of black political power, coupled with the increased flow of return migrants, gave the region and its cities a progressive mystique, as Atlanta's self-characterization as the city "too busy to hate" was extended to the region as a whole.

However, the lived reality of race in and beyond the South renders such bracketing difficult at best. While Latino and Afro-Caribbean immigrants have replaced African Americans as disproportionately represented in service-oriented jobs like health care and child care in other regions, in the South—and in particular in the "Old South" of Memphis, Mississippi, Alabama, and Louisiana—the vestiges of Jim Crow and the black/white paradigm abound. From the bus that leaves inner-city Memphis early in the morning with black domestics headed for the suburbs, to black women pushing white babies in designer strollers, to all-black janitorial staff at white private schools, to black servants at white dinner parties, it is difficult to ignore twenty-first-century Jim Crow, even for middle-class blacks.

Beyond these obvious vestiges, unequal wealth and power arrangements speak to the legacy of Jim Crow in the post–civil rights South. Black and poor residents have little access to educational choice and therefore are shut out from the expanding job opportunities available in the city. Poorer African Americans are more often the political bogeymen in local politics than they are even in American national politics. Spatial segregation in housing, schools, and public spaces bolsters the construction of lower-income African Americans as the city's untouchables. Overall, African Americans in Memphis are likely to have the health, wealth, and quality of life outcomes as their counterparts in rural communities in the Mississippi Delta, despite the relative availability of resources in the city, from research hospitals to nonprofits, to address these disparities.

To manage the stigma and reality of race, respondents employ a number of strategies born of a country cosmopolitan worldview. Two key strategies—the a priori judgment required to "not study them white folks," and taking the moral high ground—dominate my respondents' approaches to racial interaction. First, rather than allow white people to exist as individuals, they fix them within the category of whiteness, rendering them therefore stable and always intelligible. By assuming that white people have the hegemonic and oppressive characteristics of whiteness, respondents hope to avoid the inevitable disappointment of a "good" white person gone "bad." This strategy draws on the country cynicism of Granddad in *The Boondocks*, but instead of finding a white man to lie to in the middle of the night, respondents do not proactively seek to manage white people's impressions of them. Respondents are able to use this strategy *and* maintain a range of relationships with whites, from coworker to friend to romantic partner. Still, even when prepared for the worst, many respondents' narratives demonstrate that racial disappointment is unavoidable.

Second, regardless of their relationship to spirituality or religion, respondents draw on decidedly religious and/or spiritual language to navigate race, class, and regional tensions. They contend that a divine power orders their interracial steps. This includes not only keeping white folks in their prayers and leaving it up to a higher power to get justice but also serving as some white person's one black friend/acquaintance, saving whites from racial faux pas, and giving white folks the opportunity to atone for their racial and regional sins through their interactions with black people. This strategy is in line with philosophies of non-violence with which King came to be so closely associated. As such, respondents' endurance of the psychological suffering that accompanies racial micro-aggressions and more overt forms of racism leads many of them to righteousness and a closer walk with their higher power. Further, they hope, their sacrifice simultaneously leads whites to salvation and atonement as well. However, the forgiveness inherent in this strategy conjures images of passive, country southern blacks not indignant enough to extract real change from whites. Respondents that adhere to this strategy, however, disagreed with this view; forgiveness, they argued, is action.

In the New South, then, Old South methodologies of negotiating race and racism prevail. Denial, avoidance, trickery or pretense, and "giving things over" to a higher power are all key to managing the disappointments from "good" and "bad" whites. Yet, while Old South strategies may help southerners deal with the increasingly complex task of understanding and naming racism, the work of performing these negotiations has become more deliberate and more difficult.

CHAPTER FOUR

Belles, Guls, and Country Boys

Perhaps the most infamous scene from the 1997 film adaptation of John Berendt's *Midnight in the Garden of Good and Evil* occurs when black female impersonator The Lady Chablis arrives at the Savannah, Georgia, African American debutante ball and disrupts the uptight black middle-class tradition with her gender-bending and distinct performance of the lady. The Lady Chablis is juxtaposed with the southern ladies at the table to which she invites herself, parents of the young belles and gentlemen waltzing at the ball. In many ways, she is more of a black steel magnolia than are her more conservative counterparts, southern embodiments of a politics of respectability that reserves comment in favor of politeness. Throughout the film, The Lady Chablis serves as a foil for southern womanhood, black and white. Her presence at the debutante ball demonstrates that performative disruptions of gender and racial norms can be useful tools for challenging those norms in interpersonal and structural contexts.

Her disruption also serves as a metaphor for black southerners' bold appropriation of traditional regional gender archetypes—belle, gentleman, lady, and steel magnolia—regardless of class, sexuality, or gender identity. Black southerners, like The Lady Chablis, perform these white archetypes, giving new meaning to the categories and unsettling the racialized foundations of those categories in the process. The Lady Chablis's interruption of an exclusively African American ball highlights the class and sexual rigidity of the black elite, offering a space for critique of the normative center of black identity and authenticity. Like The Lady Chablis, black southerners challenge oppressive systems through the embodiment, performance, and co-creation of those systems. As such, they carve out a space from which to speak as legitimate participants in southern and black gender cultures.

Black women have long been denied access to the categories of womanhood available to white women. As slaves, black women performed work anathema to "ladies," which was at once an elite and white formulation available only to slaveholding women. As historian Elizabeth Fox-Genovese demonstrates in her examination of regional and gender conventions in southern slave society, the racialization of slave labor meant black women lacked the protections afforded to ladies.¹ Not only did black women work in fields alongside men, but their rigorous work in the detached kitchens of plantation households was explicitly racialized as "nigger work" as well. While black women covertly and explicitly snatched at the protections and benefits of ladyhood, from attempting to acquire and don clothing of fine fabrics, to challenging the ill treatment based on moral mores governing the treatment of ladies, to asking consistently through their resistance, "Ain't I a woman?," they were regularly constructed as outside of traditional gender categories. Not men but not quite ladies, black women continued to demand access to the protections and privileges of ladyhood.

Over the course of the twentieth century, elite black women challenged the gendered and racialized nature of their oppression, including rape and lynching, through political activism and by ensuring their performances and representations of the race adhered to dominant gender conventions. Still, what Patricia Hill Collins has called controlling images of black women persisted, expanded, and proliferated, constraining black women's abilities to extricate themselves from the confines of white patriarchal boxes. For working-class southern black women, toiling in white ladies' kitchens continued white southerners' abilities to deny them access to traditional regional forms of gender identity, performance, and protection. Elite southern black women developed their articulations of regional forms of gender identity in the confines of a segregated "separate city," spatially isolated from whites but still in many ways subject to white power. These complicated intersections of race, class, gender, and region still inform performances and representations of black womanhood in the South.

For some respondents in this study, the baggage of the categories of belle, gentleman, and lady is too heavy to be useful as identity categories or performative tropes. When I talked with my mother over the course of the research for this book about my findings along lines of gender, she frequently recounted a story, one that I remember her telling quite often when I was younger as well, about a conversation she had once with a white woman acquaintance. The woman had referred to herself and my mother as southern women and asked if my mother was going to the Southern Women's Show, an annual event that travels to southern cities and features local vendors and various southern fare. At my request, my mother is happy to recount the story—again—this time for the record: "And I told her, 'I don't consider myself a *s'uth'n* woman. *I* am a woman from the South.' My idea of a southern woman was the southern belle and mint juleps, Scarlett O'Hara. I know it wasn't the 1800s and no one dressed like that, but that southern drawl and all of that. Hurl."

My mother actively rejects the notion that her womanhood could be similar to that of southern white women, although she readily acknowledges the ways in which all women share certain burdens of gender. Although when I was a child, the finer points of the distinction she made—between being a woman from the South and a *s'uth'n* woman—were lost on me, I understood at least that the distinction was important. The derision with which she said *s'uth'n* was noticeable; the number of times I had overheard her telling the story (an excessive number even for her) to her black women friends made its significance clear. While I am still unable to articulate those finer points with absolute certainty, I know the distinction is similar to the one Alice Walker makes between womanism and feminism and between purple and lavender, or the one E. Patrick Johnson makes between quare and queer, throwing shade and reading.[2] That is, race complicates and changes how one relates to, experiences, and inhabits categories of being. And while I may not be able to articulate those finer points, I know that a "woman from the South" is another instantiation of a "southern black woman," emphasis on "southern black."

Gender is perhaps the most central site in which country cosmopolitanism is played out, challenged, and reformed, as ideas about "country" and "cosmopolitan" collide with traditional gender norms and preoccupations with snagging a suitable mate for the night, a spell, or a lifetime. Gender allows the respondents in this study to ascribe concrete, seemingly natural meanings to country-ness that sometimes reinscribe patriarchal privilege. However, despite our tendency to see gender as a more "natural" category than race, among my respondents, gender is the site of the most resistance against not only gender norms but also the racialized regional norms of gender behavior. It is through gender that country cosmopolitanism enters terrain that resists the existing social order through strategic appropriation and performance.

Candace West and Don Zimmerman, whose ideas about "doing gender" I referenced in the introduction, remind us that the performance of gender, like the performance of any identity category, always already exists within a structural context. As such, gender performances respond to, challenge, and reify existing ideas about gendered behavior that are perpetuated in and through popular culture and social institutions. Although gender performances, like other performances, also never exist in a vacuum, we cannot think of them as separate from performances of race. Thus, the structures that govern race intersect with the structures that govern gender to inform racialized performances of gender and gendered performances of race. On a structural level, the intersection of race and gender functions differently for black folks, whose racialization and hypervisibility place them on the margins of normative gender categories. The structural intersections of race and gender, and the performances they inspire, combine with regional norms and mores to form the bases of black southern gender archetypes.

This chapter explores the tension between respondents' unabashed inhabiting of gender categories meant to exclude them, as well as their rejection of those categories and the history of oppression they conjure. Race and notions of regional membership complicate respondents' theorizations of gender and gender performances. In addition to presenting analyses of ethnographic findings, I return to critical content analyses of key black South films to highlight how popular culture shapes and represents ideas about region, race, and gender. I am attentive to the ways in which gendered presentations of self are informed by and signify performances of class status, highlighting the ways in which tropes of the southern belle and the southern gentleman always already nod toward elite class statuses. Like The Lady Chablis, respondents' racialization of southern gender archetypes, as well as their creation of distinctively black southern gender forms, pushes the identity and performative boundaries of class, gender, and region.

Better Hair, Better Women

It was a pretend-winter Saturday morning, and I was in a beauty shop, or "salon," as I was corrected twice, in a formerly suburban neighborhood in a northeastern part of the city. I was waiting for Miriam, as I had agreed to meet her there and give her a ride back to her apartment in North Memphis for our second interview after her hair appointment. Although I believed that I had timed my arrival perfectly, allowing plenty of leeway, my black-woman-in-the-beauty-shop-on-a-Saturday-morning clock was off. Miriam had just gone under the dryer when I entered the shop.

I settled in for the wait, sitting perpendicular to the dryers and across from the row of black leather chairs, all occupied, in front of a row of mirrors, all reflecting the backs and sides of the clients' various coiffures. The pungent smell of oil sheen and burning hair was thick in the air. Kim, the head stylist, was putting the finishing touches on a client's wrap. As she flat-ironed a few stray pieces and sprayed the client's hair with a finishing spray, Kim invited the client to shake her hair. She yelped with glee at the first shake, and Kim encouraged her, "Go on, shake that hair, girl!" Kim then invited the other stylists and clients to watch her client shake her 'do. Above the "oooooh"s and "ummm-hmmm, that's nice"s, Kim said, "Now, see? That's some real hairstyling right there. That is some real hairstyling. I need to take this on the road, take it up to the White House. I'd have Michelle's hair right. This ain't no Chicago styling right here, no ma'am. This is some down-home southern styling, some 'go get your man' hairstyling up in here!" The salon erupted in laughter, claps, and "go 'head, girl" as the client shook her hair all the way out the door.

Black women's hair—how much they spend on it, how much of it is really theirs, natural hair versus chemically processed hair—is often the subject of conversations in and out of black communities. Yet, the conversation happening in the salon that Saturday morning reflected commonly held assumptions about the superiority of black southern hair and hairstyling and, by extension, black southern women's performance of normative gender presentations of self. Hair, respondents argued, is one of the key elements that contribute to southern women's overall superiority to non-southern women. On our expressway ride to her apartment, I learned from Miriam that the part of the conversation I heard was the tail end of an hour-long discussion of First Lady Michelle Obama's hair—the length, the texture, the body, and more. There was also talk, Miriam added, about First Daughters Sasha and Malia's hair, with contention among the women about whether or not the children could or should walk around with less-than-perfect hair. Prevailing sentiment about black women's hair is that it should always be in place for beneficial outcomes, both in interactions with other black folks and in interactions with whites. As comedian Paul Mooney famously quips in Chris Rock's documentary *Good Hair*, reprising one of his routine lines, "If your hair is relaxed, white people are relaxed. If you hair is nappy, they're not happy."[3]

Having observed a number of beauty shop spaces of varying types, from natural hair salons to beauty shops at the back of people's houses to high-end salons, I was especially intrigued by what I saw as explicit discussions of sentiments at Kim's salon that I had observed implicitly at other salons. For instance, beauty shop conversations were inherently regionally inflected—specific discussions of weather and humidity levels, women requesting hairstyles that would be conducive for a trip down to the Delta, discussions of cutting-edge weaving techniques developed in Atlanta, Charlotte, or Memphis—but focused less explicitly on regional distinctions. In one beauty shop, a cousin visiting from up north was given looks of sympathy as if her mother had died as a stylist shook her head slowly and ran her fingers through the offending hair with a sour grapes face. The whispers of "How did they let that child's hair get like that?" were also regionally inflected, with the "they" referring to northerners derelict in or incapable of taking care of their daughters' hair.[4]

These discourses affirm gender-based intraracial distinctions that situate southern women as fundamentally different from—and in some ways better than—other women. As the *Ebony* article on the diversity of southern belles referenced in chapter one contends, black southern women are "renowned for their warm, earthy, and full-bodied appearance . . . [and] possess a charm and sophistication rarely found elsewhere."[5] Southern black folks are seen and in many cases see themselves as qualitatively, and subsequently quantitatively, distinct from non-southerners in gendered presentations of self. Further, because gender is more likely to be viewed as a natural category—women simply are wired to do this and men are simply wired to do that—respondents typically saw regional distinctions in gender performance as enshrined and relatively immutable.

Nonetheless, they were aware of the ways in which their articulations of southern gender archetypes—the belle, the gentleman, the country boy, or some other normative formulation—were separate from hegemonic white articulations of those same archetypes. That is, even middle- and upper-middle-class African Americans, thought to have opinions and outlooks on the social world similar to those of their white counterparts, saw their use of southern belle/lady or southern gentleman as largely different from white uses of those terms. Still, from blues women and pimps to the ladies and gentlemen of debutante balls, black southerners have forged a relationship to the gender norms and mores of the region. They have, as much as possible, intertwined them with racialized experiences of marginalization and exclusion from those norms and mores to create a distinctively black and southern cultural understanding of gender performances and gender roles.

Down on Belles

Of the normative regional archetypes, the belle is perhaps the most fraught. Accordingly, among respondents, it was simultaneously the source of the most criticism and admiration. Respondents most often critiqued the belle for unfair beauty standards. Cassandra, a stay-at-home mom active in a collective of stay-at-home mothers of color, described belle beauty standards as "regular black beauty standards, but ratcheted up to here [stretches her hand far above her head]." I met Cassandra at a park I frequent with my daughter, and while the girls played, we often shared conspiracy theories about Hurricane Katrina and discussed *The Real Housewives of Atlanta* and the best places to raise black children. She is wholeheartedly resistant to the belle and highlighted childhood battles with her "red," or lighter-skinned, cousins:

> When we were younger, they would call me black, midnight. When they would play dress up, they would say I was the maid and they were the belles and princesses. I just thought it was mean at the time. Now I know they saw me as, like, a mammy or slave or something . . . less than. It was because of my skin tone. So now, anytime I hear someone say, "I'm a southern belle," or I see that on somebody's Facebook page or something, I'm like . . . "ugh." Not everybody can be hazel-eyed and light-skinned and long-haired!

Cassandra, who works as a personal trainer on the weekends, grew up between a small town in the next county east of Memphis and a well-to-do black community in Whitehaven. She said neither space was an escape from colorism, although she credited her mother and maternal grandmother with encouraging her to dismiss her cousins and arming her with ammunition, quips and comebacks, that she rattled off with a fond laugh. While women of a range of colors identify as belles, for Cassandra, belle carries with it the baggage of the color privilege.

The hazel-eyed, light-skinned, long-haired belle or southern lady is certainly an archetypal instantiation of a trope of black southern womanhood, one that is reflected in popular culture.[6] International pop star Beyoncé is perhaps the most recognizable and controversial embodiment of this trope. The cornerstones of popular recognition of the singer as beautiful include her light skin; long, generally straight hair; proper level of voluptuousness; lighter eyes; and keen features. While these markers of beauty may be the same for women regardless of region, race, class, or even nation, they take on special significance in the South, where traditional beauty expectations are heightened by the demands of regional norms. Indeed, while light skin is privileged worldwide, respondents, like Cassandra, contended that the perils associated with darker skin and the entitlements of lighter skin are particularly pronounced in the South.[7]

Beyond her physical attributes, Beyoncé's belle status is bolstered by her skillful integration of down-home and sophisticated presentations of self. The singer's respectable heteronormativity—she married longtime boyfriend and rap mogul Jay-Z and only then became pregnant with and gave birth to their daughter—and the media storm surrounding it signals "old-school" southern values, religiosity, and proper rearing. She notes on several occasions in song lyrics how men from outside of the South prefer "country girls," a combination of beauty, rural wit, southern accent, and naïveté. Still, her seemingly sexually liberated alter ego "Sasha Fierce," her dogged dedication to her career (which, by her own admission, leads to benign neglect of her husband), and the lifestyle afforded by her wealth—how many "country girls" know about Audemars Piguet watches and diamond-cream facials?—place her squarely within cosmopolitan confines.

While Beyoncé incidentally possesses physical attributes associated with the belle, in *Welcome Home Roscoe Jenkins*, casting choices give credence to the belle's association with lighter skin. The romantic conflict in the film centers on a battle between dark and light reminiscent of Spike Lee's campy "Good and Bad Hair" number from the 1988 film *School Daze*. Roscoe Jenkins's brown-skinned fiancée, Bianca (played by Joy Bryant), is depicted as a shallow gold digger famous for exchanging panties for food on a season of *Survivor*. She does yoga, adheres to a vegan diet, and is sharply critical of the size and food choices of Roscoe's family members. Bianca's counterpart, Lucinda (played by Nicole Ari Parker), is southern, light-skinned, and hazel-eyed. A veritable Beyoncé in a rural context, she is Roscoe's unrequited love and undoubtedly sacrifices a number of eggs in her baking business.

While we might expect Lucinda's lighter skin and relatively soft-spoken tone to indicate fragility and the delicateness associated with white southern belles, she is clearly the tougher of the two women. Rebuilding after a breakup, starting her own business, and picking up a snake with no fuss, Lucinda is the model of independence and folk ruggedness central to the requirements of black southern belle status. In fact, Lucinda's positive and unthreatening masculine qualities—running in the woods, being unafraid of the snake when citified Roscoe is terrified—distinguish her as the more desirable partner.

Despite her toughness, though, Lucinda is also feminine. She is presented as effortlessly beautiful and therefore unconcerned with her looks, a quality in high demand, as men may have to sacrifice time, money, and, according to Chris Rock's *Good Hair* documentary, sexual intimacy for a woman whose looks require too much labor. Further, while Bianca is at best a nag and at worst a tyrant, Lucinda provides a gentle tough love that facilitates Roscoe's growth and maturity. In contrast to Bianca, who uses sex as a behavior modification tool to control Roscoe, Lucinda's beauty and goodness largely serve as stand-ins for her sexuality until the end of the film, when it is hinted that she and Roscoe have consummated their newfound love.

Finally, Lucinda is the proverbial independent woman, which means she can support herself financially and is both ingenious and a hustler in her career enterprises. This independence is both cosmopolitan and country, in that Lucinda's financial independence does not threaten Roscoe's masculinity. The gender balancing act Lucinda represents—rugged but delicate, beautiful but humble, attractive but chaste, independent yet affirming of men's masculinity, a firm nurturer but nonetheless supportive— is a best-of-both-worlds, country cosmopolitan gender performance and the stuff of men's dreams. Women, aware of the ways in which they are expected to embody or represent this balance, attempt the performance, despite structural constraints that inhibit such a performance and despite its patriarchal underpinnings.

Most respondents were critical of this gender balancing act. For them, the problem with the belle is not her skin color or hair length requirements. Instead, the major problem with the belle is that she is merely a prettier, nicer, sweeter version of the "strong black woman" controlling image. In short, the belle is a veritable superwoman whose additional amazing power is that she, like Lucinda, does not emasculate the men in her life and has proper southern manners. Michelle, a forty-one-year-old director of a nonprofit organization, highlighted this tension in her self-identification as a belle and in the way in which potential suitors perceive her. While most respondents had a discernible southern accent, Michelle's speech had the lilt of authenticity missing from the faux accents of HBO's *True Blood* actors.

> I certainly see myself as a southern belle and always have—you know, the manners, the politeness, the hair, the smile, the clothes—particularly when I'm traveling outside of the South. But wherever I go, Atlanta, Chicago, Los Angeles, Charlotte, the men see that—they find out I'm from the South—and are like, "Ooooh, she smiles, she's not loud-talking, she cooks and cleans, *and* she works for a living." So they want you, because you aren't some woman sitting and fanning yourself all day or shopping all day or whatever, but you aren't all hard and mean. So, it's like the best of both worlds. For *them*. You have to be superwoman, but do it quietly and expect nothing substantial in return.

While Michelle playfully lamented the unplanned hiatus her dating life has taken, she asserted that she cannot be a superwoman without a return, in the way her mother and aunt were. Before taking the position as director at the nonprofit, she cared for her dying aunt and mother in succession, contending that cancer might have been their disease, but caring for ungrateful men was the underlying cause of death. For Michelle and other respondents, traditional expectations of the belle's submissiveness were coupled with black women's domestic and remunerative capabilities to disadvantage women on the dating scene and in the long term. Several respondents likened this to the "five-star chick" paradigm, referencing a song by Memphis native and rapper Yo Gotti that imagines a college-educated, credit-worthy black woman with culinary and good fellatio skills as a five-star chick.[8] Far from women's expectations being too high, as a plethora of books aimed at single black women suggest, respondents asserted that men's expectations of women, especially southern women, are unreasonable.

Other respondents offered more direct structural critiques of the belle, rejections akin to my mother's nausea at the notion of Scarlett O'Hara and southern belles more generally. Wanda, a day care instructor, said she "sho' ain't no belle, wasn't one, won't never be one, and ain't no *lady* neither." When I initially encountered her at a jamboree, she was yelling from far up in the bleachers for the performing drummers to launch into a particular cadence, one she remembered from her high school days. She grew up in Memphis and lives alone in the tiny blue house in Orange Mound in which she was raised, fighting with four boy cousins and two older brothers, in addition to one girl cousin and a younger sister. The street is jammed with similar tiny houses with neat porches, concrete planters, and oil stains in the driveway. She said she still cannot believe how quiet the house is sometimes, given how loud it was from 1972 to 1990, the year her mother died and her younger sister graduated high school. She told me in our first interview:

> Belles are white, straight, no children—you know, young and carefree, and got a rich man or some riches from they daddy. They ain't no black, no poor, or gay, old, or got a bunch of kids to feed, and they certainly ain't got the problems we [African Americans] face. And most of the black folks I know do got problems, and most of them fit into one of those groups—broke, got some children and a baby daddy, or *some* babies' daddies, you know. Them gals running around calling themselves *belles* [said with a *Gone with the Wind*-reminiscent accent and several blinks of her eyes] need to get a wake-up call. Because if they think about it, and they honest, they fits one of them things that makes them not be a belle at all.

She elaborated further on the characteristics of the belle, carefully explaining why black women do not fit the list. For Wanda, class, gender, race, sexuality, and parental status marginalization exclude most women she knows from the category of belle. Her assertions also filled in the blanks, at least partially, of the differences between "a [white] southern woman" and "a [black] woman from the South." Given the untenable requirements of gender performance writ large, why should southern black women, or black women from the South, trouble themselves with the additional corsets of southern white gender archetypes, norms that partially subsidized systems of slavery and institutionalized racism? Further, black women already have a set of race-specific controlling images to manage, including the "strong black woman", the lady, the bitch, the baby mama, and the earth mother. As a master status, does not race apply stricture enough on identities, performances, and outcomes without the addition of region?

Regardless of the theoretical and structural untenability of the belle as an identity and performance, most women respondents did not see the belle as inaccessible performative terrain as a result of their membership in status categories that, as Wanda contended, prevents them from accessing the belle. In fact, most women respondents who self-identified as belles reject these categorical exclusions: they are single mothers with baby daddies, many are working class, and most lead lives that could hardly be characterized as carefree. Further, respondents that identified as belles wore their hair in every style from straight to kinky and described their skin colors as everything from extra chocolate to milk with a little coffee. By drawing on the belle, for performative or identity purposes, in praise or critique, marginalized women disrupt normative southern gender categories, racializing and remaking the belle into something useful rather than something that wholly supports racial and gendered oppression.

Debut(ante) Blues

In my second interview with Wanda, I gained some more perspective on her indictment of the belle as a regional gender formulation unavailable to most black women. Although it did not come up in our first interview, Wanda's niece, Tara, had been preparing for a cotillion, with her debut scheduled for the spring. Wanda said that she had been "mentally blocking" it out of her mind during our interview the previous December, hoping that if she just did not think about it, Tara would change her mind about participating. Our second interview took place a few weeks before her debut, and Tara had not, in fact, changed her mind. Further, Wanda had reluctantly been roped into making her gown, since "her mama ain't got it to buy her one like all the other gals." However, as might have been expected, she was critical of the process, a vestige of black middle-class communities in general and southern black middle-class communities in particular. Upon the fitting pedestal, Tara, a gangly ginger-colored girl, fidgeted as Wanda adjusted and pinned the waist. She begged for the third time for a bathroom break, and Wanda acquiesced, mumbling to herself. She turned to me and said: "You know about these things, right? These balls? Well, they have to raise money, you know. For 'charity.' And Niecy [Tara's mother] can raise some money, sho' 'nough. But she and Tara need to face that Tara is not the cutest thing to ever walk the planet, she ain't no belle, and she ain't no doctor's child like these girls. She can pretend all she want, but she just ain't."

Wanda glanced toward the hall down which Tara had disappeared. Satisfied that she was not returning yet, she continued:

I just don't agree with it, you know. It's a fantasy. We are just simple working people. But Niecy always wanted more. Fake it 'til she make it. But she ain't never made it. So now she's trying to use Tara to get in with these people. They laughing at her. Those other people aren't asking for money from church members. They just plopping down the $10,000 right there. And what's gon' happen after she "come out"? She don't need no dresses, manners, and etiquette like that. She got plenty of what she need. She gon' get a basketball scholarship. Ain't no lawyer's son gon' be marrying and taking care of her!

Although Wanda described herself as working class and her family as just simple working people, she lives in a community of mostly older homeowners, friends and neighbors of her mother's, most of whom she has known since she was a child. Still, she disagreed with the cultural aspects of the cotillion and bristled at the thought of waltzing or being in the company of people who encourage waltzing. Her last words were in a rushed, hushed tone, as we both heard Tara bounding back to the sewing room. She hopped back on the pedestal, recounting, in perhaps too much detail, her triumph of urinating without removing the dress's hoop. For her part, Wanda continued working, glancing back at me occasionally to gesture, humph, or jerk her eyes toward Tara and back at me in response to something Tara said or did. After Wanda finished, she joined me in the kitchen, where I asked her about her experiences with debutante balls.

All I know is, they are full of these *bourgie* black folks, these rich Memphis folks, and they let Tara in because they can't just turn someone down. They think they're going to make her into some kind of lady. They don't know anything about poor or working black folks. And I know what Niecy has been going through. You can bet the rest of them ain't having to jump through such hoops because they just got the money like that. [Snaps her fingers.] Plus, they all know each other. Tara just an outsider, trying to get in. They had to *assign* her a boy to be her escort. *None* of the boys there volunteered to do it. Because, like I said, she ain't no belle, see.

I started to chide Wanda for her lack of enthusiasm and fervor for the underdog, and her flesh and blood, no less. However, I thought better of it. Although guest tickets for the ball were prohibitively expensive, I contacted the debut's coordinator and offered to play my violin as prelude music for the guests' arrival, a prospect at which she was extraordinarily excited. She told me breathlessly over the phone, "Oh, we've never had such at a debut! The parents will be so pleased. How rare!" She told me the color scheme for this year's debut and asked politely if I might wear something to complement the gold, green, and pale blue theme. I have never known cotillions to have color schemes, and I was not keen on blending in with table decorations.

I arrived especially early for the spring event, held at a downtown Memphis hotel, slightly self-conscious about my simple performance black and even more self-conscious about my locs, which I had tamed as much as possible and pulled into a bun so tight that I gave myself a mini facelift. I rarely pull my locs back, even while performing, but I wanted to ensure that my hair was not a topic of conversation among the middle-aged and upper-middle-class women on the board and the parents in attendance. Wanda's protests, commentary, and side glances had affected me, and I felt extraordinarily out of place. I was relieved that I blended in as background help amid the buzzing hotel caterers, decorators, and audiovisual technicians. As I set up across from the ballroom platform, a fair-skinned woman in a white skirt-suit, white hat, and white pumps whisked up to me and hugged me tightly, introducing herself as Mrs. Williams-Spate, the cotillion coordinator, and thanking me for offering my services. She looked me over, and I thought I met her approval. She asked, "Did you ever debut?"

"No, ma'am."

"Well, it's never too late to be involved! We could use you on the board!" She whisked away as quickly as she came, politely ordering the decorator to place the centerpieces "directly in the center of the table, not slightly off-center" because everything had to be "balanced."

Parents and guests began to arrive, and my prelude performance was frequently interrupted by their questions and comments. Like Wanda had assumed, many of the parents were members of Memphis's black upper-middle classes, as politicians, lawyers, doctors, and business people. When Niecy, Tara's mother, arrived, smiling, speaking, and waving in her fuchsia skirt-suit and matching fuchsia-sequined hat with flowing fuchsia mesh—an outfit that Wanda had bet me twenty dollars in our second interview that she would wear to the debut—the woman talking with me did a double-take and said, "Ooooh, Jesus. That must be Tara's mother." She quickly added, "Lovely speaking with you, and be sure to give me your card," rushing to her assigned table and leaning over to her counterpart, glancing relatively conspicuously toward Niecy but refraining from pointing and prolonged whispering.

The ball proceeded as most balls I have attended do, and when Tara emerged from behind the curtain and onto the platform, Niecy tapped her husband, let out a small but audible squeal, and quietly clapped her hands, then clasped them together as she stared up at the platform. Tara was quite lovely, and Wanda's craftsmanship rendered her dress a higher quality than most of the other store- and boutique-bought dresses to come down the platform. Tara beamed somewhat nervously but proudly, and her escort managed a bit of enthusiasm as well. At the end of the platform, Tara curtsied to the front, left, and right, losing her balance a bit but nonetheless continuing her winning smile, uninterrupted. Tara's usually corn-rowed hair had been relaxed to perfection and swooped up into a crown of curls accented by a glittering tiara, which Wanda had also prepped me, without a wager, to expect. At other tables, parents and guests exchanged looks, and a few stifled smirks.

While Wanda was skeptical that Tara could "pull it off," for the most part, she did. She waltzed with more ease than some of her counterparts, and her response during the question and answer portion, while given in a southern working-class speech that caused more stifled smirks and looks, was more well-reasoned and thorough than those of her counterparts, winning her an award. Further, ultimately, Tara, through Niecy's diligence and persistence, had raised more money than her counterparts and received special recognition for her efforts—which also raised some eyebrows. She gave a practiced wave as she received her plaque. I could not discern whether the gesture was a mocking wave, a genuine performance, or some combination of both. After the presentation of the girls to society and the close of the ball, Tara came up to me, beaming craftily, during the post-debut mingling. She had taken off her dainty walk and returned to her usual bow-legged, basketball walk, which nicely betrayed the hoop-skirted gown she was still wearing.

TARA: How did I do?

ZANDRIA: You did good, girl, you did it! Congratulations!

TARA: I told Auntie I could do it! Ha! I put it on! She didn't think I could be a *belllle* [bats her faux eyelashes], but I did it. Academy Award, please? [Holds her hand out, giggles, and fans herself.]

Although I did not formally interview Tara, the few interactions we did have as I spent time with Wanda made clear that she was not a cultural dupe doing her mother's bidding, although pleasing Niecy and going along with her desires was certainly part of Tara's motivation. Her comments to me after the debut indicated that she was well aware of the performance and took pride in her performative capabilities, although being a belle—or "doing the belle"—is more than likely not the terrain she wants to travel. She may or may not have access to the powers of the belle. However, her ability to "put it on" and defy it, even if only a bit, despite doubts about her and her mother's class(ed) place in the debut, speaks to the malleability of belle as a performative category—despite Aunt Wanda and Scarlett O'Hara.

Gangstas and Gentlemen

Black men's relationship to the southern gentleman as a gender archetype is rife with much the same tension as black women's relationship to the belle. Conversely, as some respondents argued, other southern black masculine forms, like gangsta, playa, mack daddy, and pimp, are more recognizable and accessible.

While the archetype of gentleman necessarily carries with it ideas about wealth and elite status, in many African American formulations of the figure, working-class men, combining the styling of playas and pimps with the manners of the gentleman, assume the mantle of übergentlemen. Like their women counterparts, gentlemen are strong nurturers and supportive partners, handsome and kempt. As a symbol of patriarchy and heteronormativity, as well as of racial stability and progress, the gentleman figure is essential to understanding black southern womanhood.

Despite the significance of the gentleman for constructions of black womanhood as well as of black manhood, contemporary popular images of southern black men are more likely to consist of gangstas, playas, and pimps. As African American and southern studies scholar Riché

Richardson points out, the proliferation of these latter representations are the consequences of southern black men's responses to a history of marginalization by white racism and of their southern residence. In southern rap iconography and presentation of self in particular, gangstas, playas, and pimps take on special significance as markers of an authentic and masculine masculinity. Still, both within and outside of southern rap, gentlemen discourses—as well as discourses of gentlemen gangstas—abound.

No culture producer is more directly central to recent popular images of black, although not necessarily southern, gentlemen than Tyler Perry. Especially invested in redeeming representations of African American men, and working-class African American men in particular, as gentlemen, Perry erects a controversial instantiation of good versus evil that ultimately vilifies black middle classes, especially churchgoers, and exalts working classes. Although the regional affiliation of Perry's African American characters is not necessarily signaled by their accents or dress, Perry situates his films in a recognizable South complete with church choirs, lush lawns, and references to counties in and around Atlanta. Drawing on the spatial iconography of the South, Perry invites viewers to read the southern experience as a universal black experience, or at least as an alternative to usual representations of black life.

In Perry's work, gentlemen are often directly contrasted with ungentlemanly characters or fallen gentlemen, whose general failure as men is exacerbated by their ill treatment of women. For instance, in *Tyler Perry's Madea's Family Reunion* (2006), wealthy Carlos (played by Blair Underwood) is juxtaposed with bus driver Frankie (played by Boris Kodjoe). Carlos is controlling, manipulative, and physically and emotionally abusive and has made promises of financial benefits to his fiancée's mother in exchange for her cooperation in facilitating the marriage. Conversely, Frankie is a single dad who politely pursues one of his frequent passengers, a single mother whose experiences with sexual abuse have rendered her distrustful of men.[9] Unlike Carlos, Frankie is a nurturer who wants to protect and care for this woman and her children as his own, in addition to being a financial provider. While it is Tyler Perry's Madea, as protective gentleman and steel magnolia, who encourages Carlos's fiancée to exact revenge and obtain her freedom from his abuse and her mother's manipulation, Frankie functions as representative of those unsung southern and black gentlemen whose only desire is to provide for and protect their female partners.

Perry rehashes this juxtaposition in most of his films, where a bad black man is contrasted with and eventually bested by a good black man, even when that good black man comes in the form of Madea. In *Daddy's Little Girls* (2007), Idris Elba plays a good working black man with a trifling and despicable baby mama. The showdown between him and the bad black man, an infamous drug dealer played by New Orleans native Gary Sturgis, involves an old-fashioned street beat-down that not only protects his daughters but indeed saves an entire black (Atlanta) neighborhood from the ravages of drug trafficking. In *Tyler Perry's Why Did I Get Married?* (2007), the evil black man is Mike, played by Richard T. Jones. His emotional abuse of Sheila, played by Jill Scott, and his public philandering are contrasted with the inherent goodness of Troy, sheriff of a small mountain town in which the characters are vacationing. Rather than chide Sheila about her weight or agree with her internalized negative assessments of herself, Sheriff Troy supports her by exercising with her and stands up for her against Mike's abuse. In each film, the gentlemen trounce, physically or verbally, the bad black men, restoring the social order.

Similar juxtapositions of bad black men and good black gentlemen are central to most of Perry's work. While most melodramas require villains and heroes, Perry's villains exist to highlight the goodness of black working-class men, whose relative lack of wealth and socioeconomic power is overcome by their value as family men, providers, and protectors. Through a resurrection of the black gentleman, Perry gestures toward a black community supported by a benign, rather than outwardly violent, patriarchy.

Although the genealogy of Perry's gentlemen is often unclear—Perry's characters are necessarily underdeveloped—male respondents in this study were clear about how and why they identify as gentlemen. Among the male respondents in my sample, gentlemen's genealogy is simple: rearing is responsible for their identities and performances of the southern gentleman. David, a lawyer who described himself as a southern gentleman, declared like many respondents that he was just "raised right":

I have the utmost respect for women. My mom was a single mom, and she was my everything. She's still my everything until I find that special lady, you know? But yeah, how some people say that only a man can raise a man and all of that? That's not true. To be a good man, a gentleman, you have to have that strong woman to raise you so you can really understand and respect what women go through. It's not just the door opening stuff either. It's being a partner and not always trying to be "the head" or be in charge.

Raised in the Hickory Hill community until the neighborhood began to show signs of a racial shift, David spent weekends with his grandmother in South Memphis, code switching between what he called the "mean streets" of South Parkway and Mississippi Boulevard and the makeshift skateboard ramps and small-town street lights of his new East Memphis neighborhood. When she could, his mother switched David from the neighborhood public school to a predominantly white and private Christian high school. There, he said, ideals he learned from his mother were reinforced through the school's interaction with the students at its sister school, also a private Christian institution. While the figure of the gentleman is not explicitly associated with feminist ideals, most men that self-identified as gentlemen were well versed in feminist ideals and could reflect and articulate them. Admittedly, I was skeptical of male respondents' feminist contentions, which ranged from black playa trickster lines to complex reflections on patriarchy as a barrier to male-female relationships. As such, I confronted David, like I confronted other respondents, with the stereotypes of black men behaving badly—especially single young professional black men with no children—as highly sought-after commodities. In our conversation, David cried foul: "I know some men are like that, but I know a lot that are not, you know? That's just a stereotype. Most men down here—if they have *any real* respect for their mamas, sisters, and cousins—are gentlemen, and they don't want to be running around with multiple people. They just want some reciprocity and don't want to deal with the drama."

Again, David pointed to the influence of and respect for women as central to not only the development of a gentleman's identity but also the adherence to gentleman behavior. David, who is "not a Jesus freak," though he attends church regularly, is not unlike many men with whom I spoke, regardless of class, occupational, or parental statuses. Even when men explicitly admitted philandering or other ungentlemanly behaviors, they contended nonetheless that they strove to be gentlemen, from opening doors and pulling out chairs to protecting women emotionally and financially.

Still, other respondents countered my skepticism with critiques of women's unreasonable expectations of men. Keith, the English teacher, was happy to run down his observations of southern women:

KEITH: It's like, you have to be a gangsta and a gentleman. You have to be able to farm, and you have to be a corporate lawyer. You have to be able to fight, and you have to also walk away from fights. And break up fights. And you have to roll a purple Cutlass with 24-inch rims and an S-Class Mercedes. Also with the rims.

ZANDRIA: But Keith, aren't you yourself a gangsta *and* a gentleman?
KEITH: Well, yes. But that is beside the point [. . .].

Although Keith was, as usual, only half-serious, most men respondents pointed out what they saw as women's unreasonable best-of-both-worlds expectations of their masculinity. Here, Keith signified different kinds of masculinity with nods toward the rural-urban divide and black southerners' infamous car culture. While black men across regions, or perhaps men in general, might contend that women unreasonably desire both a "bad boy" and a "family man," respondents argued that this pressure is more explicit in the South. Cain, who grew up in one of Memphis's historically black neighborhoods and cares for his aging aunt in the family home, described himself as having the looks of a crunk rapper but the barista skills of Seattle's finest. He discussed the regional dimensions of this pressure: "So, there's a fine line you have to walk [in the South] because there isn't a whole lot of space to be a different kind of dude, like a [skate]boarder, punk, you know, because people won't understand that. Your choices are gangsta or church dude, and if you're neither, you gotta figure out how to be part of one so people will know what to do with you. Thankfully for me, I have the gangsta looks."

Cain and other respondents spoke to the limited masculine identities available in the South, with "church dude" here approximating gentleman. In Cain's case, his "gangsta looks"—which consist of a gold front tooth and long braided locks—attract a variety of women whom he feels his Afropunk musical tastes and skateboard transportation would otherwise drive away. While he shied away from the notion of gentleman for its roots in white men's oppression of black folks, he, like Keith, embraces and blends both a gangsta identity and that "something else" masculinity. "When I'm outted as *not* being a dope boy—living in [my neighborhood], having the gold [tooth], and talking that talk be confusing people—I'm still gangsta with an extra something else that won't land my ass in jail. Punk is hard, too."

Cain implied that the social and financial capital attached to drug dealing is helpful to his masculine presentation of self. Yet, when some women find out he does not, in fact, possess that capital, he needs to quickly introduce that "something else" to make up for the loss. He argued for an interpretation of punk as hard and perhaps financially lucrative, although he admitted that the latter is rarely convincing in practice.

Travis, who works for a mobile car detailing business, also reflected on the dichotomy of gentleman and gangsta. I accompanied him on his rounds to drop his freshly printed business cards and flyers—bright white and shiny with blue and black writing—to coffee shops, bulletin boards, and other places that allow free advertising. He was certainly a door holder, the universal marker of gentleman status, outmaneuvering and dashing ahead of me several times to open doors, although I had insisted in each instance that he need not open doors. The twenty-four-year-old sees himself as a gentleman and thus would not relent on his commitment to dooropening, despite my protests. His parents, entrepreneurs with a massage business, raised him to be polite and respectful of women and to have what he called a general sense of right and wrong. Yet he, like other respondents, talked about the always already present gangsta in southern men's masculine identities. He described the gentleman/gangsta binary in regional and historical terms: "See, down south, we're more like lovers rather than fighters, although we will fight and shoot a nigga. But we're really, like, slower to anger than some dude in the Bronx like [barks like rapper DMX], so then women—well, not just women, really, people in generally who don't know—misinterpret that like we some punks. Dudes from the Dirty [South] be gangstas, but that's not our mode all the time."

When I asked Travis to elaborate on why he has couched his statement in regional terms, and specifically a barking New Yorker and a slower-to-anger southerner, he explained, "It's like our history. We had to be slicker down south. We ain't just gon' up and start a riot and burn down a city or something. You couldn't do that. You had to protect your family on the low and wait for your revenge on a cracker that's done did something to your family. Move too fast, your whole family dead and your house blown up. [. . .] Why you think all them niggas from up north come down here for dope? We know how to be cool when we breakin' the law. Ruthless, too, when necessary."

Like the Nappy Roots' admonishment to southerners and others to not "bring it round here 'less ya know fo' sho' it's jumpin' off,"[10] Travis articulated a southern masculinity that acts only when necessary and gives fair warning beforehand. Travis, who volunteers at his southeast Memphis high school alma mater, said that he does not exactly tell the group of freshmen young men he is mentoring the exact narrative that he has given me, but he insisted that he encourages them to be proud of Memphis and the South. Travis sees southern men's history of Jim Crow racial oppression as an important training ground for an expedient masculinity—one that is not impulsive and reserves action for the most opportune time.

However, popular logic links black men's hypermasculinity with the cumulative emasculating effects of slavery, Jim Crow, and institutional racism. This emasculation, the argument continues, was especially pronounced for southern men, who could not protect their wives and children from the oppressive capriciousness of white racism and often did not have the earning power to provide better lives for their families. "Southern" encapsulates much more than just regional residence in this argument, extending in particular to class and space. However, the simple dichotomy of black urban masculinity versus a lesser country black masculinity displaces marginalization and emasculation onto the South, leaving black urban masculinity outside of the South intact.

Respondents rewrote this popular logic as Travis did, claiming a historical relationship to the gangsta figure in much the same way they credit their mamas for their gentlemanliness. Hasan, the Brooklyn transplant who suffered with me through Keith's rap historiography, also attributed the strength of southern black masculinity to the history of racial oppression. "You ever heard somebody say, 'He got that old man strength'? Like, he an old black man but he picking up cars? I had never seen anything like that until I came South. That's slavery and sharecropping and Africa in these cats' blood." Not only did Hasan locate black übermasculinity geographically in the South and rural space, he also linked the South with Africa as a marker of racial authenticity and purity. To be sure, even southern respondents referred to "old man strength" as something unique to a generation of black men who had grown up farming and translated that strength to the trades they picked up and perfected in the city. Yet, Hasan implicitly extended this to younger southern black men as well, who will eventually develop "old man strength" by virtue of the sharecropping—real, fictive, or remembered—in their blood.

While respondents talked about other masculine forms, negotiating a balance between gangsta and gentleman, both for purposes of identity theorization and interaction with others, was central to their management of the complexities of black masculinity in popular and interpersonal contexts. Most respondents imagined a continuum between these poles but asserted nonetheless that these were key points on the map of black southern masculinity. Further, by refashioning the southern gentleman to reflect gangsta and genteel sensibilities, respondents racialized a category from which they were excluded because of race, class, and geography.

All the Single (Southern) Ladies and Gentlemen

As respondents moved from theorizing identities to performing them, they highlighted the difficulties of making certain formulations, like the traditional southern belle, work in practice. Valencia, a twenty-five-year-old elementary school teacher, is representative of respondents who self-identified as southern belles but offered critical perspectives on their performance of the belle, their intentions, and their desired outcomes. A majorette in her prestigious black high school band, Valencia is the stuff of southern rap songs—light-skinned, very pretty, petite, and with hair, whether in a short crop or a long weave, always done. She is busy and impatient but unendingly gracious when the spotlight is on her.

As expected, she blew into our second interview session at an East Memphis café late. As she bustled around setting down her oversized bag and a smaller clutch, she said, half to me and half to herself, "This one just has to be fired. Just got to be." When I asked her what she was talking about, she apologized and flashed her usual toothy smile, as if on cue at halftime at an HBCU football game. She paused and then declared, "He doesn't understand me. I am a true southern belle. I like men, money, and manicures. He couldn't hang with any of that. So he's in the fired pile. *Fiyered*." She went on to talk about how this man, a young postal worker, was "insecure" about her number of "suitors" and frequently expressed frustration with her seeming unwillingness to "sit down and actually tend to his needs." For his part, Darius, thirty-two, did not disagree. He had agreed to an interview with me before Valencia had communicated to him his status in the fired pile.

> She had a number of guys that would call her, and I was wanting her to really try to see where *we* could go. She didn't want to stop talking to them, like she wanted to have all of these, like, "suitors," and I wasn't going for that. I asked her about it, and she said that she liked men. I told her, "I like women, but I'm not calling or going out with or accepting gifts from them while we're supposed to be trying to be exclusive." She told me she was supposed to get gifts from different men until she had a ring on her finger.

Darius told me that his "biological clock was ticking." The oldest of five brothers and sisters and the oldest boy in a host of cousins, he had clear ideas about his desire to start a family. And while other men respondents did not explicitly point to a "biological clock," they often had clear ideas of where and how a black southern (and implicitly middle-class) life should unfold.

> I'm not interested in running around. I'll be thirty-three next year. If I want to have some time without children just for me and my wife, I need to get married soon, so we can travel and so forth, you know. Then we have the kids, because I don't want to be an old man still raising kids.

Buy some land in the country down by where my father's people live so the kids can have some summers in the country. And my parents will be happy to have some grandkids. Mama been pressuring me ever since [I started with the postal service six years ago].

Darius's sentiments reflect southerners' supposed premium on "family values," which include at least bearing and raising children. While it was clear that both his biological clock and his mother's grandmother clock are ticking, perhaps the latter more loudly than the former, other single men without children also hint at a biological clock. Key to heeding the clock's call and solidifying the southern American dream, men respondents argued, is a particular kind of southern woman.

Valencia's expression of her desires for multiple male companions, access to the economic resources of those companions, and regular spa pampering might in other contexts put her squarely in the category of the much-maligned gold digger, rendering her outside of the parameters of a suitable southern woman. However, respondents, including Darius, shied away from the gold digger description if the woman in question was gainfully employed, good looking, and domestic. Darius did not see or frame Valencia's desires as gold digging, contending that "women should have nice things, whatever they want, if they're good women." He explained further: "As men we are supposed to not just provide and protect, but give women what they want. As long as your woman is taking care of home and has a job, if she says she wants that bag or shoes or whatever, you'd better get it, or if she has her own money, which is what most women have these days, you had better let her get it, encourage her even, or you're going to be in trouble."

Darius's narrative reflects many respondents' feelings about this "new southern woman," one who is economically empowered, expects cooperation on domestic duties, and does not necessarily want a large family. While these characteristics are reflective of generational shifts in social norms that affect middle-class women across the global West, the South has been notoriously further behind national trends, with men and women still marrying and having children at a younger age than their counterparts in other regions. Still, even southerners have been waiting to marry, and respondents rightly correlated these changes with women's changing and expanding economic power. Yet, the pressure to marry, from parents and peers' Facebook status updates, persists.

Ubiquitous marriage pressures and the regional dynamics of partner choice affect men's dating practices in ways that contradict conventional wisdom. I asked Darius about the supposed abundance of women there are for black men and why a man—particularly a young, childless, federal employee who loves his mama—simply would not move on to the next woman who might demand less and give more. He responded: "That's not necessarily true about there being a bunch of women. Well, I see what you're saying, that there are a lot of women, but not *these* kind of women. These women are educated, beautiful, keep their hair and nails done, *and* are willing to let you take the lead."

Darius's statement hints at the gender balancing act that defines country cosmopolitanism. It also confirms some prevailing ideas about men's desires to feel like they are taking the lead in the relationship, financially and otherwise, and reflects the sentiments of most of the men in the sample, regardless of educational level. These kind of women, Darius and other respondents contended, are in high demand, and men see them as the perfect combination of the gentility of the belle and of the domestic and remunerative labor of southern black women, despite their perceived social and financial maintenance costs.

While Valencia and most women in my sample either described themselves as progressive, womanist, or feminist, or could be described as such based on their attitudes toward women's roles and gender equality, they also frequently reported engaging in performative feminine helplessness, an illusion they argued was central to a successful dating portfolio, as Michelle termed it. Here, Valencia testifies to the performative labor that goes into letting men take the lead in a relationship:

> I think most women make men think they're in control in the relationship. But southern women go way beyond with it. That's why we keep men. I say, "Oooh, baby, can you help me open this? Can you do this for me? I just am not strong enough. Can you go out there and chop that firewood?" Men want to feel like they can do something that you can't do, and you have got to do that work and play that role. You can walk right over them as long as you play it right. It's really hard for me, too, because I'm not like that at all. But I just laugh and kee-kee-kee, and say, "Oh, thank you so much, honey," and he's grinning from ear to ear.

It is difficult for me to imagine Valencia as performing, though she clearly acknowledged the performative aspects of her identity as a southern belle, because she does embody the essential qualities of black versions of the archetype. Although Valencia's family has lived exclusively in the city for several generations with few ties to the rural South, she is no stranger to physical labor, having worked overnight for FedEx during college. Nonetheless, her manicures obscure this reality.

Although I did not let Darius in on the secret during our post-"firing" interviews, Valencia had expressed in and out of context on a number of occasions that she is not now and may never be interested in raising a family. She cited her busy work schedule and eventual plans to pursue a graduate degree as the major factors, but I pushed her to resolve the belle's domesticity and relative fragility with her independent woman ontology. "Well, let's just say I'm a 'new' southern belle, then. All the looks, except for with air conditioning and no kids. And a lot of shoes. And I'm not going to be cooking and cleaning by myself. Fifty-fifty, nigga, or you can't be with me."

Valencia's career aspirations, coupled with what she deemed the slavery of raising a family, are not unlike those of a rising segment of women attempting to balance work, societal pressures to bear children, and minimal access to resources. For black women, this is seemingly exacerbated by the lack of "marriageable" black men. Amber, a slender flight attendant whom I met on one of her layover breaks in Memphis, scoffed at the marriageable black men argument. After high school, she knew she wanted to travel and quickly signed up to be a flight attendant. Although she intended to return to college sooner, at twenty-eight, she did not seem to be ready for a shift from work to school. Her travel for work includes destinations in the South, Midwest, and Eastern Seaboard, and she can rattle off every discount and outlet store east of the Mississippi.

In our first interview one early spring at her aunt Jessie's South Memphis home, Amber told me matter-of-factly that lack of available marriage partners is not the issue. We were competing with the intermittent flap of a screen door because of an occasional chilly breeze and her aunt Jessie's interjections. "Oh, no, that's just a myth," she told me. "It's literally raining men. We all need umbrellas." Her aunt, fifty-four, agreed, emerging from the kitchen to yell, again, directly into my recorder. "I have to sweep the mens off my porch! [Gestures with a sweeping motion.] I can't leave the house because they are all over me! They even be eyeing me in Sunday school!"

While there was perhaps some hyperbole in Aunt Jessie's claims, they were a dominant theme among respondents, even with men aware of the competition. While the male respondents were more likely to express disbelief in the magnitude of women's claims, they nonetheless adjust their performances of masculinity to ensure that they are perceived as gentlemen, regardless of what other forms their masculinity might take. Further, while women were critical of the belle and her performative requirements, they nonetheless participate in crafting gendered presentations of self to ensure a stream of interested marriageable partners, even if they are not yet ready for or interested in marriage.

Southern Guls and Country Boys

Many respondents, like Amber and Valencia, thought very explicitly and carefully about their regionalized gender performances, including thinking of them as regionally distinct and inspired. Still others did not explicitly claim regional distinction as a performance, even when pressed. Amber described this latter group of women as natural southern belles:

> AMBER: Some women don't even put it on at all. They don't have to. They are just naturals because that's, like, how they are, how they were raised, cornbread, pig feet, that kind of stuff.
>
> ZANDRIA: What makes them naturals? How are they raised differently from the way you were?
>
> AMBER: I mean, we didn't eat those kinds of things. We had Sunday dinner, but Ma'dea' and Mama did most of the cooking, so I'm finding that I need to learn how to cook those things. I'm in the kitchen every Sunday now when I'm home, watching. And some girls are just born *looking* that way. You know, pretty, thick, brown eyes. I'm just glad that skinny is in now, too, because I've always been tall and lanky. I couldn't compete with these pig feet butts if skinny wasn't in!

For Amber, being a natural southern belle is tied to consuming stereotypical southern foods, like cornbread and pigs' feet, and having a certain body type, thick or full-bodied, as the August 1971 issue of *Ebony* asserted. Valencia also contended that some women are naturals, counting herself among them. However, she also is quite conscious about her performance of the belle. Still, she argued that some women "don't even know it, or at least they pretend not to." She told me about her friend Tyana: "Tyana looks the part. Big booty, small chest, big smile, country talking, all of that. But she doesn't even know it. The dudes fall all over her, girl, I'm telling you. Some man is always buying her something; she doesn't even *have* to ask or tell him what her expectations are. I'm serious! Her nails done, hair done, everything, she got a car, and everything. I tell you what she is, though. She is a country girl. A *country* girl. That trumps a belle any day."

While self-identified southern belles do not employ tactics that are in themselves distinct from what all women, and black women in particular, are taught about the requirements of gender work and play, the deliberate execution of these tactics is regionally inspired. Respondents, like Valencia and Amber, who talked explicitly about their management and maintenance of their identities as belles, saw themselves as qualitatively distinct from country girls, or southern guls. Imani, a financial secretary for a church who also described herself as a belle, explained further:

> A country girl is one that really, actually knows about the country. They might have planted something before in their life, or picked cotton, or killed a chicken; they know how to clean chitlins and all of that. They are wide-eyed and kind of slow, but I don't mean they're dumb. Just, like, they're country, so they ain't trying to get the latest shoes and bags. I don't know about no country. I'm a city girl. And me? Killing a chicken? Girl, no. Never. Mama tried to take me down to Coldwater [Mississippi] where she grew up and tried to show me how to kill a chicken when I was seven or eight. I was traumatized. Fo' real. I knew back then I would have to be . . . a different kind of woman when I grew up. Not no chicken killer.

Imani, whom I first encountered donning a wide sun hat and fanning herself at an outdoor festival, editorialized her chicken experience in Coldwater as a pivotal moment in which she decided—in childhood, no less— to be a belle. A debutante in the late 1990s and a sorority woman, Imani contended that some women are born to be belles while others are born to plant things and kill chickens. The culinary symbols she and Amber summoned to make their respective points about urban/rural distinctions, including chitterlings, cornbread, and pigs' feet, highlight important class and experience distinctions in southern black life. Further, she assumed, as did many respondents and as do even popular culture representations, that country women's lack of knowledge about the world means they will not desire the latest material possessions. Migration from parts of the rural and small-town Mississippi Delta continues, and African American Memphians have close ties to the Delta. Although some, like Imani, resist the country life their parents attempt to introduce them to, others grow up shuttling back and forth between Memphis and Mississippi, the city life and the country life. Still, Imani's assumptions about country girls were not altogether accurate, particularly for women raised primarily in the city. The distinctions between country life and city life are not as strong as gardening, picking cotton, and cleaning chitterlings might imply.

I tracked down Tyana to get her perspective on Valencia's assessment of her as a country girl. She was traveling back and forth between Memphis,

Greenwood, Mississippi, and Houston. I met her at her apartment in Houston, where she and her son, age seven, are living while she finishes a fast-track six-week summer course toward her teaching licensure. When I told her what Valencia said, she let out a full laugh, eventually wiping away tears that had formed from the amusement.

> That's just Valencia. She thinks there's some magic to it. She'll have her makeup, her little heels, her little clothes, girl, and she walks into the room, like, "Come to me, men, I am Valencia." I'm just me. And I will say she is right about the country part. I don't know if that's what the guys like or are attracted to with me or not. Since I've been here, a lot of guys have come up to me and actually said, "Ooooh, where are you from? You're not from here, are you?" So, I've thought that was different. And I guess there is something about it. But I'm not just country. Even though I went to Greenwood a lot, I grew up in Memphis, went to college in Memphis, and now I'm in the *big* big city. So, I think guys maybe like that I'm somewhere in between. I'm a country girl, but I'm a little citified, a little belle, too. Like Erykah [Badu] say, I'm a [sings] "southern gul"!

Tyana is representative of the best-of-both-worlds country cosmopolitanism, although she denied having direct experience killing a chicken. Valencia's description of Tyana, as well as Tyana's conceptualization of herself, points to the joining of the best characteristics of the city and the country. Some articulations of regional differences in gender, then, are not only performative practice but also reflective of actual, or sincere, intraracial distinctions in African American life.

In Erykah Badu's "Southern Gul," her signification on a 1980 Frankie Beverly hit, the narrator offers several simple declarations about herself and the region that best encapsulate the dynamics of the black southern identities inhabited by country boys and southern guls. In it, she argues that the South is home of "the burnin' church," "pocket stones," "booty songs," and "fingerwaves that last all night long." She claims to eat everything fried, including her tofu; to not "know much about the world"; and to have friends who "don't know about the Internet . . . radio . . . [or] television." Badu's southern gul is "fly as a bumblebee" and has a "dirty way 'cause [she] got a dirty mouth."[11] The result is a distinct and alternative southern femininity informed by region, race, and class sensibilities.

The cover for the "Southern Gul" single features a close-up of the singer's mouth, which features the letters *B*, *A*, *D*, and *U* in faux gold across the front of her teeth. As a manifesto on black southern culture that is both accomplished performance and sincere cultural product, "Southern Gul" points to the kinds of southern blackness rooted in the blues tradition. The South that Badu conjures is one of games of dominoes, two-piece chicken meals with a jalapeño pepper or two on the side, fingerwaves, booty songs, and gold teeth. While she declares that she doesn't know much about the world, this may in fact be a ruse designed to forward a simple, country exterior and to conceal more complex identities.

Although Badu is speaking as, through, and for a southern gul, she is also speaking more broadly for country boys and southern guls. Further, she is speaking for a particular kind of black southern life that arose and functioned in the shadows of the black middle-class prosperity of the New South of the 1970s and 1980s. Inheritors of the blues tradition, Badu's southern guls and country boys are Zora Neale Hurston's "folk," modernized with gold teeth, trues, and vogues. The Dirty South that Badu references is certainly a South with the post-soul blues: home to memories of the burning churches of Jim Crow, drug trafficking (pocket stones) and concomitant violence, and relative poverty, as the narrator has to go to work to help her household.

Like the gangsta, whose tendencies toward violence and criminal activity are born of the intersection of rural and urban values, southern guls cannot always claim the best of both worlds. While performance of the belle is predicated upon middle-class performance if not membership in the middle class, the southern gul signifies on the dirtiness of the South. Southern women rappers, for instance, continuing in the tradition of blues women, frequently emphasize using what one has to get what she wants, countering the pimp/playa narrative that characterizes much of southern rap. If men are pimps, rappers like Florida's Trina argue, then as the commodities for sale, women must shift the power dynamic to control the market and simultaneously ensure their own sexual pleasure. Yet, women's inability to always control the gendered circumstances they encounter might transform spaces of empowerment to spaces of oppression.

Like southern guls, country boys can marshal the best or worst of both urban and rural life. As a distinctly southern gender form, the country boy combines elements of the gentleman and the gangsta under an umbrella of rurality. When appropriated by southern rappers as an articulation of identity and regional distinction, the country boy is most like the gangsta. He drives brilliantly painted Cadillacs and Cutlasses with specific rims and wheels, dons gold or platinum teeth, and will most certainly have the last word—or action—in any dispute. As a proud articulation of an underdog identity and a claim on southerners' right to contribute to hip-hop music and culture, the country boy is a southern gangsta. Unlike gangstas from the East and West Coasts, country boys supposedly operate according to a higher moral code, responding to violence only when it comes to their front door and engaging in only as much wrongdoing as necessary to protect themselves, women, and children.

While southern rap's version of the now iconic country boy certainly represents one facet of the intersection of urban and rural sensibilities in black southern masculinity, among male respondents, the country boy took on somewhat different characteristics. First, respondents were just as likely to draw distinctions between themselves and other kinds of southern men as they were to draw distinctions between themselves and black men from outside of the South. Thus, while southern rappers are invested in drawing space and regional and place boundaries around their masculine identities, respondents were more likely to be reconciling their identities vis-à-vis the nearest competition—different kinds of southern men.

Men were less likely to self-identify as country boys than to be identified as country boys by women. For women respondents, a country boy is desirable as much for his perceived simplicity as for his exhibition of standard levels of chivalry. Kiara, the Mississippi native who loves Jackson enough to wear an airbrushed T-shirt declaring as much, told me how to spot a country boy.

> KIARA: All the boys open the doors, these days. I mean for the most part, especially when they're first dating you, they know the routine. But a country boy goes beyond that. A country boy will check and if necessary change your oil on the first date, cut your grass, fix a squeaky door, and will be just smiling the whole time. He don't talk that much and he don't really argue because he really just want to make you happy.
>
> ZANDRIA: Umm, like a robot?
>
> KIARA: No, not a robot! A country boy is just contented with being with you, so nothing else really matters.
>
> ZANDRIA: So, like a dog?

Several respondents rendered similar descriptions of the country boy, and in each instance I countered those descriptions with what men respondents told me a country boy was like. Indeed, Raymond told me that some women really just want a handyman. "They just want someone to fix stuff when it's broke. You know, and fix *other* stuff, too. See, a country nigga won't talk back. That's why [women] like them. He'll just be like, 'Yessum' and 'No ma'am,' see? Just like slavery with a black mistress." In both men's and women's estimations of the country boy, respondents imagined a man who was endlessly handy and entirely compliant with women's requests because, implicitly, he is not a real man. Raymond more explicitly linked the country boy with the image of the hapless enslaved field hand, implying further that the country boy's sexual availability to fix other things is not entirely consensual. Other respondents imagined the country boy in this way as well, as essentially an emasculated object for consumption. Interestingly, for Raymond and other respondents, educated or upwardly mobile black women become the mistresses controlling gullible black men, whose naïveté engenders unreasonable expectations among women.

I had Kiara introduce me to an acquaintance of hers who in her estimation is a country boy. She had talked about him at length, and though I knew intuitively what she and others meant by "country boy," I was curious to meet Walter, whom Kiara hailed as an exemplar of the type. When we met him at an arts event, he was putting up a tent for an organization and hammering stakes into wet ground at a North Memphis park. As we walked up, carefully picking our way through the wet grass in our sandals, she whispered loudly to me, nudging me sharply, "I told you he was a worker! Look at him! And look how he's smiling." As we approached the tent but not before we reached a comfortable conversation range, Kiara began to shout, "Hey, Walter! I want you to meet somebody. She wants to interview you. I told her you were a country boy, but she doesn't know what that is."

Walter responded with pleasantries but raised an eyebrow at Kiara. "You told her I was a what?"

"A country boy."

"Oh, is that what I am?"

"Yes, boy, you know you country. Stop playing and give her your contact information."

After we exchanged information, Kiara analyzed our exchange, from the size of Walter's smile to his politeness to his skepticism at the label of country boy, which she called his "country shyness." In our interview a couple of weeks later, Walter flashed his wide smile and was reserved as he carefully considered my questions and prompts. Raised in a historically black neighborhood between Midtown and East Memphis, his father pastored a small church and his mother stayed home with Walter, his older sister, and his two younger brothers. He tried to make sense of Kiara's and other women's construction of him. "I mean, I'm not actually from the country. Neither are my parents. My grandparents on both sides were from the country [Alabama and Mississippi], so I'm second-generation city. And before [I got this job with the arts organization], I was not a very nice person. I was what you'd call a troublemaker and I ran with the wrong crowd, trying to be a gangsta. I think, you know, because I sort of talk slow and I have more of a heavy accent than some other folks, young ladies think I'm a country boy. I'm really not, though. I'm pretty sophisticated."

I asked Walter to elaborate on his statement, and to discuss in particular why talking slow and having a heavier accent translated into country boy for the young ladies. "Well, so, you know the stereotype is that a country boy has his overalls on and his straw hat, and the accent and talking slow just go with that. But you won't catch me in overalls and a straw hat. I know about the fashion trends and I like to dress well. I'm not obsessed with it like some guys; I'm understated, as they say. But I just know how to dress."

Walter highlighted some of the pejorative iconography of country, such as straw hats and overalls, that signify provincialism and backwardness. Northern blacks once used country, and all of its concomitant signifiers, to distinguish themselves from southern blacks, especially those migrating north with their country ways that underscored their green-ness. Urban southerners also frequently used country to draw distinctions between themselves and their counterparts in the small-town South. This usage of country by southerners has increased as the familial and intergenerational links between the rural South and the urban South have decreased. Still, despite the negative ideas attached to country-ness in general and to the country boy specifically, most respondents contended that retaining some marker of rurality was useful for drawing identity and performative distinctions.

Traditional southern gender forms are not always attainable or desirable for southern guls and country boys. Thus, in popular culture and everyday life, southern guls and country boys create a racialized regional identity that rewrites, and in some cases completely supplants, the belle and gentleman. Yet, these formulations go beyond challenging traditionally white gender norms. Moreover, southern guls and country boys open the space for cross-class participation, highlighting the exclusionary practices of the black middle classes—like the snickers at Tara's cotillion demonstrate—and offering gendered presentations of self that are not so directly tied to middle-class membership. Ultimately, the country boy and southern gul read traditional southern gender norms through a post-soul lens, facilitating alternative interpretations of gender identity and performance as well as non-heteronormative outcomes. At their most democratic, then, formulations of country cosmopolitanism allow for the maximum number of people to participate in shared racial and regional cultures.

I turn now to an examination of how black southern gender forms are articulated, reinforced, and challenged in popular culture through a consideration of gender, and women in particular, in *ATL* and *Hustle & Flow*. While respondents negotiate and conceptualize their everyday identity performances on the ground to maximize the benefit of interactive outcomes, popular culture producers have a vested interest in representing these identity performances and framing the context in which they occur. While these films do not always offer promising alternatives to the strictures of existing gender norms and archetypes, they push at the regional and racial boundaries of gender performance.

A Gul in *ATL*

As the unofficial home of post–civil rights black America, Atlanta is a prime place in which to examine the extremes of wealth and poverty among African Americans. While Atlanta has a significant black underclass, it is also home to some of the wealthiest blacks in America, who occupy exclusively black upper-middle-class neighborhoods or are significantly present in traditionally white neighborhoods. *ATL* uses intraracial class conflict and class passing as both the backdrop and foreground of a narrative about black youth in a southern urban context.

Protagonist Rashad's (played by Tip "T. I." Harris) love interest in the film, New-New, also known as Erin (played by Lauren London), is the daughter of a successful, self-made CEO, John Garnett. Garnett, raised in Mechanicsville on the "bad" side of town, has distanced himself from the impoverished community from which he hails and outwardly expresses disdain for the neighborhood and its inhabitants. Erin lives in Buckhead, attends a private school, drives an expensive car her father bought her, and, by her parents' account, is headed for an Ivy League institution after high school. She is the embodiment of the promise of New South progress for African Americans, and in particular of the black wealth narrative forwarded by Atlanta.

Erin's performative alter ego represents the other Atlanta, one spatially and socially separate from her life in Buckhead. Telling her parents that she is visiting her white girlfriend Holly, Erin ventures each weekend to the South Side, where she transforms from the daughter of an entrepreneurial elite to New-New, a southern gul from the 'hood. The diegesis follows

New-New's budding romance with Rashad through his discovery of her cross-class performance and beyond.

ATL offers New-New, with her perfectly laid hair, dangling hoop earrings with "New-New" scrawled in cursive across them, and southern twang, as representative of the youthful black southern everywoman, an African American answer to the belle. New-New frequents the skating rink and the neighborhood swimming pool and attends house parties with working- and lower-middle-class African Americans. Donning the latest fashions— "the new, new shit"—she passes her acquisitions off as the product of felonious actions rather than her father's wealth. She is quick-witted with her male and female counterparts, encourages Rashad to pursue his art, and exudes the unapologetic self-confidence of the southern gul.

In fact, the audience does not learn about New-New's home life, or her given name, until halfway into the film, when one of Rashad's friends, seeking a recommendation from Erin's father, visits the Garnett household. Whereas New-New's hair reflects the latest in urban styling, from side ponytails to swoops, Erin's Buckhead hair is conservatively flat-ironed and straight, conspicuously lacking the extra shine of her southern gul hairstyles. As Erin, she is dressed simply in jeans—of the non-booty-hugging variety— and a T-shirt. As New-New, her dialect is black southern gul twang with concomitant gum popping, neck rolling, and, when necessary, loud talking; as Erin, the southern twang completely disappears—as someone commented in the Memphis audience where I saw the film once, "Aw, mane, she talkin' like a white gul now!" Her clothing is different, her friends are different, and the entertainment in which she engages—skating rinks and trips to the neighborhood pool versus tennis and elite dinners—is different. As Erin, in fact, all markers of regional difference are removed, and she emerges as an ordinary upper-middle-class American teenager.

Erin's life as New-New is regionally spiced—her gender performance, clothes, hair, and activities are more exciting, she says, than tennis and studying with Holly—and she draws on New-New to access parts of African American class, racial, regional, and gender cultures from which she is cut off. The film argues for two forms of authentic black southern reality and uses tropes of regionalized and racialized gender performance to move between these two realities. First is the reality of elite blackness, embodied by the Garnetts. Rather than condemning John Garnett's wealth, the film condemns his inability to engage his impoverished upbringing, share his full history with his daughter, and help people from his community, like Rashad's friend Esquire, to succeed. The second is the reality of working-class and lower-middle-class blackness, which the film implicitly presents as the more enriched, or exciting, blackness. Rather than attend an Ivy League institution, Erin attends Spelman, elite in its own right but still in Atlanta, still black, and close to the skating rink Cascade. Through Erin's character, then, the film offers a lens into black southern youth working-class cultures vis-à-vis elite southern blackness. It resolves intraracial class conflicts through her as well, as Erin's gender performance at the end of the film straddles the boundaries between elite and working-class southern blackness.

Ladies and Sex Workers

While *ATL* highlights class and culture differences through Erin's gender performance and class passing, *Hustle & Flow* erects a seeming moral dichotomy between characters along the lines of gender performance and occupational status. It takes the figure of the black lady and contrasts it with the notion of the hypersexual black woman, embodied by pregnant sex worker Suge (played by Taraji P. Henson), dancer and sex worker Alexis (played by Paula Jai Parker), and sex worker Nola (played by Taryn Manning), who is racialized as black because of her class and occupational status. However, while lady and sex worker might seem to be completely opposite in formulation and in practice or performance, through the lens of regional culture, director Craig Brewer offers a different interpretation of the social distance between these roles.

Clyde (played by Anthony Anderson) and Yvette (played by Elise Neal) represent the respectable, middle-class voices in the film, operating as constant signifiers of black religiosity, with Yvette's references to church and prayer before supper and Clyde's work recording and playing piano for church choirs.[12] Each night, Yvette cooks and the couple sits down to dinner together at a table, praying before each meal. Yvette is always conservatively dressed in business casual clothing, speaks with a proper southern accent, has a proper southern job in middle management at a retailer, and is endlessly polite. Despite the contrasts between her respectable ladyness and the sex workers' unacceptable womanhood, the women's mutual understandings of southern gender norms decrease the awkwardness of their exchanges.

As a good southerner, Yvette is polite and hospitable to all people, even to Nola and Alexis, who accompany their pimp, D-Jay, on an evening visit to Yvette and Clyde's home. Perhaps the most laugh-out-loud moment of the film occurs when Alexis and Nola are sitting on Yvette and Clyde's sofa, and like a good hostess, Yvette sits across from them in a chair, prim and conservative, and engages them in conversation. In addition to sharing some small talk, Yvette even defends Nola's hairstyle—blond-weave cornrow extensions to match her dyed-blond hair—against Alexis's attacks, although this is a representation of the southern propensity to lie before offending. Alexis attempts to relieve Yvette of her hospitality duties—"you don't have to be nice to her just because she's sitting on your couch," she tells Yvette about Nola. Yvette's combination of conservative politics of respectability and southern hospitality renders her more comically uncomfortable and naive, rather than disgusted with the women and their profession. Yet, when the nature of the women's conversation has thoroughly rattled Yvette, she seeks out her husband, whom she finds in the kitchen with D-Jay and a Casio keyboard fervently rapping, "Shake it shake it real fast / put your hands on your knees / shake it shake it real fast."

As the movie proceeds and Clyde begins to spend more time at D-Jay's to complete the rap album that is the driving force of the film, the conflict between Clyde and Yvette escalates. Yvette expresses her discomfort and anger with Clyde's disruption of custom and fraternizing with sex workers and a pimp. After yet another night preparing dinner without Clyde showing up to eat it and praying alone at the table, Yvette does what any southern, middle-class, respectable woman would do: she makes a plate of tiny sandwiches, crusts removed, places a container of dill sauce in the center, and takes it over to D-Jay's house, where she is invited to listen to the recording session.

Thus, *Hustle & Flow* uses contrasting gender performances and identities and southern culture staples, including food and religiosity, to resolve class and morality differences. The film deliberately utilizes an African American woman for the figure of respectable lady, highlighting the intraracial class and epistemological differences at work in black southern communities. Its use of black and white sex workers underscores the class dynamics of southern cities, making the white working poor visible through Nola. Further, despite Suge's status as a sex worker, one impregnated by a john, no less, she exhibits the stand-by-your-man thoughtfulness of a steel magnolia and the wide-eyed beauty of a southern belle, albeit without the spoils. Through an appropriation of southern gender archetypes in an unlikely context—rap, pimps, and prostitutes—*Hustle & Flow* attempts to represent a black southern experience in an urban context.

Gender Performance and the Always Already

Despite the hegemony of race and the strict boundaries between black and white in the South, blacks southerners refashion categories from which they are excluded in service of racial progress and existential free-dom. Respondents were not naive about their appropriation of these cat-egories, nor were they unaware of how they are placed in both racial and regional identity boxes. Moreover, they frequently think about how their self-identification, as well as how others perceive them, affects their per-formances and interactions with others. Armed with their re-creations of traditional southern gender roles, respondents create, shift, and remake the parameters for cross-gender interaction. They challenge the arche-types of southern gender proliferated by popular culture as well as the strictures in which they feel they have to operate in cross-gender interac-tions. In and through these interactions, they also revisit and reform their own identity conceptualizations and performances.

Despite black women's relative inability to occupy the belle archetype, whether because of their race, color, class, or presentation of self, across self-reported measures of class, many respondents referred to themselves as belles or ladies. Moreover, they see themselves as adhering to many of the behavioral norms of those archetypes, even if the adherence is largely perfor-mative. For some respondents, like Tyana and salon-owner Kim, the care and deliberate planning that go into hair, nails, and clothing are standard prac-tice, and southern accents, wide smiles, and batting eyes are unrehearsed and unconscious. For others, like Valencia, southern presentations of self are well-theorized performances, crafted to shape interaction outcomes.

Central to these gender formulations, whether performed or sincere, is a balance between the traditional and the progressive, the country and the cosmopolitan. Women who identified as belles work to sprinkle the right amount of country on what are their otherwise citified identities to achieve a construction of an authentic southern woman—relatively defer-ent, hardworking, pretty but not pretentious, and simple but sophisticated. While men were less likely to think of themselves as engaging in a gender performance, performance of gentlemanly behaviors and gratuitous ref-erence to Mama signaled men's awareness of the kinds of performative tropes necessary for success with women, even with those they were not explicitly trying to court. These formulations, like the cotillion, always al-ready signaled elite class status, despite the amount of folk country-ness marshaled to down play the function of class in these performances. Even when respondents' income, wealth, or educational status do not coincide with the belle or the gentleman, they compensate for this lack with perfor-mance and presentation of self.

Still other respondents see themselves as outside of the traditional southern gender norms of the belle and the gentleman, or at least as outside of the standard behavioral expectations of these norms. These country cosmopolitan alternative formulations are most often articulated in popular culture, like southern rappers' regionalized version of the gangsta. However, respondents pointed to different formulations of black gender identities in the South, highlighting the ways in which these identities challenge traditional white southern norms as well as black reconfigurations of those norms. I suggest that these country boys and southern guls are a post-soul iteration of blues women and men—the post-soul folk, increasingly segregated, spatially and perhaps ideologically, from the normative black middle classes. Although middle-class blacks might see the country boy and southern gul as sources of gender failure or shame, they nonetheless appropriate some of the elements of those identities to forge more authentically southern and authentically black identities.

It is in and through gender work that the Old South meets the New South in black southern experience. Further, it is in and through gender work that region and race are most intricately intertwined. Indeed, a host of social problems, from HIV to infant mortality to teen pregnancy, are linked to public health and social institutions' inability to conceptualize the intersections of gender, race, and region. Respondents work diligently to both explode and inhabit southern gender archetypes, and in the process reinforce the existence of those categories. Through their appropriations of and challenges to normative regional gender roles, respondents highlight the intersections of race and class to which their identities, theorizations, and performances always already point.

CHAPTER FIVE
Southern Is the New Black

On the eve of the film premiere of *Madea's Big Happy Family* in April 2011, director and producer Tyler Perry temporarily misplaced his southern manners. Apparently exasperated by fellow director Spike Lee's ongoing and vocal critiques of his work, Perry reportedly responded to a query that referenced those critiques with indignation. "I'm so sick of hearing about damn Spike Lee. Spike can go straight to hell! You can print that. I am sick of him talking about me. I am sick of him saying, 'This is a coon; this is a buffoon.' I am sick of him talking about black people going to see movies. This is what he said: 'you vote by what you see,' as if black people don't know what they want to see."[1]

For Perry's critics, his characters are twenty-first-century coons, hardly updated versions of Amos 'n' Andy or Stepin Fetchit and grotesque reminders of an oppressive southern past. Likening their debate to the iconic philosophical debates between Booker T. Washington and W. E. B. Du Bois, Richard Wright and Zora Neale Hurston, and Langston Hughes and George Schuyler,[2] Perry counters the idea that his work caricatures or misrepresents black people. In other contexts, he has argued that neither his characters nor his audiences are coons or cultural dupes. He contends instead that the characters he imagines are drawn from a particular African American experience. While Perry acknowledges that his representations may not reflect the experiences of all African Americans, he nonetheless vehemently defends his right to present and articulate the southern black experience, a black American experience different from that presented by Spike Lee and his fellow black Brooklyn bohemians.

The differences highlighted by the Perry-Lee debate are not simply a matter of artistic disagreement or even genuine differences over the more thorny politics of racial representation. At its core, the debate is about the place of the South in the landscape of black identities and black respectability. It gathers together related sets of intraracial politics, from the politics of respectability to class distinction, under an umbrella of regional difference. Distinctions between southerners and northerners—between Perry and Lee, Washington and Du Bois, and unrefined country folks and their more cosmopolitan counterparts—operate alongside and sometimes overlap with class-based politics of intraracial difference. Black southerners loathe their northern counterparts' negative characterizations of their lives. New Orleans native Lil' Wayne captures this collective frustration: "This is southern face it / If we too simple, then y'all don't get the basics."[3]

Public discomfort with images and representations seen as detrimental to the race is rooted firmly in class-based respectability politics that date back to the late nineteenth century. Respectability politics were undergirded by the notion that if black people only demonstrated their morality, thrift, and humanity to whites, then whites not only would stop systematic campaigns of violence against them but also would recognize their shared humanity and eventually accept them as equals. Because blacks across class statuses tend to see their fates as linked with that of other African Americans, raising the moral standards of behavior and quality of life for blacks at the lower end of the socioeconomic ladder became central to a broader racial uplift strategy. These politics have taken on a number of forms but most often consist of wealthier African Americans directly policing or critiquing poorer blacks' behaviors, choices, and presentations of self. When policing fails, either in its attempts to improve the behavior of poorer blacks or in its ability to manage white people's impressions of black people, more elite blacks draw boundaries between themselves and other blacks, as comedian Chris Rock's famous routine about the differences between "niggas" and "black people" evidences.[4]

In a 2007 Pew Research Center survey that found that many African Americans did not think they could or should be thought of as "a single race," responses showed a convergence in the values of the American middle classes across race and a perception of increased within-race class differences among blacks.[5] These differences are reflected in Rock's observations as well as in eruptions of interclass vitriol—like when Bill Cosby tells an elite group of blacks that poorer black people spend $500 on sneakers but won't spend $200 on educational resources to help their children learn the King's English.[6] Further, they are structured by racialized and class-based systems of privilege and oppression that yield differential outcomes in neighborhood residence, occupational and educational attainment, and income and wealth.

While class differences among blacks have been present since slavery, racialization meant that even free blacks were subject to unequal treatment, despite their class or servitude status. After slavery, a tiny but growing and vocal black elite built wealth, political power, and communities, drawing boundaries between themselves and their poorer brethren but nonetheless recognizing the structural power of racialization as a fundamental constraint on their lives. As the gains of the civil rights movement yielded socioeconomic advances for these elite and facilitated the entry of more African Americans into the middle class, these groups used their social capital to advance themselves individually and to distance themselves physically from the racialized disadvantages of blackness.

Institutionalized racial disadvantage is almost inescapable for the black middle classes, who are often spatially tethered to poorer black communities even if they do not live in such communities. Although black middle classes express racial solidarity in terms of linked fate, the collective identities that govern school and neighborhood choice are often based on both race and class similarities. Further, differences *within* the black middle class underscore the salience of nuance in understanding the intersections of race, class, and capital in black middle-class identities.[7] Thus, class, as a *process* that ascribes sets of behaviors to particular groups based on their access to socioeconomic resources, intersects with racialization to disadvantage poorer black people and to facilitate boundary work by the black elite. As a quantifiable set of economic and educational achievements, class provides a clearer boundary line between haves and have-nots, posh private schools and public schools abandoned by city and state governments, and safe neighborhoods and violent communities.

Class, race, and gender intersect on structural and discursive levels, as a social process and in and through people's performances and everyday interactions. Discursively, and in performances and interactions, regional tropes encapsulate these intersections, simultaneously signifying race and class, and sometimes gender and sexuality, identities. Further, regional tropes function as convenient shorthand for intraracial differences, and intraracial class differences in particular. To talk about the South, then, is to talk about specific race and class identities, mythologized and constructed in social memories, interpersonal interactions, and popular culture. Versions of black identity associated with the South, whether forwarded by Tyler Perry or Erykah Badu, form a robust but contested basis for black identity in American culture.

Southern versions of black identity have most often served as a source of shame for the race, hearkening back to a past of servitude, racialized violence and degradation, and forced minstrelsy. Further, southern blackness is implicitly linked to an essential, authentic blackness, which counters recent political and philosophical pressure to abandon rigid performative and identity requirements and notions of authentic black selves.[8] Yet, although southern identities have been challenged, the South as a social memory, fixed in rural space and civil rights time, has proven a useful trope for accomplishing broader black political goals. As a physical and spatial reminder of the continuing significance of race, as well as of the usefulness of the black American experience for demonstrating its significance, the South functions as an enduring symbol of domestic and international black struggle.

This chapter considers how black critiques of southern identity are part of a broader respectability politics that not only polices the behavior of the lower classes but patrols the boundaries of blackness as well. These critiques are resurgent in popular culture and rehearsed in film, television, blogs, and music. In these critiques, "country" is negative, representing stagnation or backpedaling, ignorance, and impotence. Regional outsiders blanket the entire region, perhaps with the exception of Atlanta, with the country label, such that "southern" has become synonymous with "country." Like Tyler Perry, respondents in this study reject these critiques, unearthing the positive aspects of country-ness even as they trade insults among themselves to draw and reinforce class boundaries.

The various meanings that the respondents, cultural elites, and popular culture producers attach to country and cosmopolitan help delineate the boundaries of an authentic, native black identity in the context of increasing national, political, cultural, and epistemological diversity among the group of Americans racialized as black. Discussions of the South, region, and regional identity obscure this intraracial diversity in service of a unified collective black identity and experience. Respondents navigate negative ideas about the country, backward South; the appropriations of ideas about the South by corporations; and their everyday experiences to think through the relationship between class, race, region, and identity. By marshaling a country cosmopolitanism that holds fast to certain country ideals but is just as cosmopolitan and progressive as any Brooklyn bohemian, respondents push back against critiques of the South by non-southern blacks and appropriations of the South by corporations. Through the process of articulating a country cosmopolitan worldview, respondents highlight, and sometimes performatively exaggerate, a better blackness, rooted in the region.

Rapper Racists and Region Haters

Nowhere are debates over the place of the South in black identity more prevalent than in hip-hop culture.[9] As early as 1995, southerners endeavored to carve a space for the region in black cultural production. When rap duo OutKast took the stage to receive the award for Best New Rap Group at that year's Source Awards, amid boos from attendees, André 3000 blurted famously: "The South got something to say."[10] As southern artists became more prevalent on the national scene beginning in the early years of the new century, the debate reached fever pitch, exposing both spatial, generational, and identity fissures in hip-hop and black American culture writ large.

In addition to the usual critiques of southern hip-hop as lyrically bereft, emphasizing the physical—namely, booty, beat, and bass—over the cerebral, critiques of southern hip-hop by aging East Coast artists have gone further.[11] In a 2006 MTV interview, rapper 50 Cent reportedly criticized southern hip-hop as poor in quality, lacking in creativity, and moreover detrimental to hip-hop music: "A lot of the music that comes out of the South is kind of simplified and I think it's kinda 'cause they just wanna have a good time. But when they don't take the time to make it the highest quality possible, it hurts the actual hip-hop [genre]."[12] Asserting both spatial and intellectual privileges to hip-hop, 50 Cent simultaneously delegitimizes southerners' claims to speak in and through the predominant black cultural form. Moreover, he displaces responsibility for the quality of southern music solely on the artists, only implicitly hinting at the broader class, power, and corporate structures organizing and influencing rappers' actions and available choices.

Similarly, RZA, actor and member of the New York–based Wu-Tang Clan, reportedly claimed in a 2007 interview that "hip-hop culture [was not] really in [southerners'] blood." RZA postulated why southern hip-hop had been so successful despite the absence of a biological link to the genre and culture: "Those brothers came out representing more of a stereotype of how black people are, and I think the media would rather see us as ignorant, crazy motherfuckers than seeing us as intelligent young men trying to rise and take care of ourselves."[13] Here, RZA rehearses a standard objection to southern hip-hop: the idea that southerners are unwitting Uncle Toms who perpetuate negative stereotypes of black folks for money. Although southern music and history arguably provide the foundation for most black American music forms, from blues to hip-hop, RZA argues that southerners do not have the ontological or experiential bases to participate in hip-hop culture.

Still, RZA had conveniently forgotten, through a discursive displacement of a different sort, the function of the South in his own work. The famously haunting chromatic sample for Wu-Tang Clan's 1994 hit "C.R.E.A.M." comes from Stax Records' 1967 song "As Long as I've Got You," by the Charmels.

Further, RZA's comments indict southern artists for perpetuating stereotypes, although he reflectively acknowledged that the Wu-Tang Clan's corpus contributed to stereotypical notions of African American men as angry and violent. The implication, however, is that perpetuating stereotypes of blacks as coons is quantitatively and qualitatively worse than the politicized anger and violence that East and West Coast rap had come to signify.

In 2008, Cop-Killer-turned-television-cop Ice-T also entered the discourse, taking to a mixtape to accuse Batesville, Mississippi, native (by way of Atlanta and Chicago) Soulja Boy Tell 'Em of "single-handedly [killing] hip-hop." In addition to scolding Soulja Boy for "looking happy," he demanded that another rapper, Hurricane Chris of Shreveport, Louisiana, remove the beads that adorned his cornrows.[14] Ice-T's rant, as well as responses to it, became so popular on YouTube and other social media outlets that Aaron McGruder parodied the issue in a season 3 episode of *The Boondocks*,[15] with fictional rapper Thugnificent prompting a beef with the satirized Soulja Boy stand-in, Sergeant Gudda. Beyond the relationship between hip-hop beef culture and album hype, as well as the obvious generational dimensions of Ice-T's critique, the rapper underscores broader resentment of the perceived coonery of southern rap. Ice-T reinforces southern rappers' perceived illegitimacy as hip-hop culture producers by tying them to markers of emasculated minstrelsy. Citing happiness and hair beads, Ice-T draws the regional boundaries of authentic hip-hop by operationalizing common intraracial tropes of black southern inferiority.

Other assessments bypassed tropes altogether, instead drawing direct connections between southern hip-hop and blackface minstrelsy. In 2010, *America's Got Talent* host Nick Cannon and comedian Affion Crockett teamed up as "Shuck" and "Jive." Donning blackface, dreadlocks, multiple gold chains, and gold teeth—clear references to southern hip-hop artists, and Atlanta-based rapper and producer Lil' Jon in particular—Shuck and Jive performed "Eat Dat Watermelon."[16] The video of the song begins and ends with a public service announcement from rapper Nas, who warns that the "ever-mounting forces of ridiculous dances, ignorant behavior, and general buffoonery" will result in the death of hip-hop and its usefulness as a tool of political empowerment. Nas posits corporations as responsible for these "ever-mounting forces," rewriting hip-hop's historical relationship with corporate forces. Not only does Nas negate southern artists' agency by locating the hip-hop corporate plantation in the South, but he also excises corporatization from East and West Coast hip-hop historiography—this despite the fact that southern artists' marginalization necessitated the perfection of independent, artist-owned labels in the region.

Minstrelsy functions as a particularly powerful trope in the routine. The nonsensical "Eat Dat Watermelon" features a synthesized banjo accompanied by a replicated snap-crunk beat, another blatant reference to Atlanta crunk rap. Donning blackface and red lips, Shuck and Jive do a hambone dance, smile, buck their eyes, and respectively hide from "massa" inside two watermelon halves. In "Eat Dat Watermelon," southern artists are constructed as cultural dupes unwittingly controlled by an ominous white power structure, represented in the video as a looming shadow. While there is reference to the corporatization of hip-hop, southerners are still explicitly held responsible for perpetrating negative images of black folks. Taken together, the video and Nas's narrative cast southern hip-hop as the new slavery, a threat to real hip-hop, and detrimental to black culture, identity, and power.

Beyond the professional jealousy that belies these sentiments, these artists, not unlike Tyler Perry's critics, are attempting to address a discursive power shift in contemporary black identity. By engaging in a strategic transference that sanitizes their own problematic relationships to corporatization, representation, and respectability, non-southern artists erect a pure hip-hop at the expense of southern artists. Tropes of minstrelsy and emasculation bolster this strategic transference, attacking the race and gender authenticity of southern artists. These assessments also situate the South as rural, backward, and still enslaved, thereby effectively placing southerners outside of the black urban crises that inspired East and West Coast rap and outside of progress of history.

Further, by conflating southern hip-hop with negative country tropes of southern racial complacency, namely shucking, jiving, watermelon eating, and hiding from "massa," such critiques obscure the legitimacy of southern artists' claims to hip-hop culture and black identity. In many ways, non-southern hip-hop artists' reaction to the rise of the South reflects the conservative backlash to the modernization of the South. That is, just as southern hip-hop emerged as a formidable and viable force in the hip-hop industry, mainstream hip-hop gained a conscience about the effect of hip-hop on representations of black folks, conveniently forgetting its participation in the shaping and framing of those representations.

Finally, in a context in which the intraracial fissures in black identity are both more often publicized and public, these critiques serve as a proxy for intraracial class differences. However, region hating is a more accessible discourse that can be easily deployed across class without implicitly denying the existence of institutional racism and linked fate. That is, while wholesale critiques of the black poor, like those forwarded by Bill Cosby, require at least some dismissal of the power of institutional racism in affecting African American life chances, black folks, from Tyler Perry to Lil' Jon, ostensibly have the power to control how they are represented as well as the conclusions white people draw from their representations. When they choose to "shuck and jive" instead of to forward positive representations of the race, they have deliberately violated the rules of respectability and therefore deserve public criticism. In defending the South's right to speak, black southerners not only claim a right to represent a segment of African American experience but in some cases also situate the southern black experience as *the* black American identity.

Returning to a Better Blackness

Malcolm D. Lee's 2008 film *Welcome Home Roscoe Jenkins* imagines black cross-class and interregional contact in perhaps the most widely plausible way—through relationships between a man who left the South and his country cousins. Several films, like *Sweet Home Alabama*, for instance, capitalize on this narrative strategy, usually to bring a reluctant protagonist closer to a better version of himself or herself. *Welcome Home Roscoe Jenkins* ostensibly performs this same labor for the title protagonist but layers region, race, intraracial class distinctions, and culture over the standard narrative to construct an archetypal better blackness—one rooted in small-town southern culture, food, family, and sound, reasoned interpersonal relations.

Roscoe Jenkins (played by Martin Lawrence), carrying unresolved demons from his childhood, has moved to Los Angeles, changed his named to R. J. Stevens, and launched a successful career as a television talk-show host. He has a nine-year-old son, Jamaal, whom he is raising as a single father and has not been back to visit his rural Georgia home since shortly after Jamaal's birth. When he returns to Georgia with fiancée Bianca and Jamaal, the cross-class mayhem, packaged in the film as regional distinctions between South and non-South, as well as spatial distinctions between city and country, ensues.

Almost immediately, distinctions are drawn between Roscoe and the small-town southern life he left behind. He no longer eats meat, per the Hollywood diet that Bianca has instituted for him, but quickly succumbs to his brother and cousin's encouragement to eat the ribs being grilled as part of the family barbecue. Jamaal does not know how to play baseball, cast in the film as an enduring southern and family pastime, but instead plays soccer, which the film characterizes as a bizarre sport implicitly racialized as white. Further, Roscoe's attempts to earn recognition from his father, such as by purchasing him an expensive flat-screen television, are seen as misguided material attempts disjointed from the Jenkins family values. When Roscoe returns home, he finds the television still in its box. During his nine-year absence, Roscoe, the film argues, has become disconnected from a legitimate black identity and key southern values.

Relatively minor distinctions—including barbecued pork versus veganism; large, old country mixed-breeds versus purebred toy dogs; baseball versus soccer—function as comic relief juxtapositions of regional and class differences among African Americans. The most heated scene, however, includes an epistemological confrontation between Roscoe and his brother, Otis (played by the late Michael Clarke Duncan). The conversation begins simply enough, with Roscoe commenting that if Otis had not sustained a career-ending knee injury, he would have been drafted into the National Football League and be living in a mansion and driving a Mercedes. Otis responds to his brother's comment with familiar southern and black religious rhetoric: "It wasn't in God's plan for me."

From there, the conversation escalates into confrontation. When Roscoe implies that Otis is a failure, Otis explicitly calls Roscoe a failure, citing Jamaal's inability to play baseball and both of their absences from the family as proof. Roscoe contends that, to the contrary, he "made it." The conflict intensifies, and there is an increasingly clear distinction between a down-home upbringing and a city upbringing. Otis urges gently, "Don't let money raise your kids," to which Roscoe retorts, "Don't let cornbread, chitlins, hamhocks, and cheese sticks raise yours!" The conflict ends with an emboldened Roscoe being knocked unconscious by his big, country older brother.

Roscoe spends the rest of the film being schooled, down-home, southern-style. He is beaten up by his sister for being pretentious, blackmailed by his cousin in exchange for his silence about a sexual liaison between the old family dog and Bianca's toy dog, and harassed by his fiancée's jealousy of Roscoe's childhood sweetheart, southern belle Lucinda. Ultimately, Roscoe reconciles his resentment of his father and his cousin and sees the value of his southern upbringing. At the close of the film, he dumps Bianca, representative of the shallowness of non-southern black urban life, and begins a romance with Lucinda. He returns to Los Angeles and his talk show with renewed perspective on "what really matters" in life.

Welcome Home Roscoe Jenkins argues that true "making it" is in the non-material social goods that can be afforded to one through family, community, humility, and happiness. Specifically, the film locates these social goods and the better blackness they beget in the close-knit communities of the small-town black South. Although class distinctions are not evident in talk or dress, the intersection of class and region are highlighted through Roscoe's attempts to distinguish himself as successful relative to his unmarried and underemployed sister, his hustler cousin, and his small-town sheriff brother. The film actively trumps Roscoe's material definition of success, which is rejected by his family, sometimes violently, at every turn. In the end, *Welcome Home Roscoe Jenkins* situates black life at its best when it is connected to the South, and the rural and small-town South in particular, which in this formulation tempers the pretention and disconnection from good family and personal values that come from material success in an urban context.

Protecting Us from Evil

Respondents in this study made authenticity and superiority claims based on at least some of the same dimensions of intraracial spatial difference represented in black South films, particularly those that center around a rural or small-town southern reality. Specifically, respondents often made distinctions between the South and the North, especially in tandem with their own critiques of the Memphis community or the South more broadly. Keith, whom I had to physically stop from doing the Parchman Farm field hollers each time we met, was reflective about the South's shortcomings, particularly when juxtaposed with what he called the "happy nigga singing South" of Tyler Perry movies. Keith was generally energetic and upbeat, so when he arrived at one of our interview sessions frowning and flustered, I was unsure how to respond. He started talking before I could click on the recorder. When he caught his breath and settled a bit, he looked me directly in the eye and said, "These Southern chu'chfolk are making me lose my Jesus." Keith rarely referred to Jesus, especially not with a possessive pronoun, and like many respondents was frequently critical of black southern churches and Christianity more generally. He had explained to me previously that "all black southerners have Jesus, even if they don't want him. Haven't you been to the Nation of Islam mosque? They in there praying from the Bible."

He relayed to me that his attempts to start a condom basket—"a discreet one, mind you, in the counseling office"—at the predominantly black high school where he works had been thwarted by "some rabid Bible thumpers."

These ain't no southern belles we talking about here, some white girls who marry rich and young and have babies young. These are young girls in my class who may or may not be able to finish [high school] now because they're knocked up, and who might—just might—use a condom if we talked about them and made them available. But oh, no, your goody southern *chu'ch*folk won't hear anything of it, talking about "pray over the kids." I mean, other cities, up north, out west, they got condoms for teenage kids. And those programs do help some to keep down teen pregnancy. But these folks would rather keep their *s'uth'n* morals than to acknowledge these children's *s'uth'n* sexuality.

He drawled "southern" especially long, rolling his eyes each time, which many respondents did some version of during critiques of regional culture or racism. I teased him about his condom campaign, arguing that he should take it up north or somewhere with some more liberal values. Retorting several times that the North is "further away from God," he finally articulated why he is committed to the South.

Okay, seriously, though. No and yes. But, fo'real, black life is different outside of the South now. Or, should I say, black life for the average black person. This is not the Chicago heyday or the Harlem heyday. You have to have money, good money, or you can't live a good life. Obama got a million-dollar house in Chicago. Oprah got who knows what. When I visit [my cousins in Detroit], even the ones that are schoolteachers and all of that, it just seems they don't have that quality of life. In the South, you can still not have a lot of money, but be connected to other folks in a way that is valuable in your life.

This notion that black life is different outside of the South now was echoed in many respondents' sentiments, as folks contended that the Great North of the Great Migration disappeared sometime around the 1970s. Further, Keith emphasized the value of personal social networks in the South, perhaps over and above the relative value of financial capital. While respondents were critical of the South's backwardness, they saw the South somewhere along the spectrum of the lesser of two evils and the best of both worlds. Yet, regardless of their personal feelings about the region, respondents defended the South from critiques even as they downplayed the severity of the area's battles with poverty, drugs, and reproductive health and justice. Keith was genuinely critical of what he saw as the detrimental aspects of black southern culture, even if he would not fully articulate a critique without also highlighting the South's superiority—in this case, its proximity to God.

Other respondents, however, actively constructed a South with few of the social ills of the urban North, even if they have participated in or succumbed to such ills in the South. Mr. Johnson, employed at the local Veterans Administration hospital as a medical assistant, has a quality of orneriness rivaled only by the lengthiness of his narratives. Having served in the Vietnam War, Mr. Johnson, who grew up in the Arkansas Delta but moved to Memphis shortly before being drafted, spent much of the 1970s drifting between relatives' homes in the urban Midwest and West. He attributed the decline of black folks in cities outside of the South to drug trafficking. He told me:

> Heroin started it, see. At one time, all the niggas was wearing zoot suits and the finest furs and all of that. Then, wasn't nobody but the dealers wearing it because everybody else was on drugs except for the goody-goodies, and they were busy trying to take care of the folks on drugs, see. Meanwhile, we [southerners] were the ones helping funnel the dope up there. All of that "go to Chicago, go to Detroit" stuff was over, see, because it was just a dopehead wasteland up there. Then niggas was getting high and rioting and whatnot. Then that's when they started all coming back here, trying to get clean. I had two cousins, twice removed, went north in the '70s talking about they gon' get a good education away from us. They mama always thought she was better. They came back here with an education, all right. An education in dope.

I was skeptical of Mr. Johnson's sweeping history, if only because we have had several discussions about the Nelson George–produced documentary series *American Gangster*, which chronicles notorious African American drug dealers. Still, he insisted that he witnessed the ravages of drugs in black communities in the urban North and Los Angeles after he returned from the war and shuffled from city to city in search of work. I asked him if he knew people who began to use drugs around the same time in the South as well, and if he was familiar with their outcomes.

After some wrangling, between drags on a cigarette, which he eventually put out on the cement table we were sharing in a South Memphis park, he still insisted that the South was different. "The effect of dope in the South wasn't like the effects was up there, never has been, never will be. The South in a certain kind of way . . . it kinda, it protects you from evil. I mean, I'm not saying evil things don't happen down here. What the kids say? [This is the] Dirty South. I'm just saying that everything always works out, see."

For Mr. Johnson, the disparate effects of drug use on African Americans in the South relative to non-southern places was evidence of the South's "protection from evil," which he said comes from "people praying about so many things [that] some of the prayers gets on you even if you don't deserve 'em." Mr. Johnson suggested that somehow the South offers a metaphysical protection from the structural impact of inequality, embodied in his narrative by the effects of drug use and trafficking in black communities. While by some empirical measures, African American outcomes, especially for lower-income African Americans, are exacerbated by southern regional residence, many respondents insisted on the South's singular ability to protect, heal, and renew as an ancestral and maternal space.

Several respondents expressed familiarity with this mystical South that can heal—like Loretta's daughter is "healed" from autism in *Down in the Delta*—and/or shield from harm, particularly respondents who have returned to the South. Rebecca, who works in administration at a local institution of higher education, returned to the area after having lived in Detroit since she finished college in the South. She grew up in Coldwater, Mississippi, a few miles south of Memphis. Although she remembers her twenty-four years in Detroit fondly, she insisted that she feels more "at home and at peace" in the South:

> Well, the life there is different because it's not where our [African Americans] roots are. Lots of folks there, their grandmothers and great-grandmothers came up there, you see, but they are disconnected from the values here. This is where real black values are formed. That's why so many of them still send their kids down south for the summer, or if they're acting out. They come back acting right, I tell you that much. And it's not just because they're with family, because they got family, you see, wherever they are, Detroit, Chicago, Milwaukee, New York, wherever. But this South, it gets them right, spiritually, mentally, everything. Every black child who hasn't been south should come south.

For Rebecca and other respondents, the South is the site of the formation of "real black values," which I asked Rebecca to say more about.

REBECCA: You know, like, respect for elders, appreciation of, you know, the natural world, don't be throwing trash everywhere, and [respect] people's property, respect yourself and put some clothes on and pull your pants up, love of the Lord, you know, churchgoing.

ZANDRIA: Black people in other places don't teach their children those values? Or people in general?

REBECCA: No, they sure do not, not like they do here. Or if they do, they children are not mindin' at all. Up there, you may have a few [children who exhibit real black values]. But even the ones with sense that got a little money or something, they ain't humble, and that's something you *got* to have. None of that [material belongings] is yours; it's the Lord's. And if you go around not speaking to people and looking crazy at folks, you gonna be a lonely old shrew with nothing.

ZANDRIA: Well, there are some children around here who don't know all of that or follow those values. Where are the children who are acting out here sent to get some "real black values"?

REBECCA: Further down south, down in the Delta somewhere, Coldwater or Greenville or the like. If that doesn't get 'em straight, then you have to send them to the backwoods of Georgia or those Carolina islands.

ZANDRIA: And if that doesn't work?

REBECCA: Then it's back to the Delta with 'em, this time to Sunflower County [laughs].

ZANDRIA: It's to the penitentiary for them if they don't get right?

REBECCA: Exactly. They'll be model citizens or fit for the electric chair one when they come out of there [laughs].

I gathered that Rebecca was only half-kidding about sending wayward southern children to the Mississippi State Penitentiary if they cannot be "healed" by any other part of the South. However, her sentiments suggested that, the farther south one gets, the closer to middle-class values he or she is. The values Rebecca asserted, many of which were also highlighted by other respondents as distinctly southern, included some southern cultural norms, like emphases on greeting people and showing humility, but many of these values are middle-class norms across race and region. Further, her notion of values speaks directly to a politics of respectability that polices black parents and children on social behavior and presentation of self. Still, even when respondents were critical of the South, they held tight to sets of myths about southern values and southern superiority that they could prove through lived experience.

Intraracial Dichotomies of Regional Distinction

Just as regional differences are played out in the public sphere between powerful culture producers, they are also reflected, shaped, and reinforced in everyday interactions. Although most of my respondents had lived in the South all of their lives, a few folks who did not fall into this category snuck into my sample. One of these respondents, Malcolm, was quick to tell me in our first interview, "You know I'm not from the South, right? Well, not really." Malcolm, who returned to Memphis to be with his elderly grandmother in the 1990s, came of age in the 1970s and 1980s in the Bronx—incidentally, home to a number of rapper racists. Now a successful entrepreneur, Malcolm lamented what he sees as southern men's laziness: "If I find out they're from Memphis, I just don't return their phone calls. They don't want to work. They've got excuses, and I don't have time for excuses. They're lazy. It's because they're country, and they've been coddled and taken care of by women—mothers, grandmothers, girlfriends—and they would just much rather live up off some women than work. That's what I find [since being back] in the South."

Malcolm and other non-southern respondents linked southern men's feminization to the nurturing and economic power of southern women. This argument certainly seems to dovetail with the notion of southern men as either mama's boys or pimps—the most popular phrase to make out of the acronym M.E.M.P.H.I.S., after all, is "Making Easy Money Pimpin' Hos in Style." Because of women's care and willingness to take care of men, Malcolm argued, men have no incentive to work. He distinguished himself from "country niggas" by region and space—the urban North juxtaposed with the not-so-urban South. Further, Malcolm packaged a familiar class and gender critique of black southern men in the relatively benign language of regional difference, offering up southern men's dependence on women, whether exploitative or not, as a characteristic that distinguishes northern men from southern men.

While Malcolm and other non-southern respondents did little to mask their contempt for what they see as southern men's weakness and laziness, other non-southern respondents, like Hasan, sympathetically offered historical, if not entirely accurate, justifications for these differences. "Men in the South were, like, living under the oppression of Jim Crow and had their masculinity stripped, from them, you know. Men in the North and, like, out in Cali had more power, so that's where you got the Black Power movement from. While in the South, they had to do it non-violent and peaceful so they wouldn't upset the white people."

While southern respondents largely saw Jim Crow as strengthening black men's masculinity by rendering them more measured and cunning, Hasan articulated the mainstream argument that Jim Crow, in fact, emasculated black men. He further linked this emasculation to broader political and philosophical differences between non-violence and Black Power. Although he made no explicit claims about southern black men's work ethic, his assertion nonetheless situates southern men as deficient and non-southern men as better able to protect their communities from white racism, unfettered by worries of upsetting white people.

While Malcolm's and Hasan's contentions implied class distinctions rather than explicitly named them, southern respondents interpreted non-southern blacks directly in classed terms. Depending on their respective class positions, respondents cast non-southern blacks, whether they were currently living in the South or not, as either insufferably bourgie or hopelessly ghetto. LaShaun frequently told me about her "country cousins," by which she meant her relatives in Chicago. However, her husband Michael's cousins, who live in Milwaukee, received most of her scorn and pity. "I have a few cousins that live up north, and Michael has some people up north, too. A couple of times Michael's people have sent some of his cousins down to stay with us for the summer. They were rough. We spent most of that time teaching them basics they didn't get in school and getting that urban anger out of them. Their poor life is much harder than our poor life. Those kids went hungry. No one would ever let you go hungry in the South, even if you were too proud to tell anyone you were hungry. Folks knew and helped out."

Although clearly, black and poor communities across the country share this helping spirit when neighbors are in need—and communities in the South surely let people go hungry—for LaShaun, letting people go hungry is something that would simply not happen in the South. This undergirds her contention that poverty outside of the South is worse than southern poverty. These stories of southern triumph, despite marginalization, fuel the idea of a mythical South where politeness and community togetherness abound. I asked her to say more about the urban anger she said her husband's cousins had, as well as to consider the urban anger of Memphis youth. "Sure, there are a few crazy people like that Lester Street guy,[17] but the kids here aren't generally just angry on the inside. There's so much shooting and violence that goes on up there and no one is loving these children [from the North], and they're really angry. Shouting and frowning all of the time like they ain't got no sense."

LaShaun linked urban violence in the North to her younger relatives' anger, but southern cities, including Memphis, frequently round out the top ten in Bureau of Justice statistical reports for aggravated crime and murder. LaShaun's perceptions of crime in and outside of the South are likely a function of her class position. Her middle-class status and residence in a low-crime area shield her from the violence that plagues some inner-city neighborhoods. Further, cousins who need to visit for the summer are likely disadvantaged, with working parents who cannot afford summer camps and enrichment activities. Thus, differences that are more likely attributable to class are often seen as consequences of regional characteristics.

Less affluent respondents constructed northerners in less favorable terms as well, but for different reasons. Batina, thirty-nine and the youngest of five children, is the default caregiver for her mother, eighty, who suffers from dementia and a host of chronic illnesses. The rest of her siblings, save for a brother in Birmingham who is in and out of jail, live in various cities in the Midwest and Northeast, from Milwaukee to Boston. Her siblings' children and grandchildren frequently visit their grandmother/great-grandmother—which essentially means visits with their aunt/great-aunt Batina, since Batina's mother is generally incapacitated. She told me about how she always thought she would move north like her older siblings, but she did not like the social environment there when she visited. "Niggas in the North think they're the shit. Calling us country. Some of the most country talking and backward shit I ever heard was when I went to Chicago to visit my sister. And they balling, they flashing and all of that . . . they're able to do all of that because we're here holding the family together, doing all the work."

Batina saw her siblings' absence, as well as their relative wealth, as made possible by her caregiving. Batina's sentiment was both personal and general, in that it reflected a personal experience and also reflected her and others' general feelings about the North as a site of neglectful abandon.

They are living their lives, honey, all of them, all because I'm here taking care of Mama. They say I am Mama's favorite, and that Mama won't have any of them taking care of her. That's not true, though, or they don't know because they've never taken care of her. It's that they don't want to take money out of their pockets and change their lifestyles to care for Mama. My oldest brother has been in Detroit since he was a young man, since before I was born, and I've only seen him a few times. . . . They've all got money, too. Because here's their free nursing home and summer camp.

Batina's contention was that her siblings had abandoned her and that despite her pleas for at least one of them to move home to help with their mother's care, none of them had opted to move. She read this "selfishness" as caused by urban northern living. "Up north there is no community. You don't care for your own. You like . . . you for self. You put yourself before others. I don't think they were always like that. I know [the three middle children] weren't like that because they cared for me when I was growing up some. But that's what the North does to you. Makes you forget you had a family, except for when it's convenient."

Despite the particular effects of Batina's experiences on her sentiments about the North, her contentions are not unlike those of many respondents who also characterized the North as a space of abandon. Although certainly people leave home behind for other places in the South, respondents expressed the most ire toward people who have left for the non-South.

This notion of the North as a site of abandon extends beyond ideas about familial responsibility. Many respondents expressed a loyalty to region that they linked to racial responsibility and authenticity. For Keisha, the singer, it was explicitly about black ownership of the region: "Yes, black folks went off to the big cities and made it, but they were pretty much newcomers to most of the places they went. But in the South, we [African Americans] made this. From the beginning to the end. So, it's our responsibility to make sure that we make it a better place."

In other conversations with Keisha and other respondents, Atlanta frequently came up as a site that has accomplished the South as a better place, which often brought up questions about its authenticity as a "real" southern city. Like many respondents, North Memphis barber James argued that Atlanta is but one model of black ownership of a southern city:

> See, Atlanta do have a lot of, you know, African Americans in power, but them is like your celebrities, your filthy-rich *Lifestyles of the Rich and Famous, MTV Cribs* types. Then Memphis got, like, a lot of dope boys, entrepreneurs, you know, blue-collar type hustlers on the come-up. Then in Texas, in Houston, you got the dope boys, the super-smart types, like engineers and doctors . . . and you know all over the South, Jacksonville, North Carolina, South Carolina, you can pretty much choose where you wanna be based on your personality or whatever, then make a nice life around a bunch of niggas like you. Why would you go [outside the South] 'cept to visit?

Regardless of where respondents' personalities might lead them, the overwhelming majority saw themselves as responsible to and for the South. Keith, who offered a relatively balanced criticism of the benefits of and drawbacks to living in the South, nonetheless concurred with the notion of blacks' responsibility for the region:

> The South is like a big project. We all have to work on it, and do what we can to it. You build this on it, I paint this side, we all working together. Because this is our legacy in this country. Like up north and out west, you got black neighborhoods in a mostly white, or now mostly Hispanic, city. Down south, you got entire black cities. These are all the folks that came from the country, the farms, and their children. This is ours. I'm

not saying we can make white folks act better, but there can be enough of us where they got to act better.

Keith and other respondents expressed a sense of ownership over the South and often implied that blacks outside of the South do not have the same sense of ownership of place. While it is evident that place attachments abound from Bronzeville to Harlem, respondents suggested that in the South, black ownership of southern cities, rural areas in the South, and ultimately the region as a whole—"not West Virginia, though, not West Virginia," a group of respondents and taggers-along told me once at a picnic—transform place attachments into place projects. New Orleans is one such ideological project, as respondents often referenced the city as a contested site that needed to be retained in the wake of Hurricane Katrina. Discourse about New Orleans was partially a consequence of the Crescent City's expanding diaspora and influence in Memphis. However, it was moreover a result of respondents' general sense, like that of African Americans across the country, that white folks wanted to take New Orleans—perhaps by intentionally blowing up the levees—from black folks. Conversations about New Orleans often led to broader assertions about the importance of the South for African Americans in and beyond the region. Cassandra, with whom I had a number of conversations about Hurricane Katrina during our time at the park, captured respondents' sentiments about New Orleans and black folks' relationship to the South. She told me, "You know how people sometimes say that cities like Phoenix are really white and are like the last frontier for white folks? The South is black folks' territory. It's a nation within a nation. It's the home of black America. Places outside of the South are, too, but the South is where the most blacks are concentrated. So, if we lose New Orleans—which I don't think we will ever really lose it no matter how many white people move there—but still, if we lose it, that's like losing a part of a country."

For Cassandra, the black South, regardless of its diversity and despite the physical presence of white people and other racial and ethnic groups, is African American territory and should be defended like a nation-state. I asked her to elaborate on the idea of the black South as a country and how one might defend a country without borders.

You control the media, the propaganda, the messages that get out there about black folks in the South. But you don't do it like Hitler. You do it really nice and polite, kind of like subliminal messages. Like [waves her hands in my face to mimic hypnotism], "You love the South. You love black people. You love the music. Everything is so nice here. Everyone is so nice. You just want to enjoy it. You don't want to steal it and take over it. Because you need the black people. They are so nice." Next thing you know, you've got a black mayor and an all-black city council. Everybody coexisting. Bam.

Although Cassandra was only slightly exaggerating about hypnotizing white people into not stealing black southern cultures, spaces, and places, her assertions about controlling the propaganda point to a deliberate accomplishment of the South. Many respondents contended that a proliferation of black cultural products and black political power shored up the boundaries of the South and ensured that it would remain the least hostile territory for blacks in America. This narrative also imagines a world in which black political power in and of itself will yield better outcomes for African Americans despite class politics.

People affiliated with the city's art worlds, the southern neo-bohemians, were most likely to place themselves squarely at the intersections of racial responsibility and regional ownership. Cortez, a FedEx employee by night and an amateur art collector by day, quipped that Chicago, New York, and Philadelphia are where one goes when he or she has run out of ideas or "drive for the South." He explained:

> People say there isn't a market for what [artists] do here, but that's ridiculous. But I will say it takes some creativity to tap into your place in that market. A lot of people who go north, like to Chicago or New York, it's because they don't want to work for it here. You have to make art that speaks to the people in the South and that's from the people, really. In Chicago or Philadelphia, there'll always be some bourgie black or some liberal white that will buy your crap just to say they're into oil [painting] and discovered some hot, young artist out of the South.

For a few artists I encountered, the South is not a big project, as Keith said, but a hindrance to success at one's craft. These artists were not interested in both creating art and building the infrastructure of an arts community, including a market for their work. Cortez situated people who leave the South, particularly to pursue artistic endeavors, as lazy and unwilling to engage in the labor that it would take to make their aspirations possible in Memphis.

Most local hip-hop and soul artists echoed Cortez's sentiment, refusing to see their potential audience as perhaps too tied to corporate radio to develop a taste for live music with a different sound. Jamya, an emcee with a strong local following, contended that she has an audience in the South but that she has to use different motivating strategies to locate that audience.

> It's just like in any market. Not all folks in the South listen to the crunk-type, southern crunk, Atlanta-type stuff. It's just like that group Little Brother.[18] They're from the South, and they got a southern sound, but not necessarily like that Atlanta sound, you know, or that dirty Memphis sound. Some people say they sound more, like, New York or whatever, like they say about [my music]. So I let the people know, hey, there's lots of different sounds here. You don't have to go to Atlanta or Chicago or LA to make it as long as you're trying to make good music and get your hustle on. If you're trying to become a superstar [laughs] . . . well, I guess you can do that anywhere, too. Three Six Mafia had a reality show on MTV, didn't they? [Laughs.]

This you-can-make-it-right-here sentiment, while motivated on the surface by place-pride and experience, may also be the result of the lack of mobility—financial, familial, or otherwise—of many respondents. That is, it is not clear how many folks make it happen where they are because they have to, because they want to, or because of some combination of necessity and desire. Although only a few respondents couched this sentiment in economic terms, it is reasonable to assume that relative economic deprivation may be operating in articulations of local and regional loyalty, as well as in the interregional critique lodged wholesale at "the North."

Respondents frequently drew upon the language of intraracial regional difference to voice interregional resentment. What ties these sentiments together, regardless of the varied social locations of respondents, is a common racial narrative that highlights interregional differences to approximate authenticity, temporality, and identity superiority. Respondents repeatedly emphasized a folk ruggedness, loyalty, and family values as characteristics that distinguished them from other black people, despite how well such descriptions might also capture non-southern black identities. Respondents thereby returned the region-hating gaze, positioning the cosmopolitan identities engendered by the city as a social ill. Rather than seeing the northern city as a positive, modernizing force, respondents saw the North as encouraging alienation from family, lack of commitment to place, and general laziness. While they might acknowledge the fallacy of their generalizations, they nonetheless asserted them with a sincerity that strengthens the interregional boundaries of blackness and situates southern blackness as the better articulation of racial identity.

Southern Class Matters

While respondents used critiques of the North to approximate several forms of class and morality differences between southerners and northerners, they used similar language to talk about their everyday class experiences with family, friends, coworkers, and employers. Tommie, a journalist for a local publication, exemplified many sentiments about southern class matters that begin at home. At fifty, he feels he has done pretty well for himself, working and struggling to be successful at a number of things and describing himself as only happening upon journalism as a freelancer in college. Now an award-winning journalist, the third of seven children is praised by most of his siblings but resented by a loud minority. When I asked about family in our first interview, as I did with most respondents, Tommie's response quickly turned to class differences within his family:

> My two older sisters, they did fine[. . . .] Even some of the youngest siblings, they're doing all right for themselves. But the sister right under me—we're ten months apart, so that's a whole set of issues right there— she has never been anything. She never thought she had to work for anything. My parents were poor and somehow they paid for her to go off to college, to Fisk. And she came back after that first semester pregnant. They didn't pay for me [or my two older sisters] to go to college, but she just squandered that opportunity. And she never went back.

For Tommie, his younger sister is representative of the "country laziness" highlighted by Malcolm, and many respondents characterized someone they know personally, like a close friend or relative, as country or lazy. In class matters, then, country is almost always a pejorative that captures more than the stale and ubiquitous "ghetto" can. Country, in respondents' usage to approximate class and respectability differences, draws on traditional negative tropes of black southernness but imagines laziness as a function of willful ignorance. As Tommie continued, he stiffened and gripped his coffee cup as if it might run away, recounting for me their last family gathering. He had just received an award for his work and had been featured in a book of local and regional notables. He brought the award and book for his mother to see and was greeted with contempt from his sister's daughter.

I had [the awards] here in my arms like this [gestures as if carrying schoolbooks in one arm, facing inward], so I didn't come through holding them up like, "Here! Here! Look at what I did!" Her daughter, who is just like her—had two babies early, got two no-good baby daddies and is damn near thirty years old and has never worked remuneratively in her life—gon' say to me, just as nasty as she could, "Don't nobody care what you got. Don't come in here bragging and showing off. You always got to show off. You gon' upset my digestion with all of that." Now, mind you, I'm not even a braggart. She's said smart stuff like that to me before. Just no respect. I told her, "I brought this for Mama, *not* for you."

Tommie was generally soft-spoken, but by the end of this narrative, he had raised his voice considerably and looked around the coffee shop uncomfortably to see if anyone had noticed. It can be difficult to reconcile class differences within a family, and particularly in a southern family expected to be connected and supportive through church, family dinners, and family gatherings. When I asked Tommie to say more about what might have motivated his niece to react the way she did, he paused. He seemed to be searching both for the words and for the strength to maintain his composure.

Some people think that you think that you are better than them just because you want better for yourself. They take that as if you're bourgie because you want better and do better. [. . .] Just like when I left our family church because there was some ethical mess with the pastor, and [my niece] couldn't have been anymore than thirteen or fourteen then, she told me one Sunday dinner, "Our church ain't good enough for you no more? You had to go to the big nigga church?" Come to think of it, I should have whipped her tail a long time ago since her mother didn't do it.

Tommie contended that he does not understand where his sister and niece's worldview comes from. Class-based rivalries with siblings, cousins, and other relatives dominated many discussions of class, and Tommie's story is not unlike so many others that I heard. Most respondents, like Tommie, considered themselves working class or just working people, whether in jest or with sincerity, because they had to work every day to maintain a middle-class lifestyle, including making mortgage or rent payments, paying for private school or college tuition, and buying and maintaining multiple, if modest, vehicles.[19]

Most affluent respondents downplayed their class statuses and instead emphasized their connections to something humble, like a poor or rural upbringing. In order to accomplish a balance between country and cosmopolitan, and moreover between less affluent and more elite, respondents in the socioeconomic middle drew on country-ness to downplay their relative affluence. This was especially true in mixed regional company, where southernness was often mobilized to alleviate class tensions and lay blame for negative attitudes toward poor blacks on northerners: "We all [black southerners] country no matter how far we've come," boasted Anthony, a nonprofit professional, in a retort to a colleague visiting from Detroit. At a neighborhood fish fry that attracted attendees from across class statuses, Anthony and his compatriot's booming voices had become the center of attention—as much as that might be possible at a backyard gathering of nearly 100 people. "It's y'all [northerners]," he continued, "that don't want to help your kind when they a little down on they luck. Forgot where you came from!"

I was tickled by Anthony's declaration and the hearty affirmations it received, as I frequently witnessed such mobilizations of regional identity as trump cards in racial authenticity debates. Anthony grew up in a small town on the Alabama-Mississippi border before coming to Memphis at fifteen to live with an aunt after his father's death. When I interviewed him previously in exclusively southern company—a few friends with whom he had attended college—he had offered a more widely held sentiment indicative of the limits of "country": "See, everybody's running around trying to see what the *problem* is. Is it that [black people in the South] need some more early childhood education? Is it that they need some more after school programs? Or is *The Man* keeping them down? No. No. None of that. These lazy country niggas don't want to work; that's the fundamental problem."

I decided not to explicitly call Anthony on what I read as his performative racial and regional solidarity as I helped clean up after the fish fry. Nevertheless, after I asked him a series of questions attempting to ascertain the broader context of the conversation with his colleague, he began to explain, echoing respondents' sentiments across class. "Country only goes so far. I mean, I understand what it's like to be fresh out the country. I know what it's like to be poor. But I'm not there anymore. So how much can I say we're really alike and people believe that and feel like we have a genuine connection? So, sometimes I put a little extra on it. Because I ain't gon' let anybody from outside of here come challenging me about not keeping it real."

For Anthony and others, the limits of country as a performative and identity category are marked by class and achievement boundaries. Still, he admitted performatively exaggerating his country-ness—putting "a little extra on it"—to enhance his connection to his less affluent kin. Moreover, he and other respondents contended that they will defend the less affluent country folks of the South, and thereby defend themselves, their mothers and grandmothers, and their histories, from the attacks of region-hating outsiders.

The Regional Limits of Black Solidarity

An array of entities has capitalized on the packaging of southern black identities as black identity writ large, from corporations to pundits to southerners themselves. Corporations tend to draw on sanitized, positive, happy versions of country-ness to root black identity in an accessible and nostalgic home place. These appropriations of the South serve a diverse black populace longing to be grounded in native black identity in a post-black moment and endeavor to create that longing where there is none. An early advertisement for McDonald's Southern Style Crispy Chicken Sandwich and sweet tea features two African American girls in the sepia-toned past shaking a brown paper bag filled with flour to coat pieces of chicken. In the next scene, a black mother emerges from the kitchen through the screen door into a backyard with a platter of chicken. The commercial flashes to the present where a matronly African American heads to the picnic table with a platter of McDonald's chicken sandwiches to serve her family. Radio spots on black-audience stations have featured speakers reminiscing about the "good old days" and "Grandmama's fried chicken," interrupted by a friend who informs them that, in fact, they can get their grandmama's fried chicken at McDonald's.

While the McDonald's southern-style chicken and sweet tea campaign drew conspicuously on tropes of black southernness to sell chicken sandwiches and tea to black people, black-owned Glory Foods used racial, gendered, and regional tropes of black subservience, cooking skills, and mammy sassiness to sell its "authentically soulful, southern style" canned greens. In two commercial spots, Shirley, a tall, buxom black woman, rescues culinarily inept white people from their whiteness. In one spot, Shirley kicks in a door to a white couple's kitchen, gives them some greens, and solves a dinner dilemma in which the wife does not know what to cook for a mother-in-law who will arrive any minute. In the other, Shirley again bursts through a door after blatantly disrespectful white children have refused to eat their vegetables and talked in stereotypically white ways to their exasperated and clueless mother. Shirley helps the mother prepare an entire meal, complete with Glory greens, and the children are satis-fied. Although Shirley might be read as a black female stereotype without a specific regional attachment, the trope of mammy is inextricably linked to the South. Her sassiness, accent, servitude, and kindness reinforce this regional link. White southerners, and whites more generally, are encour-aged to associate Shirley's authenticity as a southern black woman with the goodness of the greens she peddles, not unlike the relationship between Aunt Jemima, pancakes, and syrup. Black southerners, and black people more generally, may find the commercials' portrayal of white ineptitude comical. However, because Shirley rescues white people from themselves in a familiar regional arrangement of white power and black servitude, they may also resist this advertising strategy as contributing to negative representations of black people and, for southerners, country-ness.

While the McDonald's and Glory Foods advertisements quickly disap-peared, the latter after a fair amount of protest from viewers, they signaled a continuing trend in corporate appropriation of tropes of southern black identity to increase profit margins. Yet, not all corporate appropriations use country, Old South tropes to inspire identification with a racial, re-gional, or national past. The now-defunct Turner South television network capitalized on a different kind of southern blackness, one focused not on returnees but on young, upwardly mobile blacks raised in the South. A poster features a black-and-white photo of a brown-skinned black woman with full lips, hoop earrings, and short natural hair. Gold words super-imposed over her face declare: "My South smells of fresh cut grass, jas-mine and sweet olive. In my South, kids still catch fireflies in mason jars. My South has tea, iced and almost as sweet as the men. My South is the best-kept secret in the country. My name is Mary Baptiste. My South is on Turner South." Although the Turner South network featured some African American programming, that Mary Baptiste's or any other black southern-er's South was consistently on Turner South is debatable. Yet, these and other compelling advertisements work to capitalize on the similarities of southern cultures across race while attempting to capture the dynamics of within-region cultural differences across race.

Culture industries of black regional tourism, from black-led plantation tours to the civil rights tours that were part of the soul patrol's *Stand* doc-umentary, educate non-southerners about the region in much the same way that West African tour guides educate relatively naive black Americans about their African homeland. Still, the predominance of the attention to the South focuses on these nostalgic, positive aspects of black southern life and fixes it in a happy, better space and place, ignoring modern realities.

This is, of course, a political and discursive move generally available only to black middle classes, and especially to non-southerners and new migrants to the South. For southerners who never left the region, the struggle is just as current as the tea is sweet.

Like other articulations of black solidarity, regional difference is connected to power and powerful discourses about the black community that privilege certain voices over others. Respondents work to present a unified southern identity, particularly in mixed regional company. Their protectiveness over the region translates into a downplaying of class differences, although this is less often the case for lower-income respondents. Thus, while expressed intraracial class differences are pronounced, they are mitigated by southern residence and a regional culture wedded, at least in a nominal sense, to tradition and a unified racial community. This unification around a collective black identity and community despite class differences, I argue, is an accomplishment that draws on politeness, or what many respondents call fakeness, to keep up racial appearances.

Within the range of class discussions I had with respondents, regionalized versions of class difference emerged far more frequently than general, nationally focused discussions of poor black folks and middle-class black folks. Region was used to mark class, as well as to make within-region class distinctions among blacks. Country and bourgie, or cosmopolitan, functioned variously to describe southerners and non-southerners but were generally operationalized as positive and negative poles, southern and northern, to account for people's attitudes and social and financial class statuses. While bourgie was most often used to describe northerners or southern folks with elitist attitudes, country functioned as a universalizing regional quality that undergirded racial authenticity. Still, some more affluent respondents' uses of country, like Anthony's and Malcolm's, reflected the appropriation of negative southern tropes, especially about men, to explain social, financial, or occupational deficiencies. Thus, more affluent southerners' racial shame is similar to that of non-southern region-haters. In general, however, respondents held fast to, sanitized, and emphasized country-ness in order to forward a country cosmopolitanism that distinguished them from non-southern blacks as more racially authentic and "down-to-earth" while maintaining a sense of sophistication and culture.

As a racial boundary, regional distinction functions successively in three ways. First, southern tropes—including fine women, men, and food; lush, abundant land; and family and church—erect a seemingly democratic and shared black community rooted in naturally occurring, non-material social goods. Second, through these tropes, regional distinction serves as a marker of authentic blackness, and in some cases of better blackness. Third, as a naturalized marker of authentic or better blackness, regional distinction masks class differences. Further, through this democratic black community relatively disconnected from material difference, regional distinction obscures anxieties about the contradictions of increasing prosperity for some blacks and continued and worsening impoverishment for others. Thus, participating in down-home black southern traditions, or in many cases simply living in the South, allows more affluent blacks to maintain a connection to authentic blackness without necessarily engaging with poor or other black communities on a sustained basis. Further, as the less-than-polite smirks and comments at Tara's debut indicated, elite African American southerners can draw on forms of blackness that exclude, or at least render unwelcome, "the folk" on which the authenticity of their identities rely.

Black Identity Redux

In his 2009 documentary about black hair culture in contemporary America, *Good Hair*, comedian Chris Rock declares that to find answers to critical questions about coif politics, he has to "travel to the place where all black decisions are made: Atlanta, Georgia." Delivered like many of Rock's punch lines, there is definitive truth in the jest. Census data from 2000 to 2010 indicate that the size of Atlanta's black population has surpassed that of Chicago and is now second only to New York City's black populace. This demographic shift, the product of over a generation of migration to the South by African Americans, as well as of immigration by Africans and West Indians, signals, as Rock suggests, an undeniable shift in the geographic center of black American identities and politics.

Tyler Perry's media enterprise, located in Atlanta, is also a testament to this demographic shift. Contributing to Atlanta's visibility as a center of black cultural identity and everyday black life, Perry writes and imagines Atlanta as the backdrop of an indistinguishable, normalized blackness. Perry downplays Atlanta's landscape and iconography to foreground a black, rather than an explicitly southern black, story. For instance, although there are a few indirect references to Atlanta in *Daddy's Little Girls*, Perry's 2007 narrative about uptight professional black women, flawed but valiant black working-class men, bad black mothers, and drug dealers is intended to speak beyond a place or regional experience to a broader racial experience. Yet, despite the relatively broad applicability of these narratives, they create and re-create southern, black, and southern black identities even as they reflect issues in the national black public consciousness.

Reality television is a broader testament to this demographic shift in popular media. Reality television and popular media enterprises weave together elements of these myriad instantiations of the region to create a space to which all can retreat to be simultaneously uplifted, revolted, and renewed. Shows like Bravo's *The Real Housewives of Atlanta* and VH1's *Love & Hip Hop Atlanta* feature a mash-up of gender, class, race, and black identity set in the elite South of dubiously wealthy, badly behaving media stars. *RHOA* is the only version of Bravo's *Real Housewives* franchise that features several African American women as main characters. While Prince George's County, Maryland, is also home to a wealthy black elite, America's fascination with Atlanta as a black mecca is partially predicated on the notion of a Deep South of peaches and pine colliding with a Dirty South of crunk, funk, and soul. Often, regional nuances are highlighted for additional spice, resulting in these series' broader functioning as representative of a certain segment, if not all, of contemporary black life.

A host of ostensibly white reality shows about the South, from the History Channel's *Swamp People* to TLC's spinoff from *Toddlers & Tiaras*, *Here Comes Honey Boo Boo*, ensures that ideas about the South are circulating in the public discourse and underscoring interpersonal interactions and are facilitating the creation and maintenance of class boundaries by a different name. Popular culture is replete with (re)imaginings of the South, many of which draw on Old South tropes in New South contexts to tell familiar stories about the South. These shows often engage the past and present, "reality" and fiction, to present a changing, yet constant, South.

While the South has risen and ridden again at several junctures since the Civil War, recent attention to the South has reified the region's lure, despite the fact that as a space, the South is evolving into something much like other American spaces: it is characterized by urban and suburban sprawl, is home to many new immigrants, and faces challenges managing the needs of economically and politically diverse populations. Anxiety about progress, homogenization, immigration, and the changing landscape of the region fuel identity alliances and articulations intended to stabilize the idea of the South—to shelter it from a perceived disruption that would decenter its values and charm.

On the ground, black southerners participate in regional boundary work, but toward different ends from those pursued by the producers of reality television shows and other purveyors of southern shock culture. Instead of drawing exclusively on Old South tropes, respondents in this study integrate rural, country behaviors and ideas with cultured, progressive, and sophisticated behaviors and ideas into a country cosmopolitan worldview. Although respondents may not have had the necessary experiences in the country to pass for black southern belles or gentlemen, there are plentiful examples from which they can draw inspiration for their performances. Further, sophisticated urban sensibilities, acquired through experiences in urban space, are just as central to how respondents see themselves as the country quips that nuance their performances of southernness and blackness. Using the varied strategies of country cosmopolitanism, respondents, as well as producers of black South film and Dirty South hip-hop, forward a

black identity that is racially authentic and rooted in an identifiable and accessible cultural heritage but not limited or constrained by those features
of the identity.

The City as Southern Future

Beyond the Souths forwarded by reality television, cultural and demographic shifts in the South mirror those across the world. Most of the
world's population already lives in an urban center or its immediately surrounding suburban or peri-urban spaces, and United Nations data indicate that an overwhelming majority of the world's population will live in
urban centers by 2030.[1] While the most rapid urban growth is happening
in the global south, the American South's urbanization patterns are not
unlike those of its global southern and industrializing neighbors. Varieties
of urban and rural space, coupled with the organization of power in those
respective spaces, affect a host of outcomes, from socioeconomic status to
quality of life. These spaces also produce meaningful identity and cultural
differences that work in tandem with the sociopolitical features of space
and place. Thus, growing differences between the large metropolises of
the global south and the hinterlands that surround them will profoundly
affect how we think about urban identities, cultures, and experiences in
the twenty-first century.[2]

In the American South, differential developmental patterns for the region's varied spaces have resulted in several southern spaces linked by
similar political, economic, and socioeconomic characteristics. These
spaces include large New South metropolises, like Dallas, Miami, Charlotte, and Atlanta, and their surrounding suburbs; what Brookings Institution demographer William H. Frey has called "the historic 'Old South'" of
Alabama, Mississippi, and Louisiana,[3] which includes a number of midsize
southern cities and their surrounding suburbs; the small-town South; and
the rural South. These ideal types do not describe all of the varied spaces in
the South, but they capture the essence of the distinctions and similarities
between southern spaces that influence cultural expression.

New South metropolises are most readily defined by their rapid population growth and relatively robust economies, even in periods of downturn.
This population growth results from people relocating from other regions
to the South, including a significant number of African Americans. However, it also includes much of the substantial growth of the *Nuevo* South,
as Charlotte, Atlanta, Nashville, and Raleigh ranked among the top ten
metropolitan areas for Latino growth from 1990 to 2008. Further, although

Asian populations are generally concentrated in the metropolises of the West and East Coasts, several New South cities, including Atlanta and Orlando, ranked among the top ten for Asian population growth over the same period.[4]

While these metropolises have familiar patterns of racial segregation, the increasing diversity of the South's racial groups shifts the traditional spatial arrangements of power. Overall, minority group middle classes are succeeding in the South, reflected by wealth, education, and income attainment. Growing Latino, Asian, and African American populations in suburbs have complicated prevailing notions of black and brown inner cities and lily-white suburbs. Still, at the neighborhood level, patterns of residential segregation endure, even if whites and racial and ethnic minorities are in closer proximity. Further, for minority groups with intersecting racial and socioeconomic disadvantages, the New South is a paradoxical place that relegates them to the shadows and margins of the New South narrative.

Whereas New South metropolises, which I have argued constitute the new urban South, are characterized by sprawling suburbs and urban core growth, population and economic growth, and population diversity, in the historic urban South, the black/white racial paradigm continues steadfastly even in the context of increased Latino populations. While many cities west of the Mississippi River have an overwhelmingly Latino majority-minority population, Memphis, Jackson, and New Orleans—and Chicago—have overwhelmingly African American child populations. The fates of these cities, then, are largely tied to African American populations, which are increasingly disenfranchised by disinvestments in public education and the urban core by political and economic elites.

Soul cities are structural reflections of country cosmopolitanism, as urban and rural problems intersect to create unique sets of disadvantages. These cities fared worse through the economic recession than the metropolitan clusters of the new urban South. Yet, even Atlanta, arguably part of both the new urban South and the historic urban South, saw paradoxical outcomes after the economic recession, and black populations fared worse in the "City Too Busy to Hate" than in other high-growth southern metropolises. The Deep South, including Alabama, Mississippi, Louisiana, and the southwestern corner of Tennessee that houses Memphis, continues to lead the nation on a number of indicators, from rates of incarceration to rates of bankruptcy to rates of teen pregnancy. The vestiges of the plantation economy, disinvestment in education and human capital, and the continued rigidness of the black/white racial paradigm ensure an enduring post-soul blues for the most marginalized populations of the historic urban South and the new urban South.

In contrast to Atlanta and other New South cities, the grit and grind perception and reality of Memphis and other working-class African American cities of the new urban South highlights the often disadvantaging intersections of race, class, gender, and region. The New South poor, like the African American communities further impoverished and marginalized as Atlanta ascended to the throne of new urban metropolis in the 1990s, are obscured by rhetoric that imagines the South as a middle-class and elite promised land, particularly for African Americans. This rhetoric is often achieved, ironically, by hearkening back to tropes of rural folk cultures, rooted in a collective memory of the South from slavery through the civil rights movement.

African American reverse migration to the urban South continues, as does Latino migration and immigration and also migration from the Caribbean. The possessive investment in a narrative of black southern life that privileges and fixes old black South tropes—Negro spirituals, food and drink, pretty women, fine gentlemen, down-home politeness—will undoubtedly increase. Further, the southern culture industrial complex readily appropriates ideas of the South to sell products to increasingly class-anxious Americans across race. In the context of these demographic changes and the region's expanding visibility, African American southerners negotiate their theorizations of race, class, gender, and region in a rapidly changing identity landscape.

Region, Race, and Intersectionality

I have endeavored here to think about regional identity as part of the constellation of intersecting identity and power categories in interpersonal interactions and structural contexts. There are certainly as many ways to be black as there are black people, and I want to defend this notion vigorously. Yet, the boundaries we draw between ourselves and others most often fall along these existing power lines, those of race, class, gender, sexuality, and, indeed, region. Further, we cannot deny the bonds of culture, history, and collective and social memory, particularly as the latter is reinforced through popular media and culture. While there may be a multitude of ways to be black, most are aware of and complicit in enforcing the boundaries of a native black identity, both to preserve the idea of links that extend beyond the bounds of shared experiences of white oppression and to resist co-optation by power structures. Once located exclusively in the migration destination urban centers of Chicago, New York, Detroit, and Los Angeles, beginning in the 1970s, a New South cultural elite, and later corporations chasing black dollars, have relocated this native black identity to its originary site—the American South.

Respondents complicated popular southern narratives while also holding firm to some discursive contradictions. Overwhelmingly, respondents insisted on a blackness that blended rural wit and charm with urban sensibilities. Specifically, this translated into theorizations of race that minimized emotional responses to racism and privileged an unflinching recognition of white racism; theorizations of gender that held fast to traditional notions of masculinity and femininity but also modernized those ideas to fit the shifting balances of work and life; and theorizations of class that drew regional lines to privilege southern blackness as the down-home blackness. Respondents experience race, class, and gender through South-colored glasses, which mediates their identity conceptualizations, performances, and accomplishments.

While anecdotally, African Americans might prefer what they perceive as southern whites' "up front" racism to the subtleties of racism elsewhere, respondents often engaged in difficult performative work to downplay the toll of racial micro-aggressions on their respective psyches. Although I believe some respondents, indeed, did not "study white folks," most respondents' discomfort with a racial experience was evident in their body language, level of agitation, voice level, and other physical indicators. However, if asked to choose between the South and elsewhere, respondents who criticized the region defended the South mightily, rationalizing their experiences of racism as public or racial sacrifice for a greater good or insisting, as Ms. Jefferies and Ms. Mae did, that white folks would be punished by a higher power—perhaps even if they cheated their way into heaven.

Across gender, respondents reported divergent conceptualizations of masculine and feminine practice, although all respondents' theorizations were informed by the southern regional logic of country cosmopolitanism. Undoubtedly, men's and women's perspectives of race, region, and gender were informed by historical archetypes of (black) southern masculinity and femininity. While respondents negotiated white tropes of masculine and feminine identity and performances, like the belle and the gentleman, they often experienced and theorized these vis-à-vis racial requirements of gender performance. Thus, the maligned history of black southern men as weak, backwards Uncle Toms and as generally failed masculine forms influenced respondents' couching of their masculine performances. Most men adhere to or feel pressure to adhere to the requirements of hegemonic masculinity, and black men's racial status may complicate the experiences of and reaction to these pressures. Still, respondents used southern gender norms of calm strength and gentility to subvert some of the more pernicious requirements of normative black masculinity. While non-southern respondents were more likely to see black southern men as failed men, and in particular as failed men who survived off the disproportionately allocated labors of women, southern respondents marshaled the legacy of Jim Crow to ground a calculating masculinity capable of both love and battle.

For women respondents, the changing nature of work and of women's relationship to work and family were central to theorizations of gender and intimate partnerships. However, as much as possible, these women attempted to forward a traditional southern belle identity, one predicated on proper appearances and manners as well as on a willingness to serve a male partner as a traditional helpmate. Several respondents begrudged the idea of the southern belle, citing it as excessive on top of the already impossible gender performance requirements for black womanhood. In particular, they cited the ways in which the idea of the belle was utilized in black southern circles as code for the usual politics of skin color, hair length, and hair texture that exists in black public consciousness and public culture. Still other respondents, like Tara's aunt Wanda, outright refused the belle as a formulation, rejecting it on both racial and regional terms.

Whatever their relationship to traditional southern gender archetypes, respondents sought to challenge those archetypes, either by racializing them, expanding traditional categories to ensure the participation of people across class statuses, or erecting new forms altogether. While white versions of the southern girl and country boy can be found at the center of new country music cultures, the southern gul and country boy exist at the margins of black gender identities. In their urban and rural varieties, the country boy and southern gul highlight intraracial class differences by diverging from normative middle-class black identities. The southern gul in particular allows for lower-income, marginalized women to take on a regionalized gender identity. In "Slum Beautiful," a record from OutKast's *Stankonia* album, rapper Big Boi defends the urban southern gul from her more affluent southern belle counterparts: "Fuck them bourgie bitches / they don't know nothing 'bout you / 'cause you push a big black Buick / so fresh, so clean on them trues."[5] Men and women respondents negotiated the requirements and conceptualizations of these alternative southern gender archetypes to claim space for different expressions of black and southern identities.

Although race, gender, and region are always already signifying on one another, class is a permanent and powerful intersecting signifier: race, gender, and region in any intersecting formulation can stand in for class. Despite the fact that the overwhelming majority of African Americans can be described as middle class, black folks' disproportionate location in the ranks of poverty and disadvantage renders it nearly impossible for mainstream America to conceptualize African Americans as sharing similar class-based interests as the nation at large. In this way, class speaks as soon as race speaks—in the case of African Americans, then, black race speaks simultaneously with lower class.

However, the rise of Atlanta and other southern metropolises as key sites for black affluence complicates how we associate the signifiers of blackness and class. Because black affluence, particularly intergenerational wealth, is contrary to normative black and American identities, affluent African American southerners offset their wealth with narratives of down-home upbringing and country rearing. While this personal historiography strategy is one operationalized across race, southern residence offers a different set of authenticity bona fides. Indeed, the South as a signifier, despite the prominence of its wealthy black elite in popular media, functions as a link to Africa, to originary black identity, to ancestral land, and to authentic black cultures. In this way, the South displaces the intraracial animosities and differences across class and wraps them in the language of regional difference.

"Southern" stands in as a signifier for class, and its symbolic meaning is contextual. Respondents talked less about poverty as a financial condition and more about poverty of culture, spirit, and values—a poverty that they ascribed to their northern counterparts regardless of socioeconomic status. This symbolic meaning is also reflected in films about the black South. As I have demonstrated, *Down in the Delta, Meet the Browns*, and *Welcome Home Roscoe Jenkins* all capitalize on a notion of the South as a (rural) healing space rich in spirit and culture. *Down in the Delta* and *Meet the Browns* forward the argument that values-richness translates into financial wealth. Both the protagonists find financial success—*Down in the Delta*'s Loretta in the form of gainful employment at the chicken restaurant and *Meet the Browns*' Brenda in the form of a house—brought on by the South's cocoon of spiritual renewal.

Accomplishing the South: Structure and Culture

As a discursive product, the South is a strategic accomplishment, both in popular media and in people's everyday lives. Black and white folks, the cultural elite acting on their behalf, and corporations are all interested in accomplishing a particular version of the region that suits their specific ends. Representing, accomplishing, and doing an authentic South, then, is integral to people's everyday negotiations of identities; to cultural elite's attempts to shape the discourse around and represent southern publics; and to corporations' attempts to sell various products, from tea, to chicken sandwiches, to television shows, to barbecue sauce, to multiple publics, southern and beyond.

While the idea of the South has long been produced by and in the hands of powerful corporate, and often non-southern, interests, the proliferation of reality television shows about the South beginning around 2008 is representative of renewed corporate focus on the region. To be sure, these corporate interests are, perhaps cynically, counting on Americans' collective penchant for southern grotesquerie. Whether bayou people are wrestling alligators or Atlanta socialites are wrestling each other, viewers cannot turn away. Yet, media corporations are also responding to the structure of the country's demographic shift southward, the South's continued and rapid urban expansion, and anxieties about class status in a long, painful recession. Southerners cry foul about reality television's perpetuation of stereotypes of the region,[6] lamenting what they see as shameful or simply untrue depictions of contemporary southern realities. However, the radical conservative arm of southern political practices—from efforts to define marriage as a monogamous heterosexual enterprise and reduce women's reproductive rights to attempts to disband unions and disenfranchise voters—reflects nicely the rednecks, hillbillies, and swamp people constructed by popular media. In the national imagination, the South endures as the repository for our hopes and fears; in fraught times, our fears are reflected in the stereotypes of regional culture as well as in our structural practices.

Corporations are also savvy about the usefulness of the tropes of black southernness for selling things to non-southern African Americans and Americans generally. Annie,[7] the Popeyes spokesperson, sells Louisiana's black and Cajun cultures; Shirley, Glory Foods' magic negress, pops up to sell collard greens in a can; and a nameless black grandmother sells McDonald's Southern Style Crispy Chicken Sandwiches. While black people have often been used as mascots, from Aunt Jemima to Uncle Ben, this new turn attempts to remove some of the traditional overt racism and replace it with familiar regional insider signifiers—food, religiosity, sassiness, and southern accents. Annie, Shirley, and backyard chicken-frying grandmothers stand in as markers of southern blacks in servitude, eager to cook for and serve white and affluent people. Usually, African American publics meet these campaigns with outrage, and corporations respond by slightly shifting the narrative. Still, blackness and southernness remain central to corporate advertising campaigns.

African American cultural elites attempt to speak back to these representations and explode the narratives perpetuated about southern blackness by corporate media advertising cultures. They also attempt to represent southern African American publics through their art, forwarding alternative visions of black history, life, and experiences in the South. With hip-hop music video director Bryan Barber's lead and script, OutKast offered up a missing history of southern black life and a new hip-hop historiography with *Idlewild*. Director Chris Robinson brought writer Antwone Fisher's story of coming of age in the post–civil rights urban South to life in *ATL*, creating one of the few urban black films set in and about a southern city—a film in and of the South.

Hip-hop artists, perhaps more so than any other category of cultural elite, endeavor to carve out a space for southernness in black identity. Emphasizing the intersections of urban and rural, of cosmopolitan and country, southern hip-hop artists articulate a best-of-both-worlds blackness that privileges southern epistemologies. In a guest verse on New Orleans native Frank Ocean's "Pink Matter," André 3000 declares that a particular woman "had the kind of body that would intimidate / any of 'em that were unsouthern / not me, cousin," simultaneously affirming the beauty and femininity of southern women and the strength of southern masculinity to remain calm in the face of intimidating physical beauty.[8] Whether riding in rimmed LTDs or donning overalls and straw hats, southern hip-hop artists, local and nationally famous, indicate shifts in southern black identities and respond first to structural changes that affect black folks in the South.

Respondents are also invested in the accomplishment of southern identity, conceptualizing race, class, and gender through a regional lens. For respondents, however, southern identity is not a set of clothes to be donned and removed as they move in and out of social situations. Imagining themselves as qualitatively different from their non-southern counterparts, respondents also advocated for a blackness that blends urban and rural sensibilities to navigate contemporary racial realities, gender reactions, and intraracial class distinctions. Although these regional differences are sometimes performatively exaggerated in interpersonal contexts, they are also sincere articulations of regional selves. Indeed, most respondents contended that these identity differences were rooted in the realities of history, social memory, and lived experience. The South's increasing diversity will only shore up these regional identity boundaries, as authentic and sincere southernness will become more difficult to name, seek, and experience.

Black to the Southern Future

Beyond the interactive and discursive level, regional differences, actual and performed, have structural consequences, not all of which can be explained away by poverty and other markers of low socioeconomic status endemic to the South. African Americans are disproportionately affected by these disparities. Southern food cultures, which often transcend class, are correlated with obesity and related chronic illnesses, including diabetes and heart disease. While high-end southern eateries have turned this food culture into refined delicacy, food deserts in the region's most impoverished communities suffer the ironic legacy of southern food traditions. The South consistently spends less on human capital investments, like education and social services, that would produce a skilled workforce. This disinvestment contributes to the inability of its citizens to compete in the global marketplace, even if the region is a magnet for corporations in search of cheap, non-union labor and comparatively low taxes in right-to-work states. Further, even in less religious urban areas, evangelicalism influences local politics, ensuring that certain voices, from LGBT communities to evolutionists, will have a difficult time being heard. As in most social arenas, those who are most marginalized, but who also have given so much to the region, are disproportionately disadvantaged in life chances and outcomes.

Increasing socioeconomic differences between New South metropolises and Deep South cities and their surrounding suburban and rural communities complicate the notion of the solid South, a fact evident in returns from the 2008 presidential election. African American experiences across the region will signal these shifts first, as HIV, infant mortality, and obesity will disproportionately affect black folks in Deep South spaces and the socioeconomically disadvantaged black and brown pockets of New South metropolises. Thus, black southern lives can tell us much about not only the character of life in the South but also the nature of black life across the United States and in marginalized black communities globally. Black southerners respond to structural and social changes through art, culture, and identity practices that affirm the region while calling out its faults. Defending the region from naysayers, especially non-southern blacks, respondents are committed to the South because of its promise, even if they are not entirely sure they will witness its fruition.

The operationalization of region as the source and shroud of familiar intraracial distinctions offers new ways of thinking through blackness in post-Obama America. Common signifiers of black American identity—from beauty salons and barbershops, to soul food, to old-time religion—unite black Americans, native and not, with a common language to speak to and through blackness. Black folks are still working to slough off the negative connotations of southern blackness, even as they hold fast to them in defiance of the shifting boundaries of contemporary American blackness. Southerners, acutely aware of the ways in which regional residence might complicate non-southerners' responses to them, nonetheless forward a regionally inflected black identity, both to claim and reclaim space in black American identity proper and to politely accent anew already existing intraracial boundary lines.

Notes

INTRODUCTION

1. Griffin, "Promise of the Sociology of the South."

2. Rushing, *Memphis and the Paradox of Place*, 34.

3. Here I am deliberately signifying on David Goldfield's 1997 collection, *Region, Race, and Cities*, with apologies.

4. The Latin Americanization thesis contends that U.S. race relations will become more like Latin American race relations, where three racial categories—"whites," "honorary whites," and the "collective black"—will supplant the black/white or non-white/white binary. See Bonilla-Silva's articles "'We Are All Americans!'" and "From Bi-Racial to Tri-Racial"; and especially Sue's critical evaluation of this thesis in "An Assessment of the Latin Americanization Thesis."

5. Anthropologist Ulf Hannerz's *Soulside*, about Washington, D.C., focuses on the largely migrant experiences of black respondents. While the District, as a slaveholding space, certainly had a sizable black population, this population was greatly increased during the Great Migration by individuals from Georgia, the Carolinas, and Virginia.

6. See, for example, Hopkinson's *Go-Go Live* as well as the op-ed by Howard University education dean Leslie T. Fenwick, published on the *Washington Post*'s online blog.

7. Silver and Moeser challenge prevailing logics about race and space by arguing that segregation in southern cities was not akin to a "ghetto" but resulted in a distinct "separate city" within a city. While they argue that in the post–civil rights era, the neighborhoods of black urban poor in southern cities have begun to resemble urban northern ghettos, the effect of the "separate city" endures.

8. See Omi and Winant, *Racial Formation in the United States*.

9. In his history of the black middle-class community Runyon Heights in Yonkers, New York, sociologist Bruce Haynes in *Red Lines, Black Spaces* demonstrates that race functioned as a unifying site for solidarity and the political organization of space, although social and spatial separation from poorer blacks was also important to this formulation.

10. For a discussion of this process vis-à-vis the HIV/AIDS crisis, see Cohen's *Boundaries of Blackness*.

11. In 1989, law scholar and critical race theorist Kimberlé Crenshaw's use of the concept of intersectionality codified concepts forwarded by both black feminist scholarship and the early work of African American scholar-activists like Anna Julia Cooper, Ida B. Wells, and W. E. B. Du Bois ("Demarginalizing"). Intersectionality, a portable articulation of the crux of black feminist theorizing, considers the ways in which black women experience what Deborah King has called "multiple jeopardy"—simultaneously occupying disadvantaged positions in the three major systems of oppression: race, class, and gender ("Multiple Jeopardy"). Sociologist Patricia Hill Collins extended this work in her 1990 book, *Black Feminist Thought*, and ushered in a broad acceptance of the mutually reinforcing and co-occurring nature of systems of oppression.

12. See Rock's HBO special *Chris Rock: Bring the Pain.*

13. After Cosby's much-publicized criticisms of the black poor, Michael Eric Dyson wrote *Is Bill Cosby Right? Or Has the Black Middle Class Lost Its Mind?* as a relatively more factual counterpoint.

14. Even among the group of people referred to as "middle-class blacks," researchers have found significant and important boundary differences. Mary Pattillo's *Black Picket Fences* and *Black and the Block,* along with Karyn Lacy's *Blue-Chip Black* and Bruce Haynes's *Red Lines, Black Spaces,* have uncovered nuances in wealth attainment, linked fate, residence, and school choice that indicate the workings of symbolic boundaries and social boundaries.

15. Historian David Goldfield argues that three factors unique to the South—race, ruralism, and colonialism—shaped and continue to shape the evolution of the region from slavery to present. The particular formulation of racial and spatial relationships in the South informs enduring struggles over power and values, from funding for public education to the structure and ideology of southern politics (*Region, Race, and Cities*). Sociologist John Shelton Reed has consistently found evidence of a relatively uniform southern white identity that endures in attitudes and public culture, despite changes in the South's social, ethnic, and political landscape (*One South* and *Southern Folk*). Further, historian James Cobb's examination of regional identity firmly roots the most signified upon instantiation of southern identity—Mississippi Delta identity—in sets of cultural practices and products that sprang from the unique conditions of the plantation, agrarian South (*Most Southern Place*). Finally, geographer Clyde Woods documents the distinctive racial and regional epistemology, which he terms *blues epistemology,* that arose from the experiences of black folks in the Delta that laid important groundwork for our understanding of marginalized black communities throughout the South.

16. Through their examination of regional newcomers' knowledge of local authors, sociologists Wendy Griswold and Nathan Wright demonstrate that new migrants tend to take their new region's culture seriously ("Dynamic Endurance of Regionalism"). As such, migrants and immigrants contribute to the institutionalization and reinforcement of regional cultures.

17. See West and Zimmerman, "Doing Gender."

18. For instance, in their *American Sociological Review* article "History Repeats Itself, But How?," Molotch, Freudenberg, and Paulsen examine how places—Santa Barbara and Ventura, California—that were similar on standard demographic measures were, in fact, quite different, as demonstrated by the cities' disparate responses to the introduction of the commercial oil industry, highways, and other twentieth-century forces of American modernization. This, they argue, pointed to the deliberate accomplishment of these distinct elements of place character and tradition.

19. See Bourdieu, *Distinction.*

20. See Gieryn, "Boundary-Work."

21. See Lamont's *Money, Morals, and Manners* for a discussion of these processes among the French and American elite and her *The Dignity of Working Men* for a discussion of these processes among the working classes of these societies.

22. See Waters, *Ethnic Options.*

23. See Dubey, "Postmodern Geographies."

24. With apologies to David Goldfield's "country cosmopolites."

25. Walker, "The Black Writer and the Southern Experience," 20.

26. See the OutKast video for "Ms. Jackson."

27. Jackson, *Real Black*.

28. While in the presentation of these data I adhere to the "holy trinity" of sociological research on inequality and identity—race, class, and gender—I also am attentive to how talking about one identity dimension means one is always already talking about, or at least signifying, the others as well.

29. One of the seminal works in this area is Peggy McIntosh's 1988 essay "White Privilege: Unpacking the Invisible Knapsack," which came out of her work "White Privilege and Male Privilege: A Personal Account of Coming to See Correspondences through Work in Women's Studies." Others, including sociologist Abby Ferber, historian David Roediger, and philosopher George Yancy, have written extensively on whiteness as well. Over the past decade, unpacking and deconstructing whiteness, culturally and structurally, has become both popular and profitable. Antiracist writer and lecturer Tim Wise has perhaps been most responsible for the recent popular attention to whiteness and white privilege.

30. See Bertrand and Mullainathan's "Are Emily and Greg More Employable Than Lakisha and Jamal?" Also, see the significant body of work in this area amassed by sociologist Devah Pager, in particular her work with coauthor Lincoln Quillian: "Walking the Talk?" and "Estimating Risk." For housing, see Fischer and Massey's "Ecology of Racial Discrimination."

31. Black folks are also inhibited in executive function after interracial interaction if they have self-reported more negative attitudes toward whites. Social psychologist Jennifer Richeson, along with coauthor Sophie Trawalter, has researched and written extensively in this area. See in particular Richeson and Trawalter's "Why Do Interracial Interactions Impair Executive Function?" and "The Threat of Appearing Prejudiced."

32. See, for instance, Sue et al.'s "Racial Microaggressions in Everyday Life."

33. On critical race stories and coping strategies, see Shorter-Gooden, "Multiple Resistance Strategies"; on racial socialization and coping strategies, see McHale et al., "Mothers' and Fathers' Racial Socialization."

34. See Collins's *Black Feminist Thought* for a discussion of controlling images.

35. For a discussion of the politics of respectability in the early twentieth century, see Higginbotham's *Righteous Discontent*.

36. As McPherson argues in *Reconstructing Dixie*, relative to white women, "Black women marshaled the figure of the lady into more imaginative formations, alternatively laying claim to the rights of ladyhood and acting out against the rigid world of southern manners over which the 'lady' presided," 20.

37. This notion emerges out of postmodern cultural studies and the work of theorists like Edward Soja. Cornel West, Madhu Dubey, and others expound upon this concept. I quote Dubey here, from "Postmodern Geographies," 351.

CHAPTER 1

1. University of Mississippi historian James Silver's *Mississippi: The Closed Society* marks the state and the region with the "closed society" moniker, which has come to stand in as more descriptive than the widely used "Jim Crow."

2. See Egerton, *Americanization of Dixie*.

3. In addition to McPherson's *Reconstructing Dixie*, other texts make this argument, most notably Kreyling's *The South That Wasn't There*.

4. See Kreyling, *The South That Wasn't There*.

5. Wright's intense disdain for what he viewed as domineering women like his mother and aunt, the backward southern dupes whom he encountered as he came of age, and his turbulent Mississippi rearing are well documented in Wright's narratives and by scholarly appraisals of his work. See, for instance, Higashida's "Aunt Sue's Children."

6. "Art and Such" was originally written for the Federal Writers Project and published in a 1990 anthology, *Reading Black, Reading Feminist*, 24.

7. The "Ethics of Living Jim Crow" is the first essay in Wright's *Uncle Tom's Children*, from which I quote here, 3.

8. Wright's less-than-stellar opinion of women is well documented. For a thorough review, see Higashida, "Aunt Sue's Children." Hurston and Wright also traded scathing critiques of one another's work—notable direct critiques were Wright's review of *Their Eyes Were Watching God* and Hurston's review of *Uncle Tom's Children*. Beyond the personal and gendered reasons behind Wright's critiques of Hurston, his core stated criticism of Eatonville's ethnographer was that her writing pandered to existing stereotypes of black folks with which whites were already comfortable—as singing, laughing, crying, and otherwise emoting. For Wright, Hurston's characters' constrained or nonexistent rage was wholly inconsistent with a South of racial degradation, inequality, and violence, a South with which he was most familiar. Of *Uncle Tom's Children*, Hurston wrote in the *Saturday Review* that Wright's characters were one-dimensional and violent and that his interpretation of black southern dialect was subpar, particularly for a son of the South. Her critique echoes the writers' intraregional distinctions as well as somewhat disparate positions on the South. While both were from the South, which produced in them a desire to preserve some notion of the folk, their differential rearing and experiences caused them to articulate that folk in different ways.

9. For a critical appraisal of the endurance and appropriation of this debate in African American arts and letters, see Maxwell's chapter on the debate, "Black Belt/Black Folk," 153–178 in *New Negro, Old Left*.

10. Ibid., 156.

11. See Estes-Hicks, "The Way We Were."

12. See Baldwin's "Everybody's Protest Novel." Ellison's strongest epistemological critique of Wright can be found in his response to Irving Howe's "Black Boys and Native Sons," "The World and the Jug."

13. Richard Wright had become acquainted with the work of philosopher Jean-Paul Sartre, whose notion of "the gaze" provided Wright the existential justification for the oppositional anger and violence of his characters.

14. A major critique of the turn South in African American literature contends that the overwhelming focus on the rural South "discursively displaced" the urban, and implicitly northern, crises plaguing cities from Detroit to Los Angeles. This argument, forwarded originally by Hazel Carby, has undergirded most critiques of turns towards southern culture. However, a generation of black literature had also strategically displaced rural folk, and by extension southerners, from the narrative of black political agency.

15. Egerton notes the "Southernization of America" in *Americanization of Dixie*.

16. See Crockett, "Now Watch Me."

17. See chapter 1 of DeFrantz's *Dancing Revelations* for a thorough, piece-by-piece description of *Revelations*. The original performance of *Revelations* on January 31, 1960, was far more theatrical and much longer than the more pared-down version, the one

presented to the nation through television debut in 1962 with which contemporary audiences are much more familiar.

18. Arthur Todd with Alvin Ailey, "Roots of the Blues," 24.

19. In playwright John Henry Redwood's *The Old Settler*, southern girl Lou Bessie has gone north to Harlem, leaving behind her country ways, values, and name; in Harlem, she renames herself the more sophisticated sounding "Charmaine."

20. The widely circulated clip of President Barack Obama singing Al Green's "Let's Stay Together" was popular not only because of the president's surprisingly nice singing voice but also because "Let's Stay Together" is a quintessential soul song. The president's knowledge and successful performance of a few bars of it, then, links him with an authentic and traditional black American community.

21. See Estes-Hicks, "The Way We Were."

22. Walker, "Black Writer and the Southern Experience," 21.

23. Ibid.

24. See Gayle, "Reclaiming the Southern Experience."

25. Johnson, "Publisher's Statement."

26. "Belles of the South," 158.

27. There are, of course, some significant and notable exceptions to this trend of looking away from Dixie, and urban Dixie in particular, in the social sciences. Sociologist Robert Bullard, a champion of the South and southern cities, produced an excellent monograph, *Invisible Houston*, that chronicles the dialectical relationship between institutional racism and resistance and cultural production among black Houstonians. Political scientists Christopher Silver and John V. Moeser also are custodians of social scientific work on southern cities. Their research on Richmond, Memphis, and Atlanta, published in *The Separate City*, is one of a few works that looks comparatively at African American experiences in southern cities in the postwar period.

28. For an important analysis of regional memory and African American culture in *Daughters of the Dust*, see Ebron's "Enchanted Memories of Regional Difference."

29. See, for instance, Adelman, Morett, and Tolnay's "Homeward Bound"; and Hunt, Hunt, and Falk's "Who's Headed South?"

30. See Dubey, "Postmodern Geographies," and the chapter "Reading as Listening" in *Signs and Cities*.

31. See Kreyling, *The South That Wasn't There*.

32. Carby, "Politics of Fiction, Anthropology, and the Folk," 77.

33. Reed, "Dangerous Dreams," *Village Voice*, 24.

34. Tavis Smiley and Cornel West, along with a number of other black male scholars and activists, participated in the 2009 documentary *Stand*, in which they situated the South as the epicenter of a transformative black politics in the wake of the Obama election.

35. In *Cultural Trauma*, Eyerman argues that the collective memory of slavery is in many ways implicated in the formation of contemporary African American identity.

CHAPTER 2

1. Various versions of this quote have been circulated, and I have reproduced it here from notes I took on the postgame interview when it aired on April 29, 2011, and in subsequent replays of the interview. See the YouTube video "Zach Randolph" for the full conversation that precipitated Randolph's statement.

2. See Royster, "Ida B. Wells."

3. See in particular Honey's *Southern Labor and Black Civil Rights*.

4. Laurie B. Green's oral history of black Memphians, *Battling the Plantation Mentality*, documents organizing in the years leading up to the assassination of King. Civil rights-generation African Americans often refer to people unwilling to agitate for their rights, particularly to gain access to resources being withheld by whites, as having "the plantation mentality." This terminology is also used generally by black folks to describe other black people unwilling to combat white racism by improving themselves and their communities.

5. From Daralik's verse in the Iron Mic Coalition's song "901 Area Code."

6. For an overview of this shift, particularly vis-à-vis predatory lending and housing, see Powell's "Blacks in Memphis Lose Decades of Economic Gains."

7. See Lloyd, *Neo-Bohemia*.

8. David Banner, "Mississippi."

9. Arrested Development, "Tennessee."

10. Spaces that were once filled, however, are now empty. The showpiece retail and entertainment space, Peabody Place, lost most of its retailers and its twenty-two-screen movie theater between its opening at the turn of the new century and the decade's end. Respondents widely cited white people's fear of the city and fear of blackness—both white patrons and white developers of the space—as responsible for the mall's demise.

11. See Hannigan, *Fantasy City*.

12. See "Flipside Memphis: Beale Street Flippers" for the Flippers' narrative of their origins.

13. Here Kiara is referring to the woman who has now become infamous for protesting the creation of the National Civil Rights Museum. She insists that King would not have wanted the museum, and she is often sitting across the street from the museum selling books and T-shirts and urging tourists to boycott the museum.

14. From OutKast's song "The Whole World."

15. The Jena Six was the moniker given to a group of African American teenagers jailed in Jena, Louisiana, for fighting with fellow white students over a noose hung from a tree. The incident drew national attention as several hundred black people converged on the small Louisiana town in protest.

16. See Harris-Lacewell, "Don't Hold Obama to Race Agenda."

CHAPTER 3

1. From Mos Def's song "Revelations."

2. For instance, when in 2013 the buttery southern food personality revealed casually that she had, on occasion, used the word "nigger," few black southerners could logically muster surprise. Still, the contradictions between a supposedly post-racist society and the Old South that looms over it all engender disappointment.

3. This conundrum plays out thusly: Do black folks never have any intention of tipping according to accepted standards, or do servers, white and black, anticipating that black patrons will not tip, give them poor service, resulting in a poor tip?

4. Sean Bell was killed leaving his bachelor party in 2006 in Queens, New York, by undercover police officers. Oscar Grant was killed in 2009 in a public transportation station in Oakland during an arrest. Tarika Wilson was killed in a drug raid on her home in Lima, Ohio, in 2008. Her infant son was shot twice during the raid. Jonathan Ferrell was shot in 2013 as he sought help from Charlotte police officers after a serious car accident.

5. See Jackson, *Racial Paranoia*; and Touré's interviewees' answers to his questions about their experiences of racism in *Who's Afraid of Post-Blackness?*

6. Jackson, *Racial Paranoia*, 87.

CHAPTER 4

1. See Fox-Genovese, *Within the Plantation Household.*

2. Walker, *In Search of Our Mothers' Gardens*, xi–xii; Johnson, "'Quare Studies,'" 125.

3. See the Chris Rock documentary *Good Hair.*

4. Similar whispers would accompany a child visiting from "the country," namely small-town Mississippi or Arkansas. However, whisperers were decidedly kinder to these offenders because they expect girls from small towns to have damaged or inappropriately styled hair. In fact, on three occasions that I observed, when visiting girls did *not* have tragically damaged hair, three different stylists at two salons waxed on about some finer point about hair care that would help the children's hair be "better."

5. "Belles of the South," 158.

6. Beyond the interpersonal level, like a disagreement between cousins, skin color has well-documented structural consequences. Lighter-skinned women are more likely to get married and have higher incomes and higher self-reported levels of happiness in comparison to their browner-skinned counterparts. See, for instance, Herring, Keith, and Horton's edited collection, *Skin Deep.*

7. Self-described "darker-skinned" respondents who had spent some time out of the South, and in large cities of the Northeast and West Coast specifically, talked at length about how they were more likely to be approached by men on the street and more likely to receive attention from men generally outside of the South. They explicitly linked these distinctions to skin color, no matter what kind of alternative reading I offered the situation.

8. "5 Star Bitch" is one of Yo Gotti's 2009 singles, which broke into the Billboard charts and remained there for several weeks. He is not the only rapper to rate potential partners on a scale, but "5 Star Bitch" is in the vanguard of a paradigm where men seek educated, financially secure, physically attractive women willing to put men's needs in front of their own.

9. What Perry intends to portray as polite pursuit of a woman unwilling to give men a chance because of her bad experiences could also be read as harassment. In the narrative, her refusal is not acceptable because it is predicated upon her experiences with other men.

10. Nappy Roots, "Country Boyz."

11. Erykah Badu, "Southern Gul,"

12. Clyde and Yvette may represent a middle-class couple by southern standards and relative to the other characters, as they both have legal jobs and attend church regularly. However, a more objective (that is, national) understanding of their class status—Yvette works in a management position in a retail/sales store and Clyde records music around town for church groups—might be as "working class."

CHAPTER 5

1. Perry, quoted on *Box Office.*

2. Perry actually cites Langston Hughes as Hurston's adversary, incorrectly attributing Wright's critique of *Their Eyes Were Watching God* to the poet. In the error, however, he

also gestures toward the differences between Schuyler and Hughes about the criteria for "black" art. Hughes and Hurston's differences were of a more personal nature, as their friendship ended in a dispute over creative ownership of a story on which the two allegedly collaborated. See Valerie Boyd's *Wrapped in Rainbows* for a detailed accounting of Hurston's relationship to both Wright and Hughes.

3. From Lil' Wayne's song "Shooter."

4. Chris Rock's most famous delivery of this joke was during his 1996 HBO special, *Bring the Pain*. Like Richard Pryor had done before him, Rock made behavioral, and implicitly ontological, distinctions between "niggas" and "black people" that spoke to everyday observations of intraracial distinction. While Rock has since ceased delivering that joke, citing white people's liberal use of the term "nigga" as a result, he has not, at least publicly, considered the ways in which the original joke erected an unreasonable hierarchy through a white supremacist, or black elite, lens.

5. The question—"Can blacks still be thought of as a single race?"—was roundly criticized by many social scientists as unclear and misleading. However, the fact remains that while 53 percent of respondents answered in the affirmative, 37 percent of respondents said no, 3 percent problematized the question with a voluntary answer, and 7 percent did not answer, perhaps because they were confused by the question's wording. See the Pew Research Center report "Optimism about Black Progress Declines."

6. Michael Eric Dyson publicly criticized Cosby for his comments and quickly wrote *Is Bill Cosby Right?* to elaborate on those criticisms.

7. See Bruce Haynes's history of the black middle-class community of Runyon Heights in Yonkers, New York, in *Red Lines, Black Spaces*; Mary Pattillo's treatment of a black middle-class neighborhood on the South Side of Chicago in *Black Picket Fences*; and Karyn Lacy's examination of black middle-class people in Prince George's County, Maryland (*Blue-Chip Black*), for sociological discussions of social capital, class, boundaries, and identity among black middle classes.

8. Philosopher Tommie Shelby advocates for a "thin" blackness that retains a sense of linked fate but not necessarily the strict adherence to racial mores, norms, and codes of conduct that he calls a "thick" blackness (see *We Who Are Dark*). Similarly, journalist Touré argues for a post-black identity that embraces the multiplicity of blackness, decentering and rejecting an authentic or essential black identity (*Who's Afraid of Post-Blackness?*).

9. On "Shooter," Lil' Wayne criticizes the payola practices of radio stations that refuse to play southern rap. He admonishes them to "stop being rapper racists [and] region haters." His comment is more broadly a critique of East and West Coast rappers' treatment of southern rap artists, highlighting establishment rap's discomfort with southernness.

10. See Darren Grem's 2006 article of the same title, "The South Got Something to Say."

11. For a different analysis of these and other similar discourses, see I'Nasah Crockett's "Now Watch Me."

12. Moss and Richard, "50 Cent Says Eminem Wants Him to Hold Off on Summer LP."

13. Perkins, "Wu-Tang."

14. "Ice T Disses Soulja Boy."

15. See McGruder, "Bitches to Rags."

16. See Crockett, Cannon, and Nas, "Eat Dat Watermelon."

17. In March 2008, thirty-three-year-old Jessie Dotson shot, stabbed, and killed several members of his family after an apparent argument with his brother. The murders received

a great deal of press and were featured in an episode of A&E's *The First 48*, which made them a topic of conversation in most interviews between 2008 and 2010.

18. Little Brother is a rap group from Raleigh-Durham, North Carolina. The group's work was lauded on Memphis's underground hip-hop scene as an example of independent success achieved without compromising the integrity of their art.

19. Lacy finds similar self-identifications of class status among her respondents in Prince George's County, Maryland, in *Blue-Chip Black*.

CONCLUSION

1. See Gottdiener and Hutchinson's discussion of these data in *New Urban Sociology*.

2. Here I borrow again, with apologies, from David Goldfield, "The City as Southern History," which argues that we can understand the history of the region only through its cities. This essay is in Goldfield's collection *Region, Race, and Cities*.

3. See Frey, "Race and Ethnicity."

4. Ibid.

5. OutKast, "Slum Beautiful."

6. See, for instance, Roger Catlin's *Washington Post* article, "Reality TV's Explosion of Southern Stereotypes," which chronicles the significant rise in rural-themed reality television.

7. Early in this advertising campaign, Annie introduces herself as "Annie the Chicken Queen." Responding to consumer outrage, her moniker was shortened to "Annie." The corporation, citing copyright concerns, has blocked YouTube videos of the original 2009 commercial.

8. Frank Ocean, "Pink Matter."

Bibliography

Adelman, Robert M., Chris Morett, and Stewart Tolnay. "Homeward Bound: The Return Migration of Southern-Born Black Women, 1940 to 1990." *Sociological Spectrum* 20 (2000): 433–63.

Alvin Ailey, with Arthur Todd. "Roots of the Blues." *Dance and Dancers*, November 1961, 24–25.

Arrested Development. "Tennessee." On *3 Years, 5 Months & 2 Days in the Life Of . . .* Produced by Speech. New York. EMI/Chrysalis Records, 1992.

Badu, Erykah. "Southern Gul." Single. Produced by Rahzel M. Brown. Motown Records, 1998.

Baldwin, James. "Everybody's Protest Novel," 1949. In *Notes of a Native Son*, 13–23. Boston: Beacon Press, 1984.

Banner, David. "Mississippi." On *Mississippi: The Album*. Produced David Banner, Bread & Water, KLC, Lil Jon, Mixzo. Universal Records/UMG Recordings/SRC Records, 2003.

"Belles of the South: Variety Adds Spice to Beauty," *Ebony*, August 1971, 158–63.

Bennett, Andy, and Richard A. Peterson, eds. *Music Scenes: Local, Translocal, and Virtual*. Nashville: Vanderbilt University Press, 2004.

Betrand, Marianne, and Sendhil Mullainathan. "Are Emily and Greg More Employable Than Lakisha and Jamal? A Field Experiment on Labor Market Discrimination." *American Economic Review* 19, no. 4 (2004): 991–1001.

Bonilla-Silva, Eduardo. "From Bi-racial to Tri-racial: Towards a New System of Racial Stratification in the USA." *Ethnic and Racial Studies* 27, no. 6 (2004): 931–50.

———. *Racism without Racists: Color-Blind Racism and the Persistence of Racial Inequality in the United States*. Lanham, Md.: Rowman and Littlefield, 2009.

———. "'We Are All Americans!' The Latin Americanization Thesis." *Race and Society* 5 (2002): 3–16.

Borer, Ian. "The Location of Culture: The Urban Culturalist Perspective." *City and Community* 5, no. 2 (2006): 173–97.

Bourdieu, Pierre. *Distinction: A Social Critique of the Judgement of Taste*. Translated by Richard Nice. Cambridge, Mass.: Harvard University Press, 1984.

———. "The Field of Cultural Production; or, the Economic World Reversed." In *The Field of Cultural Production: Essays on Art and Literature*, 29–73. New York: Columbia University Press, 1993.

Boyd, Valerie. *Wrapped in Rainbows: The Life of Zora Neale Hurston*. New York: Scribner, 2004.

Brown, Leslie. *Upbuilding Black Durham: Gender, Class, and Black Community Development in the Jim Crow South*. Chapel Hill: University of North Carolina Press, 2008.

Brownell, Blaine A., and David R. Goldfield, eds. *The City in Southern History: The Growth of Urban Civilization in the South*. Port Washington, N.Y.: Kennikat Press, 1977.

Bullard, Robert D. *Invisible Houston: The Black Experience in Boom and Bust.* College Station: Texas A&M University Press, 2000.

———, ed. *In Search of the New South: The Black Urban Experience in the 1970s and 1980s.* Tuscaloosa: University of Alabama Press, 1989.

Carby, Hazel. "The Politics of Fiction, Anthropology, and the Folk: Zora Neale Hurston." In *New Essays on Their Eyes Were Watching God,* edited by Michael Awkward, 71–94. New York: Cambridge University Press, 1991.

Catlin, Roger. "Reality TV's Explosion of Southern Stereotypes." *Washington Post,* June 7, 2012. http://www.washingtonpost.com/entertainment/tv/reality-tvs-explosion-of-southern-stereotypes/2012/06/06/gJQA3bXbLV_story.html (accessed June 7, 2012).

Chris Rock: Bring the Pain. Directed by Kevin Truesdell. HBO Productions, 1996.

Cobb, James C. *The Most Southern Place on Earth: The Mississippi Delta and the Roots of Regional Identity.* New York: Oxford University Press, 1994.

Cohen, Cathy J. *The Boundaries of Blackness: AIDS and the Breakdown of Black Politics.* Chicago: University of Chicago Press, 1999.

Collins, Patricia Hill. *Black Feminist Thought: Knowledge, Consciousness, and the Politics of Empowerment.* 1990. New York: Routledge, 2000.

Crenshaw, Kimberlé. "Demarginalizing the Intersection of Race and Sex: A Black Feminist Critique of Antidiscrimination Doctrine, Feminist Theory and Antiracist Politics." *University of Chicago Legal Forum* 140 (1989): 139–67.

Crockett, Affion, Nick Cannon, and Nas. "Eat Dat Watermelon." YouTube, 2010. http://www.youtube.com/watch?v=ooWg5ymecm8 (accessed July 18, 2013).

Crockett, I'Nasah. "Now Watch Me: The Black Dancing Body and Southern Identity." Master's thesis, University of Mississippi, 2010.

Davis, Allison. *Deep South: A Social Anthropological Study of Caste and Class.* 1941. Columbia: University of South Carolina Press, 2009.

DeFrantz, Thomas F. 2006. *Dancing Revelations: Alvin Ailey's Embodiment of African American Culture.* New York: Oxford University Press.

Dollard, John. *Caste and Class in a Southern Town.* 1949. New York: Doubleday, 1957.

Drake, St. Clair, and Horace Cayton. *Black Metropolis: A Study of Negro Life in a Northern Metropolis.* With an introduction by Richard Wright and a foreword by William Julius Wilson. The University of Chicago Press, 1993.

Dubey, Madhu. "Postmodern Geographies of the U.S. South." *Neplanta: Views from the South* 3, no. 2 (2002): 351–71.

———. *Signs and Cities: Black Literary Postmodernism.* Chicago: University of Chicago Press, 2003.

Du Bois, W. E. B. *The Philadelphia Negro.* Philadelphia: University of Pennsylvania, 1899.

———. *W. E. B. Du Bois on Sociology and the Black Community.* Edited with an introduction by Dan S. Green. Chicago: University of Chicago Press, 1978.

Dyson, Michael Eric. *Is Bill Cosby Right? Or Has the Black Middle Class Lost Its Mind?* New York: Basic Civitas Books, 2005.

Ebron, Paulla A. "Enchanted Memories of Regional Difference." *American Anthropologist* 100, no. 1 (1998): 94–105.

Egerton, John. *The Americanization of Dixie: The Southernization of America.* New York: Harper's Magazine Press, 1974.

Ellison, Ralph. "The World and the Jug." In *Shadow and Act,* 107–43. 1963. New York: Vintage, 1995.

Estes-Hicks, Onita. "The Way We Were: Precious Memories of the Black Segregated South." *African American Review* 27, no. 1 (1993): 9–18.

Eyerman, Ron. *Cultural Trauma: Slavery and the Formation of African American Identity*. New York: Cambridge University Press, 2002.

Fenwick, Leslie T. "Ed School Dean: Urban School Reform Is about Land Development (Not Kids)," published on the *Washington Post*'s online blog "The Answer Sheet," edited by Valerie Strauss, May 28, 2013. http://www.washingtonpost.com/blogs/answer-sheet/wp/2013/05/28/ed-school-dean-urban-school-reform-is-really-about-land-development-not-kids/ (accessed May 28, 2013).

Ferber, Abby. *White Man Falling: Race, Gender, and White Supremacy*. New York: Rowman and Littlefield, 1998.

Fischer, Mary, and Douglas Massey. "The Ecology of Racial Discrimination." *City and Community* 3, no. 3 (2004): 221–41.

"Flipside Memphis: Beale Street Flippers." YouTube, 2010. http://www.youtube.com/watch?v=JsaZnzbWzyM (accessed August 18, 2012).

Fox-Genovese, Elizabeth. *Within the Plantation Household: Black and White Women of the Old South*. Chapel Hill: University of North Carolina Press, 1988.

Frey, William H. "Race and Ethnicity." In *The State of Metropolitan America*, 51–63. Washington, D.C.: Brookings Institution, 2008.

Game 6 of the First Round of the 2011 National Basketball Association Playoffs, San Antonio Spurs at the Memphis Grizzlies. ESPN, April 29, 2011.

Gayle, Addison, Jr. "Reclaiming the Southern Experience: The Black Aesthetic Ten Years Later." In *Black Southern Voices*, edited by John Oliver Killens and Jerry W. Ward Jr., 556–63. 1974. New York: Meridian, 1992.

George, Nelson. *Buppies, B-Boys, Baps and Bohos: Notes on Post-Soul Black Culture*. New York: Da Capo Press, 2001.

Gieryn, Tom. "Boundary-Work and the Demarcation of Science from Non-science: Strains and Interests in Professional Ideologies of Scientists." *American Sociological Review* 48, no. 6 (1983): 781–95.

Goldfield, David R. *Region, Race, and Cities: Interpreting the Urban South*. Baton Rouge: Louisiana State University Press, 1997.

Good Hair. Starring Chris Rock. Directed by Jeff Stilson. Chris Rock Entertainment and HBO Films, 2009.

Gottdiener, Mark, and Ray Hutchinson. *The New Urban Sociology*. 3rd ed. Boulder: Westview Press, 2006.

Green, Laurie B. *Battling the Plantation Mentality: Memphis and the Black Freedom Struggle*. Chapel Hill: University of North Carolina Press, 2007.

Grem, Darren. "'The South Got Something to Say': Atlanta's Dirty South and the Southernization of Hip-Hop America." *Southern Cultures* 12, no. 4 (2006): 55–73.

Griffin, Larry J. "The Promise of a Sociology of the South." *Southern Cultures* 7, no. 1 (2001): 50–75.

Griswold, Wendy. "Regionalism and Cultural Expression." In *International Encyclopedia of the Social and Behavioral Sciences*, edited by Neil J. Smelser and Paul B. Baltes, 12935–36. New York: Elsevier, 2001.

Griswold, Wendy, and Nathan Wright. "Cowbirds, Locals, and the Dynamic Endurance of Regionalism." *American Journal of Sociology* 109, no. 6 (2004): 1411–51.

Hannerz, Ulf. *Soulside: Inquiries into Ghetto Culture and Community*. Chicago: University of Chicago Press, 1969.

Hannigan, John. *Fantasy City: Pleasure and Profit in the Postmodern Metropolis*. New York: Routledge, 1998.

Harris-Lacewell, Melissa. "Don't Hold Obama to Race Agenda." CNNpolitics.com, June 5, 2009. http://www.cnn.com/2009/POLITICS/06/05/lacewell.race.agenda/index.html?iref=allsearch (accessed June 10, 2009).

Haynes, Bruce. *Red Lines, Black Spaces: The Politics of Race and Space in a Black Middle-Class Suburb*. New Haven: Yale University Press, 2001.

Herring, Cedric, Verna Keith, and Hayward Horton, eds. *Skin Deep: How Race and Complexion Matter in the "Color-Blind Era."* Urbana: University of Illinois Press, 2003.

Higashida, Cheryl. "Aunt Sue's Children: Re-viewing the Gender(ed) Politics of Richard Wright's Radicalism." *American Literature* 75, no. 2 (2003): 395–425.

Higginbotham, Evelyn Brooks. *Righteous Discontent: The Women's Movement in the Black Baptist Church, 1880–1920*. Cambridge, Mass.: Harvard University Press, 1994.

Honey, Michael. *Southern Labor and Black Civil Rights: Organizing Memphis Workers*. Urbana: University of Illinois Press, 1993.

Hopkinson, Natalie. *Go-Go Live: The Musical Life and Death of a Chocolate City*. Durham: Duke University Press, 2012.

Hunt, Larry, Matthew O. Hunt, and William Falk. "Who's Headed South? U.S. Migration Trends in Black and White, 1970–2000." *Social Forces* 87, no. 1 (2008): 95–119.

Hurston, Zora Neale. "Art and Such." 1938. In *Reading Black, Reading Feminist: A Critical Anthology*, edited by Henry Louis Gates Jr., 21–26. New York: Meridian Books, 1990.

"Ice-T Disses Soulja Boy." YouTube, 2008. http://www.youtube.com/watch?v=tilKeoZ8B7M (accessed July 18, 2013).

Iron Mic Coalition. "901 Area Code." On *The 1st Edition*. Produced by Fathom 9. Memphis: IMC Music, 2005.

Jackson, John L. *Harlemworld: Doing Race and Class in Contemporary Black America*. Chicago: University of Chicago Press, 2001.

———. *Racial Paranoia: The Unintended Consequences of Political Correctness*. New York: Basic Civitas Books, 2008.

———. *Real Black: Adventures in Racial Sincerity*. Chicago: University of Chicago Press, 2005.

Johnson, Charles S. *Growing Up in the Black Belt: Negro Youth in the Rural South*. Washington, D.C.: American Council on Education, 1941.

———. *Shadow of the Plantation*. Chicago: University of Chicago Press, 1934.

Johnson, E. Patrick. "'Quare Studies'; or (Almost) Everything I Know about Queer Studies I Learned from My Grandmother." In *Black Queer Studies: A Critical Anthology*, edited by E. Patrick Johnson and Mae G. Henderson, 124–60. Durham: Duke University Press, 2005.

Johnson, John H. "Publisher's Statement." *Ebony*, August 1971, 33.

Killens, John Oliver. "Introduction." In *Black Southern Voices*, edited by John Oliver Killens and Jerry W. Ward Jr., 1–4. New York: Meridian, 1992.

King, Deborah. "Multiple Jeopardy, Multiple Consciousness: The Context of a Black Feminist Ideology." *Signs* 14, no. 1 (1988): 42–72.

Kreyling, Michael. *The South That Wasn't There: Postsouthern Memory and History.* Baton Rouge: Louisiana State University Press, 2012.

Kruse, Kevin M. *White Flight: Atlanta and the Making of Modern Conservatism.* Princeton: Princeton University Press, 2005.

Kyriakoudes, Louis M. *The Social Origins of the Urban South: Race, Gender, and Migration in Nashville and Middle Tennessee, 1890–1930.* Chapel Hill: University of North Carolina Press, 2003.

Lacy, Karyn. *Blue-Chip Black: Race, Class, and Status in the New Black Middle Class.* Berkeley: University of California Press, 2007.

Lamont, Michèle. *The Dignity of Working Men: Morality and the Boundaries of Race, Class, and Immigration.* Cambridge, Mass.: Harvard University Press, 2002.

———. *Money, Morals, and Manners: The Culture of the French and American Upper-Middle Class.* Chicago: University of Chicago Press, 1994.

Lil' Wayne featuring Robin Thicke. "Shooter." On *Tha Carter II.* Produced by Robin Thicke. New Orleans: Cash Money Records, 2005.

Lloyd, Richard. *Neo-Bohemia: Art and Commerce in the Postindustrial City.* New York: Routledge, 2005.

Massood, Paula. *Black City Cinema: African American Urban Experiences in Film.* Philadelphia: Temple University Press, 2003.

Maxwell, William J. *New Negro, Old Left: African American Writing and Communism between the Wars.* New York: Columbia University Press, 1999.

McGruder, Aaron. "Bitches to Rags." *The Boondocks*, season 3, episode 2. Cartoon Network, 2010.

McHale, Susan M., Ann C. Crouter, Ji-Yeon Kim, Linda M. Burton, Kelly D. Davis, Aryn M. Dotterer, and Dena P. Swanson. "Mothers' and Fathers' Racial Socialization in African American Families: Implications for Youth." *Child Development* 77, no. 5 (2006): 1387–1402.

McIntosh, Peggy. "White Privilege and Male Privilege: A Personal Account of Coming to See Correspondences through Work in Women's Studies." Working Paper No. 189. Center for Research on Women, Wellesley College, 1988. http://www.iub. edu/~tchsotl/part2/McIntosh%20White%20Privilege.pdf (accessed July 19, 2012).

———. "White Privilege: Unpacking the Invisible Knapsack." *Peace and Freedom*, July/ August 1989. http://www.library.wisc.edu/edvrc/docs/public/pdfs/LIReadings/ InvisibleKnapsack.pdf (accessed September 20, 2013).

McPherson, Tara. *Reconstructing Dixie: Race, Gender, and Nostalgia in the Imagined South.* Durham: Duke University Press, 2003.

Molotch, Harvey, William Freudenberg, and Krista A. Paulsen. "History Repeats Itself, But How? City Character, Urban Tradition, and the Accomplishment of Place." *American Sociological Review* 65, no. 6 (2000): 791–823.

Mos Def. "Revelations." On *The Ecstatic.* Produced by J Dilla, Mr. Flash, Mad Lib, Mos Def, The Neptunes, Oh No, and Preservation. New York: Downtown Records, 2009.

Moss, Corey, and Yasmine Richard. "50 Cent Says Eminem Wants Him to Hold Off on Summer LP." MTV.com, March 16, 2006. http://www.mtv.com/news/ articles/1526185/50-em-wants-him-hold-off-on-new-lp.jhtml (accessed July 18, 2013).

Nappy Roots. "Country Boyz." *Watermelon, Chicken & Gritz.* Mike Caren, Executive Producer. Produced by Carlos Broady, Mike City, James Chambers, Troy Johnson, Brian Kidd, and The Trackboyz. Atlantic, 2002.

Neal, Mark Anthony. *Soul Babies: Black Popular Culture and the Post-Soul Aesthetic.* New York: Routledge, 2002.

Ocean, Frank with André 3000. "Pink Matter." *Channel Orange.* Produced by Frank Ocean, Malay, Om'Mas Keith, Pharrell. Def Jam, 2012.

Odum, Howard W. *Southern Regions of the United States.* Chapel Hill: University of North Carolina Press, 1936.

The Old Settler. By John Henry Redwood. Directed by Lazora Jones. Hattiloo Theatre. Memphis, Tenn., January 15, 2011.

Omi, Michael, and Howard Winant. *Racial Formation in the United States: From the 1960s to the 1990s.* 2nd ed. New York: Routledge, 1994.

OutKast. "The Whole World." On *Big Boi and Dre Present . . . OutKast.* Produced by OutKast and Organized Noize. Compilation Album. Stankonia Recording, Atlanta, Ga. Arista Records, 2001.

———. "Ms. Jackson." Music video directed by F. Gary Gray, 2001. From *Stankonia.* Produced by Earthtone III and Organized Noize. Stankonia Recording, Atlanta, Ga. LaFace/Arista, 2000.

———. "Slum Beautiful." *Stankonia.* Produced by Earthtone III and Organized Noize. Stankonia Recording, Atlanta, Ga. LaFace/Arista, 2000.

Pager, Devah, and Lincoln Quillian. "Walking the Talk? What Employers Say Versus What They Do." *American Sociological Review* 70, no. 3 (2005): 355–80.

Pattillo, Mary E. *Black on the Block: The Politics of Race and Class in the City.* Chicago: University of Chicago Press, 2007.

———. *Black Picket Fences: Privilege and Peril among the Black Middle Class.* Chicago: University of Chicago Press, 1999.

Perkins, Brandon. "Wu-Tang: Widdling Down Infinity." *URB Magazine,* July 10, 2010. http://www.urb.com/2007/07/10/wu-tang-widdling-down-infinity/ (accessed July 18, 2013).

Pew Research Center. "Optimism about Black Progress Declines: Blacks See Growing Values Gap between Poor and Middle Class," November 13, 2007. http://www.pewsocialtrends.org/files/2010/10/Race-2007.pdf (accessed November 13, 2007).

Powdermaker, Hortense. *After Freedom: A Cultural Study of the Deep South.* New York: Viking Press, 1939.

Powell, Michael. "Blacks in Memphis Lose Decades of Economic Gains." *New York Times,* May 30, 2010. http://www.nytimes.com/2010/05/31/business/economy/31memphis.html?pagewanted=all (accessed June 4, 2010).

Quillian, Lincoln, and Devah Pager. "Estimating Risk: Stereotype Amplification and the Perceived Risk of Criminal Victimization." *Social Psychological Quarterly* 73, no. 1 (2010): 79–104.

Reed, Adolph, Jr. "Romancing Jim Crow: Black Nostalgia for a Segregated Past." *Village Voice,* April 16, 1996, 24–29.

Reed, John Shelton. *The Enduring South: Subcultural Persistence in Mass Society.* Chapel Hill: University of North Carolina Press, 1986.

———. *Minding the South.* Columbia: University of Missouri Press, 2003.

———. *One South: An Ethnic Approach to Regional Culture.* Baton Rouge: Louisiana State University Press, 1982.

———. *Southern Folk, Plain and Fancy: Native White Social Types.* Athens: University of Georgia Press, 1986.

Richeson, Jennifer, and Sophie Trawalter. "The Threat of Appearing Prejudiced and Race-Based Attentional Biases." *Psychological Science* 19, no. 2 (2008): 98–102.

———. "Why Do Interracial Interactions Impair Executive Function? A Resource Depletion Account." *Journal of Personality and Social Psychology* 88, no. 6 (2005): 934–47.

Roediger, David. *The Wages of Whiteness: Race and the Making of the American Working Class.* New York: Verso, 1999.

Royster, Jacqueline Jones. "Ida B. Wells: Legacies for Civic Action and Leadership from a Truth-Telling Woman." Lecture delivered at the "Civic Learning: Rhetoric, Public Address, Political Division" Conference, University of Memphis, Memphis, Tenn., September 28, 2012.

Rushing, Wanda. *Memphis and the Paradox of Place: Globalization and the American South.* Chapel Hill: University of North Carolina Press, 2009.

Sarig, Roni. *Third Coast: OutKast, Timbaland, and How Hip-Hop Became a Southern Thing.* Cambridge, Mass.: Da Capo Press, 2007.

Sartre, Jean-Paul. *Being and Nothingness: An Essay on Phenomenological Ontology.* New York: Washington Square Press, 1983.

Shelby, Tommie. *We Who Are Dark: The Philosophical Foundations of Black Solidarity.* Cambridge, Mass.: Belknap Press, 2005.

Shorter-Gooden, Kumea. "Multiple Resistance Strategies: How African American Women Cope with Racism and Sexism." *Journal of Black Psychology* 3, no. 3 (2004): 406–25.

Silver, Christopher, and John V. Moeser. *The Separate City: Black Communities in the Urban South, 1940–1968.* Lexington: University Press of Kentucky, 1995.

Silver, James W. *Mississippi: The Closed Society.* Jackson: University Press of Mississippi, 2012.

Simmons, Bill. "NBA Playoffs Are 'Wired': Part 1." ESPN.com, May 3, 2011. http://sports. espn.go.com/espn/page2/story?page=simmons/part1/110503&sportCat=nba (accessed September 23, 2013).

Smiley, Tavis, dir. *Stand.* Sivat Productions, 2009.

Soja, Edward. *Postmodern Geographies: The Reassertion of Space in Critical Social Theory.* New York: Verso, 1989.

Stack, Carol B. *Call to Home: African Americans Reclaim the Rural South.* New York: Basic Books, 1996.

Sue, Christina. "An Assessment of the Latin Americanization Thesis." *Ethnic and Racial Studies* 32, no. 6 (2009): 1058–70.

Sue, Derald Wing, Christina M. Capodilupo, Gina C. Torino, Jennifer M. Bucceri, Aisha M. B. Holder, Kevin L. Nadal, and Marta Esquilin. "Racial Microaggressions in Everyday Life: Implications for Clinical Practice." *American Psychologist* (May-June 2007): 271–86.

Touré. *Who's Afraid of Post-Blackness? What It Means to Be Black Now.* New York: Free Press, 2011.

"Tyler Perry On His Critics: 'Spike Lee Can Go Straight to Hell.'" Box Office, April 19, 2011. http://www.boxoffice.com/news/2011-04-19-tyler-perry-on-his-critics-spike-lee-can-go-straight-to-hell (accessed May 4, 2011).

Walker, Alice. "The Black Writer and the Southern Experience." 1970. In *In Search of Our Mothers' Gardens,* 15–21. New York: Harcourt Brace Jovanovich, 1983.

———. *In Search of Our Mothers' Gardens*. 1970. New York: Harcourt Brace Jovanovich, 1983.

Waters, Mary. *Ethnic Options: Choosing Identities in America*. Berkeley: University of California Press, 1990.

Wattstax. Directed by Mel Stuart. Stax Films and Wolper Productions, 1973.

West, Candace, and Don Zimmerman. "Doing Gender." *Gender and Society* 1, no. 2 (1987): 125–51.

West, Cornel. "The New Cultural Politics of Difference." In *Out There: Marginalization and Contemporary Cultures*, edited by Russell Ferguson, Martha Gever, Trinh T. Minh-ha, and Cornel West, 19–38. New York: The New Museum of Contemporary Art, 1990.

Wise, Tim. *White Like Me: Reflections on Race from a Privileged Son*. Berkeley: Soft Skull Press, 2011.

Woods, Clyde. *Development Arrested: The Blues and Plantation Power in the Mississippi Delta*. New York: Verso, 2000.

Wright, Richard. *Black Boy*. 1944. New York: Harper and Row, 1989.

———. *Uncle Tom's Children*. 1936. New York: HarperCollins, 1993.

Yancy, George. *Black Bodies, White Gazes: The Continuing Significance of Race*. Lanham, Md.: Rowman and Littlefield, 2008.

Yo Gotti. "5 Star Bitch." Single. Hot Rod, Producer. Polo Grounds Music/J Records, 2009.

"Zach Randolph 31 Points vs. Spurs Full Highlights (2011 NBA Playoffs GM6)." YouTube, 2011. http://www.youtube.com/watch?v=VOScgIwQ8Xs (accessed September 24, 2013).

Zukin, Sharon. *The Cultures of Cities*. London: Blackwell, 1995.

Index

Bo-Keys, 73, 74

Bonilla-Silva, Eduardo, 7, 95, 99, 199 (n. 4)

Booker T. Washington High School: 60

Boondocks, The: racial epistemology, 103–4, 119; fictional representation of Soulja Boy/Ice-T beef, 164

Boundary work, 15–16; and symbolic boundaries, 15, 16; and social and cultural capital, 15, 20, 23, 32, 36; and race, 29, 31, 95–96, 162; and region, 30–31, 33, 36, 58, 181, 188; and class, 161

Bourdieu, Pierre, 15

Bullard, Robert, 203 (n. 27)

Bravo (television network), 3, 187

Brewer, Craig, 73, 155

Brown v. Board of Education, 45

Bryant, Joy, 128

Bush, George W., 87–88

Call to Home, 53

Cannon, Nick, 164–65

Carby, Hazel, 202 (n. 14)

Cash Money Records, 66

Cayton, Horace, and St. Clair Drake, 40

Chappelle, Dave, 108

Chappelle's Show: black racial logic, 108; representation of coping with racism, 117

Charles, Ray, 72

Charlotte, North Carolina, 7, 25, 53, 83, 125, 129, 189, 204 (n. 4). *See also* Cities: in new urban South

Charmels, 163

Chicago: as migration destination, 2, 8, 17, 71; and demographic change, 8, 9, 187; South Side, 35, 50, 52, 54, 103; film representations of, 50–51

Chicago School of sociology, 10

Cities: southern, 7–11; in new urban South, 7–8, 190–91; in historic urban South, 7–8, 190–91; Soul, 8–11, 62, 190; and demographic change, 8–9, 189–90; Chocolate, 8–10; and Chicago School of sociology, 10; separate, 11, 122, 199 (n. 7), 203 (n. 27)

Civil rights movement: African American life since, 4–5, 26, 61, 161; and

Memphis, 5, 11, 61, 80; legacy of, 11, 35, 49, 51, 80, 87, 89

Class: and intersections with region, 18, 22–23, 26, 29, 49, 55, 59, 95, 185, 194; and intraracial difference, 153, 166, 181, 193; theory, 161; and intersections with other oppressions, 161, 194

Cleaborn Homes, 60, 76

Clinton, George, 8

Closed society, 33, 201 (n. 1)

Cobb, James, 200 (n. 15)

Coleman-Kiner, Alicia, 60

Collins, Patricia Hill, 122, 199 (n. 11)

Color Purple, The (film), 69

Colorism: intraracial class differences and, 29; and southern belle, 129; structural inequality and, 205 (n. 6); in the South, 29, 205 (n. 7). *See also* Black women: and skin color

Confederate commemorative symbols, 20, 67, 72, 88, 95

Cosby, Bill, 12, 160, 165, 200 (n. 13)

Cosmopolitan: definition of, 20, 21, 22; and the North, 25; and bourgie, 132, 178, 181, 185. *See also* Country cosmopolitanism

Cotillion. *See* Debutante ball

Country: as marker of regional difference, 16, 152, 166–67; performance of, 22, 182–83; and intraracial class politics, 29, 180, 182, 194, 198; connotations of, 31, 96, 147, 162, 173, 180; and gender, 128, 129, 141, 146, 147, 157. *See also* Country cosmopolitanism

Country boy, 148, 149; definition of, 150–51; and southern rap, 149–50; connotations of, 151, 152, 158; and class, 180, 182, 193; and race, 193

Country girl, 128, 146, 147–48, 193. *See also* Southern belle; Southern gul

Country cosmopolitanism: and "better blackness," 1, 32, 50, 72, 74, 89, 95, 106, 162, 166–67, 186; definition, 17–18, 20–22; use by black southern cultural elites, 18, 45–46, 188–89, 194–95; use by corporations, 18, 183–84, 194–95; use by respondents, 18, 20–23, 33, 65, 188–89,

Made in the USA
Middletown, DE
12 November 2020